APOCALYPSE HOW?

APOCALYPSE HOW?

BAPTIST MOVEMENTS DURING THE ENGLISH REVOLUTION

Mark R. Bell

MERCER UNIVERSITY PRESS
Macon, Georgia

ISBN 0-86554-670-3   MUP/H499

Copyright ©2000
Mercer University Press, Macon, Georgia 31210-3960 USA
All rights reserved
Printed in the United States of America

The paper used in this publication meets the minimum require-
ments of American National Standard for Information Sci-
ences—Permanence of Paper for Printed Library Materials, ANSI
Z39.48-1984.

Library of Congress Cataloging-in-Publication Data

Bell, Mark R.
    Apocalypse How? Baptist Movements during the English
Revolution / Mark R. Bell
        p. cm.
    Includes bibliographical references and index.
    ISBN 0-86554-670-3 (alk. paper)
    1. Baptists—England—History—17th century. 2. Baptists—Doc-
trines—History—17th century. 3. Eschatology—History of Doctrines
—17th century. 4. England—Church history—17th century. I. Title

BX6276 .B45 2000
286'.0942'09032—dc21

                                                    00-035512

In memory of
Martin Luther King Jr,
1929-1968,
one of America's greatest Baptists

The church must be reminded that it is not the master or the servant of the state, but rather the conscience of the state.
—Martin Luther King Jr., *The Strength to Love*

CONTENTS

ACKNOWLEDGMENTS / vii

INTRODUCTION   / 1

PART I: GENERAL BAPTISTS AND THE RETURN OF CHRIST   / 11

   1. REFORMATION AND REVELATION   / 13

   2. KINGDOM AND KINGS:
      THE BAPTISTS' APOCALYPTIC PERSPECTIVE   / 23

   3. BAPTIST BEGINNINGS:
      JOHN SMYTH AND THE GENERAL BAPTISTS   / 33

PART II: PARTICULAR BAPTISTS IN BABYLON   / 53

   4. KING JESUS:
      PARTICULAR BAPTISTS AND LONDON'S GATHERED CHURCHES   / 55

   5. DEFINITION AND DEVELOPMENT:
      THE PARTICULAR BAPTIST CONFESSIONS OF 1644 AND 1646   / 73

   6. UNEASY ALLIANCES: BAPTISTS AND LEVELLERS   / 97

   7. RESPONSIBLE MEN AND RESISTANT SAINTS:
      LEADERS AND ORGANIZATION   / 121

   8. FURTHER AFIELD: PARTICULAR BAPTISTS BEYOND LONDON   / 135

PART III: "UNORTHODOX" BAPTISTS   / 161

   9. FIFTH MONARCHISTS AND BAPTISTS   / 163

   10. SEVENTH-DAY BAPTISTS   / 205

   11. FIFTH-MONARCHIST-SEVENTH-DAY BAPTISTS
      AND THOMAS TILLAM'S PALATINATE APOCALYPSE   / 229

CONCLUSION: REFLECTIONS BEFORE THE END OF THINGS   / 255

BIBLIOGRAPHY   / 263

INDEX   / 289

ACKNOWLEDGMENTS

This book, in its first incarnation, began in 1995 while I was still at Stanford University. In the ensuing half decade the manuscript has developed a history of its own and I have accumulated a number of debts that I would briefly like to acknowledge.

This work has relied on the assistance of numerous archives and archivists, particularly those at the Bodleian Library, Dr. William's Library, Stanford University Libraries, Emory University Libraries, and the Public Record Office. I owe a very special thanks to the staff of the Angus Library at Regent's Park College for all of their assistance.

Over the past five years this project has received generous financial support from the Undergraduate Research Opportunities program at Stanford University, the gift of Mrs. Robert Golden, STA Student Travel Grants, the Carl F. Brand Fund, Balliol College, the US-Marshall Scholarship fund, and a Chappell-Lougee Scholarship. I would also like to thank the History Faculty of Stanford University for presenting this project the James Birdsall Weter thesis prize and the Prize for Advance Study in the Humanities; the award from both helped fund subsequent work on the book.

In terms of intellectual gratitude, I have tried to indicate in the footnotes where I have drawn from the work of numerous others. However, the reader will immediately recognize that my indebtedness to the scholarship of Bryan W. Ball, B. S. Capp, Murray Tolmie, and B. R. White cannot be contained in any number of notes. I hope that some of my suggestions demonstrate the provocative nature of their respective works and their influence on this presentation of the Baptists' story.

A number of other individuals have influenced the final form of this book, either through helpful and critical insights, or through the equally important function of allowing me the time and space to complete the work—and in many cases both. The briefest list would have to include Robert C. Gregg and Jack N.

Rakove, who in different ways helped to inspire and guide this project; Norman Naimark and Carolyn Lougee for the guidance they offered to a young historian; my Atlantan mentor Jeff Rosensweig; my Oxford advisors and advocates Felicity Heal and Jonathan Powis; my patient and insightful editor Andrew Manis and the professional staff at Mercer University Press; Ara Barsam who has not only taught me a great deal about theology, but also read through the entire manuscript when it was in its penultimate stage; and to my PRO buddy Bianca Camac, who has been my toughest critic and truest companion.

As for my primary advisors on the project, Paul S. Seaver and Brad Gregory, one would think that after such a wordy text, I would be able to find the words to express my indebtedness to them, but I cannot. All I can say is that it is wonderful when your heroes are also your teachers and your friends.

Finally, I am most grateful for the support of my parents, Mark and Pam Bell, who loved and trusted me even when I went to the other side of the world to study apocalyptic Baptists from the seventeenth century. I thank them for giving me both roots and wings. And to my brother, who has made the right decision by enrolling in a university dedicated to transforming the world through understanding the message of religion. May histories soon be written about him.

Mark R. Bell
Oxford
Feast of St. George, 2000

NOTE ON DATES AND SPELLING

Partly in an effort to resist the perceived evils of the Continental Papists, the English used the Old Style, or Julian, Calendar while their Continental contemporaries used the New Style, or Gregorian, Calendar throughout the period discussed in this book. The Old Style was ten days behind the New Style and in England the year officially began on 25 March, as opposed to on the Continent where it began on 1 January. In this text, all dates are given in the Old Style for the day and month, but the year is taken to start on 1 January. For the English Baptist William Allen, the execution of King Charles took place on 30 January 1648. For his Continental contemporary, Henri Mission, it took place on 9 February 1649. In this book, the date is given as 30 January 1649.

Spelling and punctuation have been modernized in quotations when possible and appropriate. Titles of seventeenth-century texts have not been altered. The heavy use of italics in the seventeenth century has largely been ignored.

INTRODUCTION:
THE STORY OF THE BAPTIST MOVEMENTS

Well before the seventeenth century had ended, and the dust had settled from a hundred years of religious turmoil, civil war, and revolution, people began scrambling to set down histories of these events. A profound transformation had forced England out of its medieval slumber and prepared it for its modern future. While it was a time of tremendous development for Britain, the same was also true for a number of movements that can be called "Baptists." This book offers a look at several such movements at a time when a new age was dawning. It is a story of compromise, betrayal, and survival amidst the religious fervor, apocalyptic expectations, and revolutionary politics of early modern England. It is a small but formative part of the Baptists' story.

In recent years a number of studies have appeared, providing fresh insight into both the Baptists and the seventeenth-century context in which they developed. While the following narrative is largely an effort to combine original research with such findings, some of the lessons learned during the last thirty years of scholarship should be mentioned from the start. Initially, denominational terminology can be dangerous. The distinctions between religious groups were amorphous in the seventeenth century. As long as there was a state church that persecuted those who stepped outside its bounds, many dissenters found common cause; often when persecution eased they found they had irreparable differences. When the English ecclesiastical system collapsed in the middle of the century, changes transpired at a rapid pace. Individuals could travel through a myriad of religious positions in a brief span of time, going from Anglican, to Presbyterian, to Baptist to Quaker and beyond. Often, there was as much disagreement within congregations as there was between them. Therefore the greatest caution must be exercised to avoid associating modern connotations with denominational names. This story is concerned with how the denominational foundation came into existence. It is a story about beginnings, about the process of development from baptists to Baptists. The group of Christians whose origins are early in the seventeenth century were not called Baptists until the end of that century. Secondly, research into early modern England has demonstrated that theological developments cannot be divorced from their political environment. The Baptists were not born fully formed in a vacuum. They were shaped by their environment and the historical context in which they developed. Finally, the process was not a linear progression from the past to the present. Neither the development nor the survival of the Baptists was guaranteed. It is precisely for this final reason that the period before there was a denomination must be considered.

Three concurrent threads comprise the fabric of this analysis of the early English Baptists. First is the context of plurality, of competing voices and sources of authority—the idea of "movements." By movements is meant a rough grouping of individuals united by similar beliefs and goals. The term is used here to denote a proto-denominational identity. From their earliest origins Baptists were diverse and comprised a variety of movements. Throughout most of the seventeenth century, contemporaries were not certain what to call the Baptists. They often simply referred to them as "Brownists" or "Anabaptists." The Baptists found both of these terms unacceptable. "Brownists" referred literally to the followers of Robert Browne and only indicated that the Baptists had separated from the Church of England. The term "Anabaptists" was even worse, since it associated the English Baptists with the atrocities of the Anabaptists at Münster. The Baptists also objected to the term "Anabaptist" because it literally meant "re-baptizer," implying that infant baptism was a legitimate form of baptism. The early Baptists were equally uncertain of what to call themselves. "Christians" seemed to be the obvious choice. Sometimes they used the term "baptized believers." When they wanted their identity to be clear to contemporaries, they had to resort to such awkward titles as "those churches often (though falsely) called Anabaptists."

What they meant was a gathered congregation of Christians who practiced believer's baptism. A gathered congregation signified a community of believers existing outside of the Church of England on a voluntary basis, constituting their own church. Believer's baptism was the practice of baptizing only those who were capable of making some profession of faith, which excluded infants. This bold move was seen as a threat to the already fading idea of a universal Christendom, in which membership was conferred to all through baptism at birth. Although most Baptists agreed on these principles, there were still differences between them that resulted in a number of different Baptist movements.

The forerunners of the English Baptists were the Anabaptists of the Continental Reformation. A few of these "re-baptizers" found their way into sixteenth-century England, where they were fiercely persecuted and, in a few instances, executed. These Anabaptists were usually foreigners and an English Anabaptist movement does not seem to have developed. Nevertheless, while these Continental Anabaptists were not active participants in the events of the 1600s, they did have a profound influence on the later English Baptist movements. This influence was largely negative as the subsequent Baptist movements tried to define themselves in contrast to the Continental Anabaptists.

In the seventeenth century the first group of English Baptists to appear were descended from John Smyth's congregation. They were later called General Baptists because they believed in a "general" atonement, that Christ had died for all people and not solely the elect. The similarity between their soteriology and that of the Dutch theologian Jacobus Arminius meant that they are sometimes referred to as Arminian Baptists. The second group of English Baptists emerged in the 1630s and are called Particular Baptists since they believed that Christ died only for the elect.

These first two groups make up the "main" or "older" English Baptist movements. In addition to being the oldest of the English Baptist movements, they also had the largest membership and the most direct influence on Baptist development. Their size, age and influence, however, does not mean that they were the only Baptists in seventeenth-century England. There were other groups, often closely connected with these two main movements. One such group that began to form congregations in the 1650s were the Seventh-Day Baptists. These Seventh-Day Baptists believed that the Bible commanded that Christians observe Saturday as the Sabbath. Some Seventh-Day Baptists were General and others were Particular. A few were not necessarily Baptist, or adopted Baptist views after beginning to observe the seventh day. In addition, this study includes attention to a group referred to in this book as the Independent Baptists. These were "mixed communion" congregations, churches made up of both people who did and did not accept believer's baptism. The presence of the these Independent Baptists forced the other Baptist movements to make a decision on the issue of open versus closed communion. Further on the periphery was another Baptist-related movement that emerged in the 1650s, the Fifth Monarchists, so called because they believed that the coming of the fifth monarchy of Christ was imminent. While many of the most visible spokesmen for the Fifth Monarchy movement were Independents (i.e. Congregationalists) and not Baptists, a large number of the supporters of the movement came from the General, Particular, Seventh-Day, and Independent Baptist movements. In addition to defining themselves in contrast to the larger society, these various Baptist movements also defined themselves in contrast to each other. The process of self-definition and identification, so crucial in the development of each Baptist group, was accelerated by the proximity of competing Baptist movements.

The second thread in the following pages is the Baptists' ideas about the end of the world, or their "collective eschatology."[1] The following presentation of the English Baptist movements begins with John Smyth's "further light" hermeneutic leading him to leave the country and, eventually, to baptize himself. It ends with Thomas Tillam's efforts to establish an apocalyptic colony in the Palatinate. As such examples demonstrate, different ideas about the apocalypse led Baptists in different directions.

Baptist eschatology will be specifically examined below, but there are two general characteristics in common among the various movements to be noted at the outset. While actions like those of Smyth or Tillam may appear odd, the eschatology upon which they were based would not have been as alien to seventeenth-century society as were the conclusions that these men drew from it. A sense of living in the final days and preparing for the establishment of God's Kingdom were prevalent in early modern England. What is notable about Baptist eschatology is its degree and direction.

The degree of millenarian enthusiasm varied among the Baptist movements. For groups like the Particular Baptists, it was generally high in the early 1640s and cooled in the 1650s. For other groups, such as the Fifth Monarchists and the Seventh-Day Baptists, millenarianism was taken to new heights in the 1650s, with some of

---

[1]While a precise distinction between terms like "apocalypticism," "millenarianism," and "eschatology," is slightly anachronistic, as contemporaries did not observe modern differentiations, a working definition for these terms can be given for clarity. The most general of these terms is "eschatology," from the Greek *eschatos* "last," meaning the doctrine of last things—particularly in relation to resurrection, the afterlife, human death, judgment, and the end of the world. In this book the term is used primarily in reference to beliefs concerning the "end of the world" and the total consummation of God's purpose, rather than the nature of life after death. "Apocalypticism," from the Greek *apokalypsis* "unveiling," also generally refers to beliefs about the end of the world, but denotes a greater emphasis on the sudden cataclysmic end of the world and the triumph of good over evil. Millenarianism, from the Latin words *mille* "thousand" and *annus* "year," means not only that the world will end, but that God's Kingdom will be established on earth and will last a thousand years (usually with Christ as the king) before God brings about the end in the final judgment. This doctrine is largely derived from Revelation 20. The same admonition concerning denominational labels applies to this terminology and throughout these terms are generally used to denote a strong sense of living in the final age.

the former advocating armed rebellion and many of the latter joining in Tillam's Palatinate migration.

Related to the degree of millenarian intensity was its direction. Some believed that their current society was leading towards the Kingdom of God, their millenarianism was directed towards society, meaning that their eschatology supported the status quo. Others thought that their society was corrupt and had to be replaced or reformed before the millennium, such thinking was directed against society. Early Baptist eschatology was largely directed against society, viewing society at large as ungodly and unregenerate. Society during the Interregnum accepted the Baptists to a greater extent and the Baptists sought peace with that society.

As a result, the direction of their eschatology changed, as some Baptists saw the government as either a force for the establishment of the Kingdom, or at least not a major hindrance. This was primarily true for the Particular Baptists, especially those influenced by the Londoner, William Kiffin. For Fifth Monarchists and Seventh-Day Baptists, however, this was not the case. They continued to see society as unreformed and "witnessed against the Beast," by criticizing it. The spectrum of degree and direction can at the one end be seen in the call for further Reformation—representing a critique of the status quo and an urgency to obey God, and on the other end, the effort to shed the title "Anabaptists," in order to be more accepted by society and achieve greater accommodation.

The concept of accommodation provides the final thread of the narrative. At the beginning of the twentieth century, the sociologist Ernst Troeltsch developed a typology of Christian religious phenomena that divided them into the two basic types of "church" and "sect." A "church-type" religious movement recognizes the society as it is, and rather than relinquishing its ability to influence society by withdrawing from it or risking a loss of status by directly challenging it, the church-type accepts the main elements of the status quo in order to retain a position of influence. Therefore it is built on compromise and claims of universality. For the church-type, the institution takes precedence over the individual in a highly organized, and therefore highly resilient, type of religion. The church-type "dominates the world and is therefore dominated by the world. . . . The essence of the Church is its objective institutional character. The individual is born into it, and through infant baptism he comes under its miraculous influence. . . . The Church means the eternal existence of the God-Man; it is the extension of the Incarnation."

The other type is the "sect," which stresses literal obedience to the Scripture, a rejection of compromise, and an indifference or opposition towards society in general and towards ecclesiastical order in particular. The individual takes priority over the institution, resulting in a low level of organization. "From the very beginning, therefore, they [the sects] are forced to organize themselves in small groups, and to renounce the idea of dominating the world." Sect-type groups claim to be a revival of the original message of Christianity, allowing for an intense and often radical movement, frequently characterized by a strong eschatological element directed against society.[2]

This typology has undergone numerous revisions since it first appeared in 1911, but sociologists continue to employ some variation because of its heuristic utility. While this study is not an exercise in sociology, one variation on the church-sect typology provides a useful way of conceptualizing the transformation that some of the Baptist movements underwent during the seventeenth century. Since the Baptist movements resembled sect-type groups throughout the period, it is necessary to view their transformation within the parameters of the sect-type. J. Milton Yinger developed a sub-typing of sect-type groups that placed them along a continuum, with the "aggressive" sect at one end and the "accepting" sect at the other, according to their relationship with society and government.[3] Where a movement

---

[2]Ernst Troeltsch, *The Social Teaching of the Christian Churches*, Trans. by Olive Wyon (New York: The Macmillan Company, 1931), vol. 1, 331, 336-338.

[3]J. Milton Yinger, *Religion and the Struggle for Power* (Durham: Duke University Press, 1946), 18-23. See also idem, *Religion Society and the Individual* (New York: Macmillan, 1957); William H. Swatos, Jr. *Into Denominationalism: The Anglican Metamorphosis* (Ellington, Connecticut: K & R Printers, Inc., 1979).

falls on this spectrum depends on its degree of tension with society.[4]
The aggressive sect opposes society and seeks to transform the world.
The accepting sect is still separate from society, but it is more
accommodating and, like the church-type, it seeks favor from the
world rather than striving to transform it. Though these categories do
not correspond to a historical reality, they are useful to keep in mind
as ideal types. The general trend that leads from baptists to Baptists
can be thought of as a movement from a more aggressive sect towards
a more accepting, or accommodating, sect.

This process of accommodation was facilitated by the development of an organization and clear theological and political leaders. As
these leaders sought greater peace with the world, the process of
accommodation accelerated. In general, mainstream Baptists moved
toward a position of lower tension with society; this was facilitated in
the middle decades of the century by the tolerant atmosphere of the
government. Even during these tolerant years, there were groups that
failed or refused to make their peace with the government. Those
groups who did not make peace with the world or develop an
organization and effective leaders—groups such as the Fifth Monarchists and Seventh-Day Baptists—failed to survive in England.

In bringing together these three threads, this approach aims to
provide a broader perspective on the development of the early
Baptists. The result is that a more holistic and less systematic picture
of the Baptists emerges. Furthermore, by re-integrating the religious
and political aspects of the Baptist movements, it can be seen that the
Baptists were capable of generating support, at various times, for both
the radical politics of the Levellers and the extreme millenarianism of
the Fifth Monarchists. On the other hand, Baptists were also able to

---

[4]Benton Johnson, "On Church And Sect," *American Sociological Review* 28 (1963): 539-
549. Johnson explains that "a Church is a religious group that accepts the social environment
in which it exists. A Sect is a religious group that rejects the social environment in which it
exists" (542). See also Armand L. Mauss and Philip Barlow, "Church, Sect, and Scripture:
The Protestant Bible and Mormon Sectarian Retrenchment," *Sociological Analysis* 52 (1991):
397-414. In this book, however, the words "church" and "sect" are not used in their
Troeltschian sense.

offer articulate defenses of the status quo and quell radical religious enthusiasts. While the Baptist story can be taken to begin around the start of the seventeenth century, it certainly does not end with the conclusion of this book near 1660. Instead the Baptist story had barely begun. The two generations that preceded the Restoration of the Monarchy in 1660 set the stage for future Baptist growth and definition. Such changes are beyond the scope of this book, for by the end of the seventeenth century the Baptist movements had differentiated themselves from one another and moved on to become denominations, each with their own history.

PART I

THE GENERAL BAPTISTS AND THE RETURN OF CHRIST

And he said unto them, Go ye into all the world, and preach the Gospel to every creature. He that shall believe and be baptized shall be saved; but he that will not believe shall be damned. . . . So after the Lord had spoken unto them, he was received into heaven, and sat at the right hand of God.
    —Mark 16:15-16, 19

Now for baptizing a man's self there is as good warrant, as for a man Churching himself: For two men singly are no Church, jointly they are a Church, & the both of them put a Church upon themselves, so may two men put baptism upon themselves . . . And as Abraham & Iohn Baptist, & all the Proselytes after Abrahams example, Exod. 12.48. did administer the Sacrament upon themselves: So may any man raised up after the Apostasy of Antichrist, in the recovering of the Church by baptism, administer it upon himself in communion with others.
    —John Smyth, *The Character of the Beast,* 1609

1

REFORMATION AND REVELATION

From the earliest time, Christian teachings regarding baptism have been mixed with thoughts of the last things. More than a generation had passed from the time Mark's Gospel recorded Jesus's commission to baptize believers until John of Patmos penned the "Amen" that closed the canon. Despite its late arrival, the Apocalypse, or the book of Revelation played a central role in the development of the message that a Mediterranean Jew had left behind. Revelation is the primary eschatological book of the New Testament and has greatly influenced the way Christians conceptualize the end of the world. Christian eschatology is in turn founded upon earlier Judaic writings. Of course, Revelation is not the only part of the New Testament containing teachings about the end, Mark 13 for example is another important source.[1] What Revelation does contain is the enigmatic teachings about the millennium, the thousand year rule of Christ and his saints: "And I saw thrones, and they sat on them, and judgement was committed to them," begins Revelation 20:4. The prophet at Patmos continues: "Then I saw the souls of those who had been beheaded for their witness to Jesus and for the word of God, who had not worshiped the Beast or his image, and had not received his mark on their foreheads or on their hands. And they lived and reigned with Christ for a thousand years." The remaining verses of the chapter describe the eschatological consum-

---

[1]The Christian apocalyptic tradition is based on earlier Jewish apocalyptic works like those in Daniel, Ezekiel, and Isaiah. Some extracanonical writings and books of the Apocrypha also contain strong apocalyptic elements, chapters 13-14 of 2 Esdras presents an example of this type of literature. Extracanonical writings such as the Jewish 1 & 2 Enoch, The Apocalypse of Abraham, The Apocalypse of Elijah, and the Christian Apocalypse of Paul, and the Shepherd of Hermas provide further examples of apocalyptic literature.

mation of God's plan with the binding, re-emergence, and final triumph over evil—the perfection of the Kingdom. The Kingdom of God became identified by many with the millennium of Revelation 20. Closely connected to the Kingdom was the idea of the church and Christ's future, present and past kingship.

John's Revelation both furthered and reflected the early Christians' urgent expectation of the completion of the Kingdom. They lived in a state of apocalyptic expectation that can now only vaguely be imagined. For the first generations of Christians, John's prophecies represented a literal prediction/promise of a future thousand year earthly rule of Christ and his saints. Harsh persecution of the small movement of Christians encouraged the belief that punishment would pour down on their oppressors. Denied the material fruits of the earth, despite a life of holiness, a thousand year rule and enjoyment of the kingdoms of the world must have consoled many minds of the ultimate justice of Christianity's cosmology. Like the Jewish apocalyptic literature that preceded it, Christian apocalyptic writings served as a comfort and a call for endurance amidst a desperate present with the promise of a joyful future. When Christians were revisited by persecution, this literature again provided them with solace.

While this view of the millennium and the Kingdom predominated for the first three centuries of Christianity, it was not an unrivaled interpretation. Among his many endeavors, Origen (185?-254?) began to reexamine the Apocalypse and speculate concerning the consummation. Instead of seeing the Kingdom as an earthly paradise flowing with milk and honey, Origen maintained that it was a heavenly Kingdom already established. He suggested that a better understanding of the Second Coming was not in terms of a literal reappearance, but rather as an unveiling within the believer's soul. "With much power, however, there comes daily, to the soul of every believer, the second advent."[2] While many of Origen's writings have

---

[2] From Origen's, *A Series of Commentary on Matthew*, quoted in L. E. Froom, *The Prophetic Faith of Our Fathers* (Washington DC: Review and Herald, 1950), vol. 1, 318. See also Arthur W. Wainwright, *Mysterious Apocalypse* (Nashville: Abingdon Press, 1993).

been lost, and his views on a number of issues are unclear, his theology reveals an innovative sophistication and maturity. He did not simply believe in a literal earthly rule.

By the fifth century, the Catholic Church had grown secure and was no longer plagued by persecutions or corresponding visions of apocalyptic judgment. In *The City of God*, Augustine (354-430) spiritualized the millennium, seeing it not as a literal future thousand years, but as the present time between Christ's first and second coming. Since he rejected a literal thousand years his position is often called amillennial. He also denied a correlation between most of the symbols of Revelation and literal historical figures, explaining instead that the Beast from the sea was the City of Man that opposed the City of God. As a result, his position can also be called ahistorical. For Augustine, the New Jerusalem and Christ's reign on earth were already present in the body of the church. He wrote:

> The second coming of the Savior which continually occurs in His Church, that is, in His members, in which he comes little by little, and piece by piece, since the whole Church is his body. . . . Therefore the Church even now is the kingdom of Christ, and the kingdom of Heaven. Accordingly, even now His saints reign with him.[3]

Satan was chained and limited with Christ's first coming, to be released for a spell at his return and then finally defeated. As for the timing, Augustine cited Jesus's own words, that it was not for humans to know. Augustine's interpretation turned Christian thought away from the second advent and back to the first. The millennium was

---

[3]Although Augustine is frequently credited with quieting millenarian enthusiasms, it is important to remember that in Augustine's eschatology there were six stages of history, "the later part of which" he believed was "now passing." Augustine, *The City of God*, in ed. P. Schaff et. al. *A Select Library of the Nicene and Post-Nicene Fathers* (New York: Scribner's, 1905-1917) vol. 2, 424, 427, 429; see also T. E. Mommsen, "St. Augustine and the Christian Idea of Progress: The Background of the City of God," *Journal of the History of Ideas* 12 (1951): 346-374.

Joachim challenged Augustine's view

placed in between. His interpretation eventually became orthodoxy. Those who followed in this tradition did not see Revelation as a way of interpreting the present, or as history of the church, nor did it predict a future earthly millennium. Augustine's ideas comprised the overwhelming orthodoxy for over seven centuries.

By the twelfth century, Joachim of Fiore (1145-1202) presented an interpretation of Revelation that challenged the Augustinian orthodoxy. Joachim saw Revelation as a description not only of the present and the future, but also of the past. In this interpretation there were three ages, each ruled by a corresponding member of the Trinity. The Age of the Father had passed with Jesus, who inaugurated the Age of the Son. Joachim believed that the Age of the Son was now ending and was to be replaced by the Age of the Spirit. This new Age of the Spirit, which he implied would begin before 1260, would see the end of the world. Thus, history was powerfully reintroduced into Christian eschatology, along with the idea of progressive revelation.

Additionally, Joachim did not resist the temptation to match symbols from Revelation with contemporary events. A consequence of Joachim's innovation was that the conception of a future millennium was revived. Another result was that interpreters building on Joachim began to see Revelation as not only prophecy but as history, with each symbol corresponding to an actual event either in the future, past, or present. The goal of the theologian and the historian were thus jointly employed in the task of cataloging those events that had occurred and speculating on those yet to come. The Beast again became a literal person or group of people. Perhaps a Jew from the tribe of Dan, or a powerful Muslim leader. Joachim's ideas did not immediately replace Augustine's interpretation, which continues in some circles even today. Different groups, however, were attracted to aspects of Joachim. The Waldensians were influenced by him and later the Oxford don, John Wycliff adopted his perspective on Revelation.

Jan Hus (1372?-1415) was influenced both by the historical interpretation of Revelation and by the writings of Wycliff. Hus even suggested that the pope might be the Antichrist or the parallel Beast of the Apocalypse, but he did so only in a metaphorical sense. The suggestion that the papacy was Antichrist had been present in earlier interpretations of Revelation. There had been the suggestion that the Antichrist might be an evil tyrant, a resurrected Roman Emperor, or an evil pope. As theologians began to re-adopt a historical explanation of Revelation and see it as a complete history of the church, many began to see the contemporary pope as Antichrist in an increasingly literal sense. Soon the idea of the papacy as an institution came under similar identification. The Waldensians, the Lollards, and later the Hussites, along with other groups that broke away from the Catholic Church increasingly synthesized the historical interpretation with the identification of the papacy with Antichrist. Therefore, while Joachim himself did not believe that the Beast of Revelation was the papacy, many who followed in his intellectual tradition did.

Jan Hus agreed to attend the Council of Constance under a guarantee of safe conduct so that his criticisms of the Catholic Church could be discussed. But the promise of safety was swiftly disregarded and he was seized as a heretic. When he was burnt at the stake, a series of Hussite rebellions erupted in Bohemia. Many of these Hussite movements had a fully revitalized millenarian perspective. One such group gathered on a hill that they renamed "Tabor," after the place where Jesus allegedly gave his eschatological teachings. These Taborites launched a program of radical religious reform and embraced an intensely apocalyptic creed. The Taborites explained their actions in eschatological terms, proclaiming that their innovations, such as lay preaching and strict obedience to the Bible, presented the final stages of the struggle against Antichrist. Movements such as the Taborites presented a mixture of active apocalypticism and revitalized prophecy. That is, while they sought to bring about the millennium, they were usually additionally inspired by prophets who claimed to be guided by the spirit of God.

The Taborites were an extreme example of millenarianism. Most of the Christians who held apocalyptic views during the Middle Ages never revolted. Instead, their eschatology helped them to understand their times. Events were compared to prophecies, biblical and otherwise, to help render the world intelligible. While devils and corresponding minions were responsible for daily inconveniences, Antichrist was seen as the moving force behind larger catastrophes, and where Antichrist was found, the Second Coming of Christ was expected to follow. The fall of Constantinople in 1453 to the Turks, for example, was seen as a clear sign that the end was approaching. Other major crises of Christendom were also explained in terms of the struggle between Christ and Antichrist. Given the late medieval tradition of correlating events with apocalyptic prophecies, it is understandable why Christendom's greatest crisis, the Reformation, was interpreted apocalyptically. By suggesting that the millennium had not fully begun with the resurrection of Christ, Joachim's work opened the door for later thinkers who would see their times as the beginning of the new and final age. As the centuries old ecclesiastical structure came under unprecedented attack and wars began to break out across Europe, many contemporaries saw their times as the final period in the battle between good and evil. With the onset of the Reformation, millenarian thinking was revived and reinforced. Newly reinvigorated, it regained a central position in the minds of most Christians.

The idea of *sola scriptura* and a priesthood of all believers had a profound impact on Christianity in general, and the later Baptist movements in particular. These concepts also further fueled Protestant apocalypticism. The Protestant emphasis on a return to the Scripture led to a massive effort on the part of individuals to understand the apocalyptic prophecies of the Bible. Martin Luther admitted that he found such sections of the Bible confusing. In his preface to the Book of Revelation in 1522, Luther confessed "My spirit cannot be sent into this book."[4] Despite his difficulty with the apocalyptic texts, eventually eschatological concerns came to affect much of Luther's thought. At the center of Luther's spiritual desire was an

---

[4]Cited in Kenneth A. Strand, ed., *Luther's "September Bible" In Facsimile* (Ann Arbor: Ann Arbor Publishers, 1972), preface to Revelation (pages unnumbered), lines 26-27.

eschatological excitement and longing for the consummation of the divine plan. By 1520, three years after the publication of his Ninety-Five Theses, Luther had concluded that the pope was Antichrist and that the Roman Catholic Church was the subtle agent of Satan, whose mission had always been to lead the people into slavery and idolatry. Since the whole papal structure was corrupt, it was no longer a matter of reforming the church; it had become an issue of rescuing the Word from the clutches of Antichrist. Once Christians began to see the Catholic Church as Babylon, they looked for the New Jerusalem outside of the traditional religious structures.[5]

While the identification of the papacy as the Beast began in some circles before the Reformation, the early years of the Reformation saw that association become one of the primary ways of interpreting Revelation. This was for two reasons. It provided a way of justifying and explaining an unprecedented break within a divine cosmology. In a related way, its forceful rhetoric and dualism meant that people either had to choose for or against the papacy, and not suggest moderations. Second, it helped Protestants resolve a major dilemma: If, as the Reformers had asserted, the Catholic Church had been so corrupt, why had God allowed it to persist for so long? The Catholic Church could point to centuries of tradition for its legitimation, but how were the Protestants to respond to the question of "where was your church before Luther?" A historical interpretation of Revelation provided the answer. As men like John Bale of England explained, there were two churches, a false church and a true church. Under this interpretation, the true church had existed since the time of Christ, but after a time it had been obscured by the forces of Antichrist. Its powerful re-emergence was evidence for Protestants that the struggle between Christ and Antichrist was nearly finished. Luther's eschatological expectancy, the degree to which he believed he lived near the end of time, was not fundamentally different from that of another contemporary, Thomas Müntzer. Müntzer was a radical reformer often in opposition to Luther. While they had numerous differences,

---

[5]Robin Barnes, *Prophecy and Gnosis* (Stanford: Stanford University Press, 1988), 36-52.

they both anticipated the consummation of the divine plan. They ultimately had a shared agenda in that they both wanted to bring about a purified church and Christ's Kingdom. However, the two men disagreed on the nature of that Kingdom. They agreed on the nature of the times, but they diverged over how to act accordingly. The question, then, was *apocalypse how?*[6]

This would be as much a question for the English Baptists as it was for the Continental Reformers. It was essentially a question of Kingdom building. Both agreed that the end was at hand, what then was to be done? Eschatological convictions, both for the early Baptists and for the early Reformers, led believers in different directions. It drove some towards radicalism and rejection of society, while it led others towards greater cooperation with the governors. Luther answered the question of *apocalypse how* by insisting that the papacy must be undone. He worked with princes and governors in the hope of reforming society by convincing the magistrates of the truth. Müntzer went beyond Luther in saying that the existing structures of authority had to be undone. Müntzer maintained that direct action had to be taken against the forces of the Beast. He gathered supporters and weapons, declared a community of goods in affirmation of the apostolic and rejection of the contemporary church. He believed that the magistrates were already too tainted by the Beast to play a role in the building of the Kingdom. Müntzer's willingness to bypass the magistrates and act independently of their authority in his pursuit of the millennium marks a distinction among the Reformers, and places Müntzer in the company of the "non-magisterial" Reformers. The English Baptists too would later be seen as in this tradition. Luther, however, desired to convert kings and have their national churches follow. In this way the whore of Babylon, the Beast, would be overthrown. Luther sided with the princes while Müntzer sided with the peasants, and for this Müntzer condemned Luther himself as the Beast. When the Peasants' War erupted, Luther denounced it while

---

[6]Barnes, *Prophecy and Gnosis*, 31.

Müntzer took to the field as a new Gideon. Müntzer, however, was soon captured and beheaded. His kingdom never arrived.

Although Müntzer never referred to himself as an Anabaptist, he was venerated by many of them. Anabaptists first appeared around the time of Müntzer's death and, like Müntzer, they opposed both Luther and the Roman Catholic Church. They believed that Luther had retained an improper mode of baptism, claiming that infant baptism was without biblical warrant. The Anabaptists sought to reject all that was not Christian and formed small communities of purity. The Anabaptists were not a single monolithic movement, but dozens of independent groups. Most of these groups were peaceful and composed of believers who were willing to respect authority as long as it did not conflict with their religious beliefs. The Anabaptists also hoped for a millennium, but were generally not violent and posed little immediate threat to their governors. But the Peasants' War had been proof that religious freedom caused anarchy, and the Anabaptists were ruthlessly persecuted. Some fled to England, hoping to practice their religion in peace, but found little relief. In an effort to understand such harsh treatment, many Anabaptists adopted an apocalyptic interpretation of events. Hans Hut saw these events as the final signs and predicted the millennium to occur within a few months. Others shared his expectation, but even so, most chose to suffer patiently and wait for the millennium.

Therefore, the Anabaptists in the German town of Münster were an anomaly. The infamous series of events at Münster began in 1534 when two Anabaptist evangelists arrived and touched off a contagion of religious fervor. In a matter of days they had re-baptized thousands of converts. When these two evangelists moved on, two more appeared. One of them was Jan Bockelson, also known as John of Leyden. The rapid increase in the number of Anabaptists frightened Münster's Lutherans and many of them abandoned the town, leaving the Anabaptists in the majority. A call was issued for neighboring Anabaptists to come to Münster since the world was to be destroyed before Easter, and Münster alone would be spared.

John of Leyden

Münster

A theocracy was established, and instead of killing the remaining Lutherans and Catholics, armed gangs ran through the town singing "get out, you godless ones, and never come back, you enemies of the Father." Others cried "repent and be baptized or else the wrath of God will overwhelm you." All the Lutherans and Catholics were expelled and their goods were seized. The next day the town was besieged by a mercenary army led by the local bishop. The presence of the mercenaries only confirmed the Anabaptists' belief that the end was near. Communal ownership of goods was established inside the town and polygamy was legalized. By the summer of 1534 John of Leyden had been anointed king of the New Jerusalem.[7]

In 1535, frustrated by their failure to take the town, the besiegers began to strangle the New Jerusalem by blockading it. Starvation soon followed. Driven to desperation, two men escaped from the town and informed the besiegers of weaknesses in Münster's fortifications. In June 1535, Münster was stormed and overrun in a fierce battle. When the fighting ended, the remaining Anabaptists accepted an offer of safe conduct and laid down their arms. The bishop ignored the amnesty and ordered them executed one by one. The process took several days.

The incident at Münster was burned into popular memory as an example of the fruits of religious enthusiasm. For a time, the events at Münster discredited millenarianism, and it was only with some hesitancy that theologians again began to examine the issue. The English Baptists also had to suffer for John of Leyden's excesses. They were frequently associated with the atrocities and dismissed as little better than fanatics. Münster cast a shadow over Baptist movements for more than a century.

---

[7]Norman Cohn, *The Pursuit of the Millennium*, rev. & exp. ed. (Oxford: Oxford University Press, 1970), 262; William Hughes, *Munster and Abingdon* (Oxford, 1657), 14-17.

2

KINGDOM AND KINGS:
THE BAPTISTS' APOCALYPTIC PERSPECTIVE

While Münster might have discredited the pursuit of the millennium, it certainly did not curb the Protestant appetite for the Apocalypse. This was particularly the case in England, where men like Bale and his friend John Foxe helped to blend the idea of the Apocalypse as key to history with England's own past. In addition to Bale's explanation of the two churches, Foxe's tale of Protestant martyrs endowed the people of early modern England with an apocalyptic instinct. Everywhere was Antichrist. Soon a quiet Oxford scholar named Joseph Mede produced an examination of Revelation which gave such endeavors credibility in intellectual circles. The result was that English culture had apocalypticism coming at it from both directions—down from the eschatology of the universities and up from the popular folk apocalypticism. While Baptist apocalypticism has been viewed as belonging more to this folk type, recent work suggests they were more in the mainstream than has been accepted. As years went on and they further developed and refined their eschatology, the Baptists' apocalyptic perspective came more in line with the respectable currents in English society.

While the apocalypticism that arrived in England in the wake of the Reformation and influenced the Baptists had been around for some time, many of its ideas were still forming. Men like Mede argued for "synchronizing" the prophecies of Revelation, that is having certain themes be represented various times in the book by different images. Others maintained that each image corresponded to a separate event. History, prophecy, and the millennium were all jumbled together. There was debate as to whether there was to be an earthly millennium or a heavenly spiritual one. The nature of Christ's presence was also uncertain—would it be physical or spiritual? Was the millennium in the future or was it present? Certain things were however generally agreed upon: the Antichrist was most often identified as the pope, his undoing was at hand, Christ's future Kingdom was near. Literal, spiritual, present, coming, were all debatable, but unlike in Augustine's theology, Englishmen in the hundred years after the Reformation looked forward to the Second Coming, whatever its form.

While such ideas were spread throughout society, they had particular currency among those who were persecuted and who opposed the status quo. For believers like the Baptists, it was easy to identify with the godly remnant of true believers described in the apocalyptic texts. Persecution became a proof of godliness. As one group of General Baptists declared concerning their maltreatment, "and truly in this we can rejoice . . . considering that God's people in no age did escape such soul aspersions: for who was accounted the troubler of Israel but Elisha?"[1] Additionally, apocalyptic language was useful because it could reveal at the same time that it concealed. The subtle use of images and reference to certain passages of Scripture avoided the detection of the censor, but emboldened the inducted faithful. The General Baptist Henry Denne prefaced his remarks in 1645 by saying, "I shall speak a riddle to some, to whom it is not given to know the mysteries of the kingdom, but you to whom it is given, will understand what I shall say."[2]

As unrest spread throughout English society on the eve of the Civil War, an eschatological framework was used to interpret the unprecedented times. Some of the bishops of the Church of England had begun to adopt a theology that appeared to many to be just short of Catholicism. The bishops, the court, and even the king himself

---

[1] A Declaration of Some of those People in or near London, called Anabaptists (London, 1660), 1.

[2] Henry Denne, Antichrist Unmasked in Two Treatises . . . the Second , The Man of Sinne Discovered (London, 1645), 11.

were suspected of being subject to Antichrist's influence. By 1642 military conflict between the king and Parliament had begun. The Puritan preachers who instructed the English Parliament explained the world in apocalyptic language intended to spur the Parliamentarians on to further Reformation. The preachers expressed two main objections. The first was to episcopacy, the second was to political tyranny. Both of these were seen as forms of oppression that were to be abolished in the New Jerusalem. Politics and religion were closely intermingled. The execution of the king's principal political and ecclesiastical advisors was a prelude for the final unthinkable act—the execution of the "man of blood," himself, King Charles.

The Baptists shared in the millenarian sentiment of the 1630s and '40s, but there were some distinctions. For Baptists in the period the overwhelming answer to the question of how to build the Kingdom was through church work. It was in his church of true gathered believers that Christ was supreme head and king. This was his primary Kingdom, his enclosed garden, even the New Jerusalem. Fellow believers were seen as his saints or the new Israelites.

Further aspects of the Baptist apocalyptic perspective were the concepts of "new light" and "further light." The new light was part of the new light that was dawning, revealing that which had been obscured by the shadow of the Beast. Further light was the idea that still more was to be revealed. The new light illuminated the past truths that were re-emerging and was therefore central to the double-movement inherent in Baptist eschatology. The double-movement was a move backwards in order to go forward. The true church that Christ had established had been lost, and for it to be found the Baptists had to search the Scriptures and recover all that had been obscured. As Hanserd Knollys said, "The Church at Rome was a true Church in the Apostles time . . . but afterwards that Church departed from the Faith, apostatized both in doctrine, and in discipline . . . and so became a false church, and a synagogue of Satan." All that had to be undone by going back to that true Apostolic church. This going back was required before they could move forward to the millennium. Knollys wrote: "You cannot come to Sion until you come out of

Babylon." At the same time, as the cloud of popery was dispersed, even broader horizons opened. The new light/further light elements of Baptist apocalypticism made it dynamic. It is also made it divisive. Light did not spread to all believers at a constant rate. As some saw themselves more enlightened than others, arguments occurred. The fierce fighting that broke out between Baptists over the observance of the smallest practices must be understood in its proper eschatological perspective. Issues such as the laying on of hands, revival of the position of messengers, or paying tithes were seen as essential questions that had to be resolved before the church could be rebuilt and the Kingdom established. These decisions were made even more urgent by the short amount of time remaining. The belief that the end was near and final judgment close at hand spurred the Baptists on. While it provided them with the strength to challenge traditional authority, it also led them frequently to fall out with one other. The idea was that the millennium was just around the corner. There were only a few stumbling blocks left, and once they were removed there would be no more barriers.[3]

Since there were so few stumbling blocks remaining, Baptists frequently associated such barriers with the last defenses of Antichrist. They saw Antichrist in two forms. In 1644 Christopher Blackwood published a text whose title amply illustrates this belief. His book was called, *The Storming of Antichrist in his two last and strongest Garrisons, of Compulsion of Conscience and Infant Baptism.* Religious persecution and infant baptism were the two surest signs of the Beast, but at the same time, they were also his two strongest fortresses. In the Baptists' battle against Antichrist, the most important practice to reinstate was believer's baptism. Baptists maintained that this was what the Bible called for and that the first Christians observed this practice, but when Antichrist crept into the church, it had been eclipsed. As John Smyth explained, believer's baptism was made "invisible when the church went into the wilderness." While this practice was obscured, the Beast introduced infant

---

[3]Hanserd Knollys, *Mystical Babylon Unveiled* (London, 1679), 20, 27.

baptism as "a stone to stumble at," in order to delay the return of Christ. Like later Baptists, Smyth also thought that the English Reformation had "in a very good degree razed the temple of Antichrist," but he insisted that "even so you should now proceed to undermine the very foundation, and to blow it wholly up at once, which is done by entertaining the baptism of Christ to be administered upon persons confessing . . . their faith." Smyth declared "the error of baptizing infants, [is] a chief point of antichristianism, and the very essence and constitution of the false church." Infant baptism was not only futile, it was Satanic. It directly thwarted the Kingdom, and for that reason Antichrist was willing to use all his deceptions to keep the practice in place. As a result of Antichrist's duplicity, many of the best reformed churches in Europe still maintained this Antichristian practice. Baptists like Thomas Collier preached and wrote identifying the Antichrist, the Beast, and the Devil as the sources of infant baptism. Antichrist and the Beast were conflated and seen as the sustaining force behind the Kingdom denying practice of infant baptism.[4]

The practice of believer's baptism brought Baptists into extremely high tension with society. It was a symbolic rejection of that society that Baptists found unacceptable. Before the Baptist challenge, infants had at birth been baptized and symbolically entered into the Christian community that was seen as comprehensive. By rebaptizing themselves, Baptists stressed that faith and piety were individual and existed between the believer and God. They signified their membership in the priesthood of all believers. To many observers the practice was seen as the final step on the road to anarchy. Tension only increased when the Baptists adopted the dramatic practice of baptism

---

[4]W. T. Whitley, ed., *The Works of John Smyth, Fellow of Christ's College, 1594-8* (Cambridge: Cambridge University Press, 1915), vol. 2, 565, 576, 659; Thomas Collier, *Certaine Queries: Or Points Now in Controvercy Examined* (London, 1645), 18-22; Thomas Edwards, *The Third Part of Gangraena* (London, 1646), 27. While Thomas Edwards, the famous heresiographer, applied high standards to his data collection and believed that the information that he was reporting was factually accurate, he tended at times to exaggerate. Thus his reports should be treated with some skepticism.

by immersion, or "dipping"—symbolizing their death to an old life and rebirth in a new. Many otherwise law abiding citizens were so threatened by the Baptists that they resorted to both symbolic and physical violence against them. When the General Baptist evangelist Samuel Oates visited Essex, he was dragged from his lodgings and thrown into a nearby river, thus "thoroughly dipping him," in a symbolic rejection of both his presence in the community and his practice of believer's baptism. Hanserd Knollys recalled being stoned out of his pulpit on account of his Baptist principles and the Particular Baptist confession complained that "men that know not God . . . if they can find the place of our meeting . . . get together in clusters to stone us, . . . looking upon us as a people holding such things, as that we are not worthy to live."[5]

Similar stories abound. Baptists logically viewed such treatment as the Beast's defenses as they attacked his final garrison. All those who persecuted the Baptists for their obedience to God were seen as supports for Babylon's walls, and the Baptists tried to inform them that if they did not leave that city, then they would be crushed as the walls collapsed beneath the weight of the New Jerusalem. The Beast then took on a dual nature—first was the baptism of infants, but second was persecution for religion. The idea developed that Christ had given temporal authority to the magistrate, but still retained all authority in matters of conscience. While it was true in the Old Testament that the magistrate was responsible for the morality of the people, under the Gospel, Christ alone was the king of the church. All who opposed his authority in this matter were usurpers, the Beast, Antichrist. Again, this perspective helped Baptists to see their persecution and alienation as a confirmation of their favor with God. As William Kiffin explained, "for the afflictions and persecutions that

---

[5]Edwards, *Third Part of Gangraena*, 105-106; Hanserd Knollys, *The Life and Death of that Old Disciple of Jesus Christ* (London, 1692), 22; William J. Lumpkin, ed., *Baptists Confessions of Faith* (Chicago: Judson Press, 1959 revised edition 1969), 155.

are imposed by the wicked men upon the Saints, causes them to see a spirit of glory reflecting upon them."[6]

Seeing the mark of the Beast in infant baptism and religious persecution was the central theme of Baptist apocalypticism. Most Baptists were millenarians, in that they believed that a future millennium was described in Revelation. They debated whether it was literal or spiritual, but they agreed that it was close at hand. They also believed that Revelation was a chart for church history. It described all of time from Christ's death to his Second Coming. In Peter Chamberlen's words, "the Revelation was of all that should happen from Christ to the end of the world."[7]

A final facet of Baptist eschatology was the idea of bearing witness against the Beast. While most Baptists did not believe in the revolutionary politics of Müntzer, they did believe that the Beast had to be combated. Soon Christ would return to judge all in their struggle against the Beast. As Knollys wrote, "Consider I beseech you, there is a world to come, and Christ will come, and everyone shall give account of himself to God." For their conscience to be clear, the saints were required to "witness" against the Beast. What this meant was often disputed. Some thought it meant to abandon all vestiges of popery, coming completely out of Babylon, and not resting until God's church had been recovered. Others believed it meant pointing out the Beast whenever his deceitful plans were recognized. Most Baptists agreed that witnessing against the Beast required some form of action. It called Christians to go beyond mere faith, to put faith into motion against the Beast.[8]

Some Baptists thought that witnessing against the Beast required radical, even military action. Such Baptists often supported the Fifth Monarchists, but most Baptists did not. There were three reasons that

---

[6]William Kiffin epistle to *Christian Mans Triall* by John Lilburne (London, 1641), sig. a1.

[7]C. Burrage, "A True and Short Declaration," *Transactions of the Baptist Historical Society* 2 (1911), 141.

[8]Hanserd Knollys, *The World that Now is and the World that is to Come* (London, 1681), part 2, 32.

the Baptists' millenarianism generally avoided the extremes of Fifth Monarchism and violent revolution. The first reason was that the Baptists wished to distinguish themselves from the Anabaptists of Münster. They wanted to prove to the world that they were not seditious but that they were capable of living peacefully within society as long as their religious principles were unmolested.

Second, Baptists' close focus on the Bible meant that they took seriously two scriptural injunctions in Romans 13:1-6 and Mark 13:32-33. The verses from Romans demanded Christian compliance to their governors.[9] These verses had been invoked by John Smyth as early as 1609, in his *Character of the Beast,* and were frequently employed subsequently by Baptist leaders as proof that God did not call them to active rebellion, but only to witness against the Beast. Additionally, the words of Jesus reported in Mark 13, that "of that day and hour knoweth no man . . . for you know not when the time is,"[10] restrained the Baptists from engaging in the perpetually disappointing practice of predicting the date of the end of the world, despite their belief in its imminence.

Finally, Baptist millenarianism was often restrained on account of their identification of the Beast as a mixed civil and ecclesiastical power. In other words, since the Baptists saw the Antichrist as attempting to hold both the sword of a governor and the sword of the prophet—that is both religious and civil power—they hesitated to do

---

[9]"Let every soul be subject unto the higher powers: for there is no power but God: and the powers that be, are ordained of God. Whosoever therefore resists the power, resists the ordinance of God: and they that resist, shall receive to themselves condemnation. For Magistrates are not to be feared for good workers, but for evil. Wilt thou then be without fear of the power? do well: so shalt thou have praise of the same. For he is the minister of God that for thy wealth, but if thou doe evil, fear: for he beareth not the sword for nought: for he is the minister of God to take vengeance on him that doeth evil. Wherefore you must be subject, not because of wrath only, but also for conscience sake. For this cause you pay also tribute: for they are Gods ministers, applying themselves for the same things." Romans 13:1-6 from *The Geneva Bible* (annotated New Testament, 1602 edition) ed., Gerald T. Sheppard (New York : Pilgrim Press, c. 1989).

[10]Mark 13:32-33 (Geneva, 1602). The gloss on the text reads "The latter day is not curiously to searched for, which the Father alone knoweth: but let us rather take heed, that it come not upon us unaware."

the same. Their advocacy for the separation of church and state meant that they did not aim to wrest political power from the Beast and take it upon themselves. What their millenarianism required was that Christ be free to be the king of his church.

Of course there were exceptions to such generalizations. As will be seen, some members of the Baptist movements did take radical action and many saw their war against King Charles in an apocalyptic light, where bloodshed was not only permitted but required. Still others came to see Oliver Cromwell as the Beast and advocated his violent overthrow. These conclusions were easily drawn in an age when politics and religion were inseparable. Such radicals, however, were pushed to the sideline, and partly as a result of their ideas the Baptists further restrained their witnessing, lest they be mistaken for Anabaptists. All these developments, however, were still far in the future when John Smyth's further light guided him into the events that were to result in the first congregation of English Baptists.

3

BAPTIST BEGINNINGS:
JOHN SMYTH AND THE GENERAL BAPTISTS

J ohn Smyth (1570-1612), one of the
first leaders of the Baptists, never intended to establish a new religious
movement. He only aimed to reestablish pure worship. For Smyth, the
completion of the Reformation was not an ideal concept, but an
immediate obligation. At first he hoped, like other Puritans, that this
could be done from within the Church of England. After leaving
Cambridge, Smyth began his public career with a lectureship in
Lincoln, but his rigorous mind and "factious" preaching created
controversy in the community and he was deprived of his post by
1602.[1] Undaunted, or perhaps embittered, Smyth's continual religious
questioning brought him four years later to Separatism. He abandoned the possibility of true reform within the confines of the Church
of England and he began to worship with a small group of like-minded
Christians. William Bradford recorded that "about a year" before
1607, a group around Smyth "joined themselves (by a covenant of the
Lord) into a church estate."[2] By autumn 1607 Smyth described
himself as "Pastor of the Church of Ganesburgh."[3]

Before his separation Smyth had appeared to be well within the
mainstream of Calvinist Puritanism. He believed in "the Lord's

---

[1] J. H. Shakespeare, *Baptist and Congregational Pioneers* (London: National Council of
Evangelical Free Churches, 1906), 129, quoted in Champlin Burrage, ed., *The Early English
Dissenters in the Light of Recent Research* (Cambridge: Cambridge University Press, 1912), vol.
1, 227.

[2] William Bradford, *Of Plymouth Plantation* notes and introduction by Samuel Eliot
Morison (New York: Alfred A. Knopf, 1959), 9-10.

[3] Smyth, *Works*, vol. 2, 331.

predestination," and "justification by faith only." He clearly rejected
Anabaptism, and subscribed to the view that "the magistrates should
cause all men to worship the true God." Furthermore, he denounced
religious toleration and he accepted the swearing of oaths.[4]

But Smyth's spiritual pilgrimage did not end with his separation.
Within a decade of losing his lectureship, Smyth went from being a
Puritan, to a Separatist, to a Baptist, to an Anabaptist. His rapid series
of religious transformations requires some explanation. Smyth himself
confessed that "it might be thought most strange, that a man should
often times change his religion, and it cannot be accounted a
commendable quality in any man to make many alterations and
changes in such weighty matters, as are the cases of conscience." The
explanation for these changes lies in Smyth's eschatological outlook.[5]

From his Puritan beginnings, Smyth adopted a "further light"
hermeneutic common among Puritans.[6] Woven into the Puritan
eschatological framework was the idea that the light of Christ's spirit
was beginning to dispel the Antichristian darkness that had envel-
oped the Bible. Smyth explained that "now Antichrist is perfectly
discovered and consumed . . . by the evidence of the truth, which is
the brightness of Christ's coming."[7] This outlook provided him with
a desire to find the truth and a radical willingness to abandon old
interpretations. If the eschatological context that Smyth inherited
from the Puritans is considered, then as Stephen Brachlow explains,
"the metaphoric character of Smyth's career is less surprising than it
is indicative of the centrifugal forces of radical Puritan thought that

---

[4]Smyth, *Works*, vol. 1, 66, 134, 140, 165-166.

[5]Smyth, *Works*, vol. 2, 564.

[6]B. R. White used the term "further light" in the context of Smyth's first forming of a
Separatist covenant and his indebtedness to previous Separatists. In the original members'
covenant statement— "as the Lord's free people, joined themselves (by a covenant of the
Lord) into a Church estate, in the fellowship of the Gospel, to walk in all his ways, made
known, or to be made known unto them (according to their best endeavours) whatsoever
it should cost them, the Lord assisting them"—White identified the phrase "or to be made
known unto them" as "what could be termed the 'further light clause,'"(B. R. White, *The
English Separatist Tradition*. Oxford: Oxford University Press, 1971, 123).

[7]Smyth, *Works*, vol. 1, 270.

sent many others like him ranging across the shifting terrain of the religious underworld in pre-Revolutionary England."[8] Because he believed that a new day was dawning, Smyth was constantly compelled to revise his faith. At the same time, his eschatology provided him with the courage to make bold moves in his effort to establish a pure church.

A further revision of his thought came when Smyth decided that his Separatist congregation had to leave England. Persecution had always plagued the Separatists, and Smyth's congregation was no exception. Smyth knew of the English congregations in Holland, in fact his former tutor at Cambridge, Francis Johnson, was the leader of a church there. There were a handful of other English churches in exile in the Low Countries and Smyth decided it was wise to try to establish his church there. Thomas Helwys, a lay member of the congregation, financed their departure. In 1607, Smyth began to shepherd his flock to Amsterdam, where the majority of the congregation arrived by mid-1608. Within a year, Smyth's constant self-revision led him to the shocking act of self-baptism. The issue of baptism had always been a difficult one in Separatist circles. Debate within Smyth's congregation and among other Separatist congregations on the issue ultimately led Smyth to the conclusion that baptism was not for infants and that "Antichristians converted are to be admitted to the true Church by baptism." Thus, Smyth's pursuit of the truth and his further light had brought him to the belief that baptism should only be for believers, and since infants could not believe, they should not be baptized.[9] Furthermore, Smyth maintained that the baptism of other churches was not valid, and so converts to the true church had to be rebaptized.[10] Smyth then sought a

---

[8]Stephen Brachlow, "John Smyth and The Ghost of Anabaptism" *Baptist Quarterly* 30 (1984): 297-298. Another informative discussion of the development of Smyth's thought can be found in J. R. Coggins's *John Smyth's Congregation: English Separatism, Mennonite Influence, and the Elect Nation* (Waterloo, Ontario: Herald Press, 1991), see also M. R. Watts, *The Dissenters* (Oxford: Oxford University Press, 1978), 41-50.

[9]Burrage, *Early English Dissenters*, vol. 1, 231-236.

[10]Smyth, *Works*, vol. 2, 574. Smyth insisted that this requirement of a rebaptism was not "Anabaptistical" (*Works*, vol. 2, 576). It is here that Smyth became a Baptist.

rebaptism for himself and his congregation. But Smyth believed that
the world had fallen into such a state of Antichristan apostasy that
there was not a true church into which he could be baptized.
However, since the spirit was pouring forth onto the earth, as it had
in the time of John the Baptist, the congregation had the authority to
baptize themselves. Smyth first baptized himself and then Helwys and
the two of them baptized the rest of the congregation.

Smyth's self-baptism stunned even the radical Separatists in
Holland, causing them to deride Smyth for his "inconstancy, and
unstable judgment and being so suddenly carried away with things."[11]
This swift denunciation pronounced upon Smyth and his congregation must have been difficult for them to bear. There had been
tension among the English congregations in Holland even before
Smyth's arrival, but his presence seemed to exacerbate matters. His
argumentativeness and confidence caused friction within this small
community of English men and women living in Holland. Now, with
Smyth's self-baptism, his congregation found themselves even more
isolated than they had been before.

It was perhaps this new isolation that soon led Smyth to be further
"carried away." Mysticism began to influence his thought and he now
viewed disputes over "carnal" ecclesiology as less important. He had
moved from a Puritanical Old Testament emphasis on an exacting
God, to a New Testament focus on a transcendental and spiritual
divine. Soon, he abandoned the idea of predestination and original
sin; thus becoming "general" in his soteriology. As this transformation
continued, Smyth renounced capital punishment, the swearing of
oaths, and office-holding. Smyth also came to the conclusion that
magistrates should not interfere with religion and that their authority
was solely temporal.

While these changes were occurring, Smyth had come into
contact with a group of Anabaptists who took the name of that part
of north-central Holland called Waterland. After the catastrophe in

---

[11]William Bradford, quoted in Keith L. Sprunger, *Dutch Puritanism* (Leiden: E. J. Brill,
1982), 81.

Münster, a former Catholic named Menno Simons, organized pacifist groups of Anabaptists who were later called Mennonites. These "Waterlanders" that Smyth met were one type of Mennonite. Upon examining their beliefs, Smyth concluded that they were a true church and in 1610 he applied for membership.[12]

Even though the Waterlanders were not eager to accept Smyth, he could not be dissuaded from his desire to join. Thomas Helwys also had strong objections to his leader's application, which to Helwys seemed like an effort to validate apostolic succession. He wrote to the Waterlanders discouraging Smyth's petition, explaining that "John Baptist being unbaptized preached the baptism of repentance and they that believed and confessed their sins he baptized. And whosoever shall now be stirred up by the same spirit . . . may according to John his example, wash them with water and who can forbid?" Smyth understood Helwys's fear that he was following Antichrist by supporting a succession of ministers. Smyth explained that he denied

> all succession except in truth, and I hold that we are not to violate the order of the primitive Church, except necessity urge a dispensation, and therefore it is not lawful for everyone

---

[12]When Smyth was first influenced by Mennonite thought is a subject of serious debate, particularly since many feel that its resolution will reveal whether the English Baptists have an English or a Continental origin. For a list of some of the major articles in this debate, see Stephen Brachlow, *The Communion of Saints* (Oxford: Oxford University Press, 1988), 150. The either/or approach to the search for General Baptist origins is not as useful as seeing the question in a both/and light, since both English Separatism and Continental Anabaptist thought were capable of generating the course that Smyth and his followers took. At all stages, Smyth's development resulted from the interaction between his own searching and larger theological developments. Since Smyth was a well educated man and was conversant with many important theological thinkers of his time, it is all but impossible to locate his influence definitively. However, the historical evidence seems to indicate that up to the time of his self-baptism, Smyth had very little contact with the Mennonites, especially since his later acceptance of the Waterlanders as a true church indicates his ignorance of their existence in 1608. Thus his baptism was more Separatist than Anabaptists. It is likely that significant interaction with the Mennonites began when Smyth's congregation rented space in the bakery of the Mennonite Jan Munter, sometime around 1609/10. Smyth's petition to join the Waterlanders demonstrates that his journey had led him to being more Anabaptist than Separatist.

that sees the truth to baptize, for then there might be as many churches as couples in the world, and none have anything to do with each other, which breaks the bond of love and brotherhood in churches.[13]

Helwys was not convinced. Believing that the succession of ministers was "Antichrist's chief hold," Helwys and about eight others left Smyth's congregation to form their own church. They did so, not because they did not want to be Anabaptists, but because they thought that they already were. Ironically, some commentators have seen Helwys's actions as a rejection of Anabaptism and the Mennonites. This is not the case. In fact Helwys had become more Anabaptist than Smyth, for while Helwys did not deny that the Waterlanders were a true church, he also passionately believed that the congregation that he and Smyth had baptized were a true church as well. Helwys urged the Waterlanders not to accept Smyth and his thirty-two followers because he thought that such an acceptance implicitly invalidated the gathered church re-established through the believer's baptism that Smyth had administered.[14]

In 1612 Helwys and his handful of remaining followers determined that it was more desirable to "lay down their lives in their own country for Christ and his truth" than to perish in exile. Once they had decided that they were prepared to give "their lives for that truth they profess, in their own" country, Helwys and his remnant returned to England that year. In August 1612, Smyth was overcome by consumption and died in Holland. After his intense spiritual journey, the last thing he shed was his "factious" spirit. He renounced all bickering about outward observance and finally resolved that such outward differences would not "cause me to refuse the brotherhood of any penitent and faithful Christian whatsoever." He had come to a resting place and on his deathbed he told his congregation that "if I live . . . I will walk with no other people but you all my days." After

---

[13]Burrage, *Early English Dissenters*, vol. 2, 185; Smyth, *Works*, vol. 2, 758.
[14]Burrage, *Early English Dissenters*, vol. 2, 185.

his death, his congregation finally merged with the Waterlanders in 1615. They were absorbed and disappeared. By 1616, Helwys himself was dead.[15]

Helwys and his companions knew that they would face persecution upon returning to England. It was a brave move for such a small and powerless group of believers. Their writing reveals that they had discussed it at length and were well aware of the consequences:

> And let no one think that we are altogether ignorant, what building, and warfare we take in hand, and that we have not sat down and in some measure thought and considered what the cost and danger may be. And also let none think that we are without sense and feeling of our own inability to begin, our weakness to endure to the end, the weight and danger of such a work: but in all these things we hope and wait for wisdom and strength, and help from the Lord.[16]

Their decision to return to England, rather than remain in safety and exile, influenced future dissenters to do the same. Helwys comforted his congregation, reassuring them that those who persecuted the true church were Antichrist. In his book, *The Mistery of Iniquity* (1612) Helwys explained that the hierarchy of most Protestant churches was actually the second Beast described in the Book of Revelation.[17] His criticism of episcopacy led to his abandonment of both the idea of a godly king and a universal Christendom. He

---

[15]Thomas Helwys, *A Short Declaration of the Mistery of Iniquity* (Amsterdam[?], 1612), 212, most of this work is concerned with the relevance of prophecy for the current times; Smyth, *Works*, 755; Burrage, *Early English Dissenters*, vol. 1, 249.

[16]Helwys, *Mistery of Iniquity*, 212

[17]A similar sentiment was expressed in a treatise signed on behalf of those "commonly (but most falsely) called Ana-Baptists." It explained that those "afflicting our bodies for conscience cause . . . are not God but . . . Antichrist." The bishops' use of censoring, imprisoning, and harassing the godly was proof that they wielded the instruments of Antichrist. The text was entitled *Persecution for Religion judg'd and Condemn'd: in a discourse between an Antichristian and a Christian* ([London] Printed 1615 and 1620, reprinted 1662), 50, 74. The text has been variously attributed to Thomas Helwys and John Murton, his successor. It expressed a sentiment with which they both would have agreed.

1612

became the first leader in England to demand complete religious liberty. He explained that

> the king is but an earthly king, and he hath no authority as a king but in earthly causes, and if the king's people be obedient and true subjects, obeying all human laws made by the king, our lord the king can require no more: for men's religion to God is betwixt God and themselves; the king shall not answer for it, neither may the king be judge between God and man. Let them be heretics, Turks, Jews or whatsoever, it appertains not to the earthly power to punish them in the least measure. This is made evident to our lord the king by scripture.

Helwys's cries for liberty went unheard and he was soon jailed. It is possible that he died in prison. Nevertheless, the General Baptists persevered.[18]

1615

By 1615 John Murton appears to have take over Helwys's role as leader of the General Baptists in England. Murton echoed Helwys's advocacy for freedom of worship by publishing *Persecution for Religion Judg'd and Condemn'd . . . that No Man Ought to be Persecuted for his Religion* (1615). By the time of Murton's death, sometime in the mid-

1620s

1620s, there were at least five General Baptist churches in England in communion with each other. While there were some differences among them, especially over christological questions, and some divisions and excommunications, the five churches laid a foundation for the General Baptist movement. In addition to occasional publications, such as *A Description of What God hath Predestined* (1620), glimpses of the General Baptist churches can be seen in their continued correspondence with the Waterlanders. The English General Baptist churches wrote to the Waterlanders for various

---

[18]Helwys, *Mistery of Iniquity*, 69, 212. There are only four known copies of *Mistery of Iniquity*. The copy in the Bodleian Library, Oxford, bears an inscription by Helwys dedicating the book to King James I and reminding him that "the king is a mortal man, and not a God" and "therefore hath no power over the immortal souls of his subjects." Helwys penned the inscription from "Spittlefeild neare London."

reasons. Their letters inquired about certain theological questions, such as strict Separatism and the nature of Christ. The letters also reveal the English General Baptists' desire to join in communion with the Waterlanders in Holland. Their attempts at union were frustrated by continued differences between the English General Baptists and the Waterlanders. A formal union was never able to occur.[19]

These letters to the Waterlanders reveal further information about the General Baptists during their decades of obscurity. They show that after the death of John Murton, another General Baptist leader was J. Toppe of the Tiverton congregation. C. Burrage notes that Toppe was likely the original organizer of the Tiverton congregation and that "though little is known about him, it seems that he became . . . a staunch millenarian." Toppe was involved in a dispute with another English Baptist over the nature of "Christ's monarchical and personal reign upon earth and over all the kingdoms of this world." Toppe foresaw a literal future reign of Christ on earth. He believed that "Christ shall reign over all the kingdoms of this world under the whole heavens during the time of the 1000 years . . . to begin after his second and next coming." His fellow Baptist opponent believed that Christ was the king of his church, which was the heavenly Kingdom of Revelation. This dispute reveals that even the earliest Baptists in England had differing interpretations of the Apocalypse.[20]

Aside from their publications, appearances in state papers, and their own correspondence with the Waterlanders, the General Baptists for a short time became almost invisible. Their correspondence with the Waterlanders demonstrate that they did not want to be cut off from fellowship with like-minded Christians, nevertheless

---

[19]For more on the earliest General Baptist churches before 1640, see W. T. Whitley, *A History of British Baptists* (London: The Kingsgate Press, 2nd (revised) ed. 1932), 45-58.

[20]Walter H. Burgess, "James Toppe and the Tiverton Anabaptists" *Transactions of the Baptist Historical Society* 3 (1913): 193-211, which makes use of Toppe's millenarian ms. in the Sloane Collection, ms. 63 ff. 36-57; Burrage, *Early English Dissenters*, vol. 1, 270-280, vol. 2, 222-257; cf. B. Evans, *Early English Baptists*, (London: J. Heaton & son, 1864), vol. 2, 21-44. See also [Whitley], "Salisbury and Tiverton about 1630," *Transactions of the Baptist Historical Society*, 3 (1912): 1-7.

they unwillingly became isolated and not until the Revolution offered the prospect for national regeneration did they clearly reemerge.

B. R. White speculates that "while there is no certain evidence that the . . . General Baptists persisted through the difficult years of the 1630s, it seems reasonable to believe that the Bell Alley congregation of the 1640s was in the direct succession of those who had returned with Thomas Helwys." The Bell Alley General Baptist congregation was to be at the center of General Baptist activity in the early 1640s. It was lively and always seemed to be bursting with energy and excitement. The heresiographer, Thomas Edwards, was fascinated by the Bell Alley congregation, and though his descriptions of their meetings were meant to denounce the General Baptists, his writings also inadvertently record how vivacious these early Baptists were.[21]

By the 1640s, the Bell Alley congregation came under the leadership of Thomas Lambe, possibly the most significant General Baptist leader after Helwys. For half a decade before coming to Bell Alley, Lambe was an itinerant evangelist, constantly harassed by the authorities and always in and out of jail. His rhetorical skills made him irresistible to the London crowds, where "yards full, especially young youths and wenches flock thither" to hear him. When he was not preaching to his own congregation, he often challenged other London ministers, even climbing into their pulpits to present his opinions. Lambe was eager to shake things up. His church gatherings were noisy and chaotic. Everyone was allowed to participate and often the congregation voted on who they wanted to hear preach. Lambe also eliminated many of the formalities of the society that he opposed.

---

[21]B. R. White, *English Baptists of the Seventeenth Century*, rev. & exp. ed. (London: Baptist Historical Society, 1996), 24 and idem, *English Separatist Tradition*, 165. A. C. Underwood, *A History of the English Baptists* (London: The Carey Kingsgate Press Limited, 1947; 3rd. impression 1961), maintains that this church lasted until the end of the nineteenth century (49).

The simplified marriage ceremony practiced at Bell Alley evidently did not even require a minister.[22]

Lambe's popularity did not tempt him to soften his General Baptist beliefs. Instead, he published a defense of them entitled *The Fountaine of Free Grace* (1645). The document is the most elaborate statement of General Baptist beliefs extant from this early period. Indeed, its intricate argument may have been written with the help of members of the Bell Alley congregation; it claimed to be by "the congregation of Christ in London constituted by baptisme upon the profession of faith, falsly called Anabaptists." The authors declared that the doctrine of general atonement was not only a fundamental Christian truth, but also that those who opposed it were the forces of evil.[23]

Lambe's success in planning and executing extensive evangelical missions demonstrates that the General Baptists had begun to develop a more sophisticated organization than the loose federation that held the five congregations of the 1620s together. The impetus for this organization stemmed from the General Baptists' missionary zeal, which was rooted in their apocalypticism. In 1644, the General Baptist Francis Cornwell published his *Vindication of the Royall Commission of King Jesus . . . Against the Antichristian Faction,* which revealed the connection between General Baptist evangelism and apocalypticism. By going out into the world and baptizing according to Christ's command, they were pushing back the Antichristian darkness that had covered England. This connection was further

---

[22]Thomas Edwards, *Gangraena: or a Catalogue and Discovery of many of the Errours.* 1st part 2nd Enlarged Edition (London, 1646), 124-127, passim; *The Anabaptists Catechisme* (London, 1645), 2-5, 10.

[23]Thomas Lambe?, *The Fountaine of Free Grace Opened . . . Providing the Foundation of Faith to Consist only in Gods Free Love, In giving Christ to Dye for the Sins of All, and objections to the Contrary Answered by the Congregation of Christ in London constituted by the baptisme upon the profession of faith, falsly called Anabaptists . . .* (London?, 1645), passim. Wing attributes the authorship of this text to John Saltmarsh. While this is a possibility, the fact that a "corrected and amended" edition appeared the year after Saltmarsh's death makes it unlikely. Cf. Murray Tolmie, *The Triumph of the Saints: The Separate Churches of London, 1616-1649* (Cambridge: Cambridge University Press, 1977), 212, Thomas Crosby, *A History of the English Baptists* (London: Printed for the author, 1738-1740), vol. 3, 56.

highlighted by the General Baptist Edward Barber in 1645 with his publication of *A true Discovery of the Ministry of the Gospell . . . according to that Royall Commission of King Jesus . . . whereby may be clearly Seen the Great Difference Between the Ministers or servants of the Churches of Jesus Christ and the Ministers or rather Masters of the churches of Antichrist.* Obeying the royal commission of King Jesus was a process of active witnessing and the most direct combat against one of the final stumbling blocks.[24]

Lambe's experience as an itinerant evangelist helped him to plan effective missionary campaigns for the 1640s and it was noted that "they send forth into several counties . . . from their churches in London, . . . several emissaries members of their churches, to preach and spread their errors, to dip, to gather and settle churches." According to Thomas Edwards, the General Baptists even developed a form of staged disputations in order to win people away from the errors of Antichrist. Their general soteriology meant that the General Baptists would have few theological allies among the other sects. This generalism isolated them and placed them in a position of high tension with society. In addition to their "Arminianism," their practice of believer's baptism was found to be equally horrifying. Finally, their intense biblicism and belief that the Bible could be interpreted by each member of the congregation was hard for contemporaries to comprehend as more than sacrilege and anarchy.[25]

---

[24]Francis Cornwell, *The Vindication of the Royall Commission of King Jesus . . . Against the Antichristian Faction . . . that Enacted by a Decree, that the Baptisme of the Infants of Beleevers, Should Succeed Circumsion . . . Which Doth . . . Oppose the Commission, Granted by King Jesus* (London?, 1644), passim. Cornwell published an interesting work entitled *King Jesus is the Beleevers Prince, Priest, and Law-Giver . . . or, The Loyal Spouse of Christ hath no head, Nor Husband, But Royall King Jesus* (London, 1645). This work drew heavily from Foxe's "Book of Martyrs" and reveals both the General Baptist's familiarity with this work, and the way in which it shaped their apocalyptic perspective. Edward Barber, *A true Discovery of the Ministry of the Gospell . . . according to that Royall Commission of King Jesus . . . whereby may be clearly Seen the Great Difference Between the Ministers or servants of the Churches of Jesus Christ and the Ministers or rather Masters of the churches of Antichrist* (London, 1645), passim.

[25]Edwards, *Gangraena* (1st part, 2nd ed.), 65-67. See also Ruth Butterfield, "The Royal Commission of King Jesus: General Baptist Expansion and Growth 1640-1660," *Baptist Quarterly* 35 (1993): 56-81.

Numerous radicals associated with Lambe's Bell Alley congregation and many of the future leaders of the General Baptists were
baptized by Lambe himself. Samuel Oates, who believed that "Antichrist's way is first to baptize, then to believe and preach," was
baptized by Lambe and closely connected to the congregation. During
his harried time in Essex, Oates "had preached against the assess-
ments of Parliament, and the taxes laid upon the people, teaching
them, that the Saints were a free people and should do what they did
voluntarily, and not be compelled, " except by the laws of Christ. He
reportedly prayed in the public meetings that "the Parliament might
not . . . meddle with making laws for the Saints, which Jesus Christ
was to do alone." When authorities arrived to break up his meeting,
the congregation jeered at them and told them to get back to "their
steeple house, to hear their popish priests, their Baal's priests." Oates
was frequently called before the authorities and was in trouble not
only for his General Baptist beliefs, but also on account of his deep
involvement with the Levellers. Like Lambe and other members of
the Bell Alley church, Samuel Oates was a vital part of the Leveller
movement.[26]

While the missionary efforts of the General Baptists in the 1640s
were successful to an extent that John Smyth and Thomas Helwys
could not have imagined, discord soon emerged among the builders
of Zion. The General Baptists' lack of a hierarchy and emphasis on
the individual's ability to interpret Scripture meant that divisions
would almost inevitably occur. The most troublesome issues were
frequently associated with "recovering" elements of the true church
out of Scripture, which had been obscured by Antichrist. The
millenarian Francis Cornwell raised just such an issue in Lambe's
congregation in 1645. Cornwell suggested that the laying on of hands
was a rite meant for each member of a baptized church. Previously,
this rite had been reserved for ordained elders of a congregation. A

1645

---

[26]Edwards, *The First and Second Part of Gangraena*, third edition (London, 1646), 106;
idem, *Gangraena* (1st part 2nd ed.), 220 (misnumbered 120); idem, *The Second Part of
Gangraena* (London, 1646), 146-148.

minority in Lambe's congregation decided that the Bible in fact required the laying on of hands for all baptized believers along with their baptism. Lambe disagreed and he was opposed by a physician named John Griffith. Unable to find a resolution for this difference, Griffith and a small group of followers separated from Lambe's church to form their own in Dunning's Alley. Griffith soon emerged as a Baptist leader of almost comparable stature to Lambe, and as the laying on of hands controversy spread among General Baptists, Griffith's church was often looked to for leadership among those adopting the practice. By 1654, Griffith was instrumental in bringing forth a confession of faith that declared that "God gives his Spirit to believers dipped through the prayer of faith and laying on of hands."[27]

Even before Griffith had decided that the laying on of hands was at the foundation of a true church, and that true Christians were obligated to separate from those who did not hold the practice, the contagion of the laying on of hands controversy had already spread to Edward Barber's congregation. Barber was another of the leading General Baptists of London, who by the mid-1640s had a considerable congregation that met in a large house in Bishopsgate. He described himself as a "freeman of England; citizen and merchant-taylor." He was a strong opponent of infant baptism and tithes from the start of the 1640s. Later, he explained that all those who paid tithes denied in doing so that Christ was to return "in the flesh." His views had already landed him in prison as early as 1641. Echoing Helwys's belief that "no man out [ought] to be forced in matter of religion," Barber published that year a "humble petition" to the king and Parliament on behalf "of many of his Majesty's loyal and faithful subjects, some of which having been miserably persecuted by the prelates and their adherents, by all rigorous courses, for their consciences, practicing nothing but what was instituted by the Lord Jesus Christ . . . and

---

[27]Henry Danvers, *A Treatise of Laying on of Hands, with the History thereof, both from Scripture and Antiquity. Wherein an account is Given how it Hath been practised in all ages since Christ* . . . (London, 1674), 58, passim; Thomas Lover, *The True Gospel-Faith Witnessed by the Prophets and Apostles, and Collected into Thirty Articles* (London, 1654), sig.a.1; Lumpkin, *Confessions*, Article XII, 193.

practiced by the primitive Christians." Like Helwys, Barber's petition received little attention. Nevertheless, the new more tolerant atmosphere of the 1640s meant that Barber was not deterred from continuing to publish his beliefs. In 1642 he published a small tract in defense of believer's baptism showing that he thought that it should be done by "dipping," i.e. by immersion. He also explained that believer's baptism brought Christians into "union with the whole body of God." Most pressing was that the Bible itself demanded that baptism be for believers only. This ancient obscured practice now had to be revived in preparation for Christ.[28]

Barber said that he was a man who loved and longed for the "appearing of King Jesus," and his insistence on going back to ancient biblical practices was based on his belief that such going back into the past would lead to the future Kingdom of Christ. This line of thinking led to Barber's position on reviving the church position of "apostle or messenger," since that position, established by Jesus, had "not ceased." These messengers were to obey the royal commission of King Jesus and go forth to the ends of the world baptizing. They were also to remember that they represented the "very presence and person of Jesus Christ." Therefore, it is easy to see how the same line of thinking that led Barber to defend believer's baptism and revive the apostolic position of messengers also led him to insist that the laying on of hands was necessary for church membership. The laying on of hands controversy was to prove a plague on the General Baptists, as it divided the congregations.[29]

---

[28]Edward Barber, *An Answer to the Essex Watchmens watchword* (London, 1649); idem, *The Storming and Totall Routing of Tythes . . .* (London, 1651); idem, *To the Kings Most Excellent Maiesty, and the Honourable Court of Parliament* (London, 1641), 1; idem, *A Small Treatise of Baptisme, or Dipping. Wherein is cleerly shewed that the Lord Christ Ordained dipping for those only that Professe Repentance and Faith* (London, 1642), 1, 10-13; Richard Greaves and Robert Zeller, eds., *Biographical Dictionary of British Radicals* (Brighton, Susses: Harvester Press, 1982-1984). For references to both the *Dictionary of National Biography* and the *Biographical Dictionary of British Radicals*, the reader should assume the entry for the relevant individual unless page numbers are indicated.

[29]Edward Barber, *Certaine Queries, Propounded to the Churches of Christ* (London, 1650?), title-page, passim; idem, *A true Discovery*, 1-15.

The thinking behind this controversy is demonstrated by Barber, whose eschatology insisted that he make no compromises in his efforts to recover the primitive church. Additionally, the lack of a General Baptist hierarchy to resolve doctrinal disputes and the ability of individuals to interpret Scripture for themselves meant that controversy often had to be settled by divisions with members voting with their feet. The laying on of hands controversy illustrates the way in which enthusiasm caused divisions, even among brethren. It also demonstrates the way in which the General Baptists were defining themselves. This controversy caused bitterness among the General Baptist churches, but it did not debilitate the movement. While such divisions were frequent and to be expected among fervent believers, the 1640s and 1650s still proved to be a period of unprecedented growth for the General Baptists.

Years before the laying on of hands controversy came to divide Lambe from some of the congregations he had helped to plant, Lambe had baptized another future Baptist leader, Henry Denne. Denne frequently associated with religious and political radicals, and in addition to becoming a Baptist leader, he was also a leader among the Levellers. Denne had long been of a dissenting opinion, and he used the opportunity provided by the differences between the king and Parliament in the early 1640s to express his radical beliefs. He preached in several districts and his open opposition to tithes was noted. He was evidently a brilliant preacher and his evangelism won many to the General Baptist cause. Thomas Edwards, not often inclined to report compliments, noted that one "Mr. Disborough saith of him [Denne], he is the ablest man in England for prayer, expounding and preaching."[30]

Denne was also instrumental in the establishment of the well-known Baptist church at Fenstation, among other important churches. Denne reassured these fledgling congregations that their persecutors were the forces of Antichrist, who would shortly be defeated. Edwards commented that, "This Denne hath some kind of

---

[30]Edwards, *Gangraena* (1st part, 2d ed.), 109.

strains in his Preaching, which affect and take the people much; as for instance, he will say thus, 'O Lord Christ, if thou wert now upon earth, and did reveal the Gospel to men, they would call you Anabaptist, Antinomian, Independent, who now call us so'."

He suffered for his beliefs and was frequently taken into custody. Once when he was apprehended, the authorities feared that Denne's popularity would spark an uprising. On another occasion, when arrested in the mid-1640s, Denne was given the choice of prison or military service. He chose the latter and played an influential role at the Putney debates of 1647, where he called for the trial of the king and a new form of constitutional government.[31]

Like most Baptists who published on millenarian themes, Denne was a former clergyman who had been educated at Cambridge. Before he joined the army, Denne published a text revealing that the basic apocalyptic perspective of the General Baptists had changed little since Helwys's return to England. In 1645 Denne published *Antichrist Unmasked in Two Treatises: The First, An Answer unto two Paedobaptists, . . . The Second, The Man of Sin Discovered: Whom the Lord Shall Destroy with the brightnesse of his Coming.* Denne believed that Jesus' promise was finally being fulfilled and that "every plant, which my heavenly Father hath not planted, shall be rooted up." Denne saw himself as an instrument in that uprooting. He recognized that he had to take an active part in the transformation of society that was occurring around him.

Denne devoted the first half of his text to uprooting the arguments in defense of infant baptism recently published by Stephen Marshall and Daniel Featley. Marshall was a member of the Assembly of Divines and a tremendously popular preacher. His arguments against the Baptists were seen as a forceful and balanced assault on

---

[31]Edward B. Underhill, *Records of the Churches of Christ, gathered at Fenstation, Warboys, and Hexham, 1644-1720* (London: Hanserd Knollys Society, 1854). Edwards, *Gangraena*, 1st part 2nd ed., 108-109; idem, *The Third Part of Gangraena*, 87; Benjamin Stinton, *An Account of Some of the Most Eminent & Leading Men Among the English Antipadobaptists*. ms. Angus Library, 36 G.A. e.10, 23-24; W. T. Whitley, "Henry Denne," *Baptist Quarterly* 11(1942): 124.

their practice of believer's baptism. Although few of his arguments were new, the publication of such ideas by a leading Presbyterian minister was seen as a serious challenge to the Baptist cause. Aside from Marshall's attack, another member of the Assembly of Divines, Daniel Featley, also produced a work aimed at thoroughly discrediting the Baptists. Featley's sensational text, *The dippers dipt. Or, The Anabaptists duck'd and plung'd over head and eares* (1645) had provided a series of arguments justifying infant baptism. Denne's realization that "the whole strength" of the Featley's book existed "in ten arguments," confirmed his belief that Featley was the mouthpiece for the ten-horned Beast. The eschatology underlying Denne's thinking—his apocalyptic interpretation of history, his "further light" hermeneutic and the importance of the apocalyptic imagery for his world view—were all revealed in the first part of his discussion.[32]

In the second part, Denne explained that he was involved "in this spiritual warfare" in which the forces of "the man of sin" were engaged in a battle with the true followers of Christ. He had long awaited "the approach of the Son of righteousness" and wondered "why stay the wheels of his chariot so long, and why is he so long in coming?" The answer was that before the full dawning of "the day of Christ, the man of sin must be revealed." Denne explained that the man of sin could be recognized by two predominant characteristics, the identification of which would help speed the return of Christ.[33]

The first was false teachings about baptism. Denne expressed his astonishment that so many false teachings concerning the true mode of baptism should still abound in England. "That such things as these should come from Rome, that the hot climate of Africa should breed snakes and serpents is no wonder: But who could have thought to have found such in England? . . . and yet this is too true." The very ministers of the nation elected by God to complete the Reformation

---

[32]Henry Denne, *Antichrist Unmasked . . .The Man of Sinne Discovered* (London, 1645), sig. a1-a2, passim.

[33]Denne, *Man of Sinne*, 2.

were in fact part of "that mystical body of iniquity, which opposes Jesus Christ." For

> we are deceived within ourselves, if we look for Antichrist, to come like the heathen Bacchus, staggering up and down in the streets, wallowing in his vomit; we are deceived, if we look for Antichrist, among the lewd sons of Belial, roaring in the taverns. No, we shall find him in the Temple, sooner find him in the . . . pulpits of England![34]

The second important "note of a false Church is persecution." "The false Church of Antichrist, the man of sin, the red dragon" is resolved to "convert all men (Mahomet like) with guns, and pistols, with swords, and staves, with fire, and fagot, with bonds, and imprisonment." All punishment for heresy should be left to God and men should obey "the command of [their] Lord, and Savior. 'Let them alone' Matth. 15.14." Denne granted that "the magistrate may punish offenders, against peace and liberty we grant, but that he should compel their conscience to be of this or that judgment in religion we cannot see." Like Helwys, Denne believed that liberty should be given to all in the belief that "Jesus Christ hath died for all men, Turks, Pagans," as well as Christians.[35]

Denne's writings demonstrate that thirty years after Helwys's death, the General Baptists still understood baptism and their plea for religious liberty in an apocalyptic context. They were fighting against the forces of Antichrist in an effort to prepare the way for the return of Christ. Of course, the General Baptists had changed in many ways. They had gained large numbers of new converts and had developed a proto-organization and an effective style of evangelism. Competent leaders had emerged and led various congregations.

The General Baptists were also taking part in the political activities of the 1640s—assisting the Levellers, joining the army and

---

[34] Denne, *Man of Sinne*, 15-17, 27.
[35] Denne, *Man of Sinne*, 20; Edwards, *Gangraena*, (1st part 2nd ed.), 109.

petitioning Parliament. Additionally, they capitalized on the collapse of censorship and published numerous texts, which helped to define their doctrines, both for the public and for themselves.

Like the Particular Baptists, the middle years of the seventeenth century marked the beginning of the General Baptists' transformation. From one small group under Helwys, to five isolated churches in the 1620s, the General Baptists had suddenly become a major movement with thousands of followers. With these changes came tension, even among the brethren, as seen in controversies such as the laying on of hands. These growing pains were an integral part of the process of self-definition that would characterize the General Baptists for the rest of the century.

PART II

PARTICULAR BAPTISTS IN BABYLON

For all nations have drunken of the wine of the wrath of her fornication, and the Kings of the earth have committed fornication with her, and the merchants of the earth are waxed rich of the abundance of her pleasures. And I heard another voice from heaven say, Go out of her, my people, that yee be not partakers of her sinnes, and yee receive not her plagues.
—Revelation 18:3-4

Thy Kingdom come, Thy will be done
On Earth as it is in Heaven
—Matthew 6:10

4

KING JESUS:
PARTICULAR BAPTISTS AND
LONDON'S GATHERED CHURCHES

T he Calvinist counterparts to the
General Baptists first appeared in the 1630s as a development within
London semi-Separatism. While they lacked the General Baptists'
association with the Continental Anabaptists, their origins were
equally steeped in eschatological enthusiasm. The most direct
expression of that enthusiasm was the gathering of churches. The
calling together of an independent congregation of saints was
simultaneously a sign and a condition for the return of Christ. John
Wilson explains that the gathering of churches in this period "must
be understood fundamentally as specific anticipation of a broader
reign of Christ."[1] By the 1640s, General Baptists like Francis Cornwell
would see their actions and beliefs as mandated and validated by
"King Jesus."[2] Years later Hanserd Knollys explained the appearance
of congregational churches as directly prophesied in the eleventh
chapter of Revelation. The single golden candlestick was "the
national church of the Jews," but the two golden candlesticks, the
seven candlesticks and the seven churches of Revelation "were a
representation of the true visible constituted churches of God in the

---

[1]John Wilson, *Pulpit in Parliament* (Princeton: Princeton University Press, 1969), 229.
[2]Francis Cornwell, *The Vindication of the Royall Commission of King Jesus . . . Against the
Antichristian Faction of Pope Innocensius the Third, and all His Favorites; that Enacted a Decree,
that the Baptisme of the Infants of Beleevers, Should Succeed Circumsion . . . which doth
Universally Oppose the Commission, Granted by King Jesus* (London, 1643).

latter-days . . . viz. congregational churches."[3] These ideas were already visible at the beginning of the seventeenth century in various Separatist groups. While there were several such groups, the one that formed around the Puritan minister Henry Jacob is particularly central to the Baptists' story. From this small church grew a number of other churches, from which the first Particular Baptists eventually emerged.[4]

Unlike the congregations of Smyth and Helwys, Jacob's congregation did not entirely repudiate the Church of England as a false church. In this way, Jacob was not a Separatist. Jacob had always shunned Separatism. Not only did he not want to give up hope in the Church of England, but he also did not want to condemn good Christians who unwittingly followed popery. Thus, his congregation existed in the limbo of "semi-Separatism," independent but not against the Church of England. Jacob desired to avoid the name of "Brownist" and "Barrowists," not only because of their negative connotations, but also because they were not accurate terms for his belief. Instead, he sought a middle way. As he wrote in 1605, Jacob was willing to remain in "brotherly communion" with the Church of England, even though he believed that the national church did not constitute a true church. Jacob's middle way did not however prevent persecution and he soon left for the Low Countries.[5]

---

[3]Hanserd Knollys, An Exposition of the Eleventh Chapter of Revelation: Wherein All Those Things therein Revealed, which must shortly come to pass, are Explained (London, 1679), 14-15.

[4]The evidence for the earliest days of the Jacob-Lathrop-Jessey congregation is primarily reconstructed from three documents that were assembled and transcribed by Benjamin Stinton at the beginning of the eighteenth century, now in the possession of Angus Library, Regent's Park College, Oxford under the title "A Repository of Divers Historical Matters relating to the English Antipaedobaptists" (Angus F.P.C.c8). These documents were made generally available by W. T. Whitley in Transactions of the Baptist Historical Society 1 (1908-9): 203-245. The relevant documents are traditionally referred to as the "Knollys," "Kiffin," and "Jessey" memoranda, not because of their authors, but because of their probable owners in the seventeenth century. The Jessey and Kiffin Memoranda can also be found in Burrage, Early English Dissenters, vol. 2, 292-305. Burrage's transcription is largely followed in the following discussion.

[5]Burrage, Early English Dissenters, vol. 1, 286, vol. 2, 146-166; Geoffrey Nuttall, Visible Saints (Oxford: Blackwell, 1957), 10; Watts, Dissenters, 50-52.

Murray Tolmie explains that around 1610 "Jacob began to emphasise the kingly office of Christ as the immediate head of each individual congregation. The rule of King Jesus over a worldly kingdom of the saints gathered in their churches was one of the most powerful conceptions of the early Separatists." Jacob had been aware of this idea, but he began to see it in a new way and by the end of the year he realized that "the kingly office of Christ could serve to liberate the gathered church from its subordination to the magistrate's consent for its very existence." In this way, the gathered church did not directly deny the authority of the magistrate over the church, but placed Jesus at the head of each gathered congregation. It was clear to Jacob that only the gathered church was a true visible church on earth. Such a church possessed the authority to dispense all divine ordinances. By 1616 Jacob had decided that he must obey Christ rather than man. He was now compelled to establish the Kingdom of Christ upon earth as it had been in Gospel times. He wrote:

> this free congregation . . . is the kingdom of Christ upon earth now [as] in the time of the Gospel. And our savior commands all Christians first to seek the kingdom of God, and his righteousness, and so all other things shall be ministered unto us. Therefore all Christians stand bound to seek his free congregation and to enjoy it, yea first, and before all other things. Otherwise they both break Christ's commandment, and also do shut out themselves from being subjects in his visible kingdom here upon earth.

The "essential order in the Gospel" for the "visible churches of Christ" upon earth consisted of a gathered church "meeting in private for the exercise of our religion."[6]

---

[6]Tolmie, *Triumph*, 9; Henry Jacob, *A Defence of the Churches and Ministry of Englande* (Middelburg, 1599); idem, *A Collection of Sundry Matters* (Amsterdam, 1616), sig. a6v; idem, *A Confession and Protestation of the Faith of Certaine Christians in England* (Amsterdam, 1616), sig. a3 and the 3rd and 8th pages of the attached petition. Springer, *Dutch Puritanism*, passim; Watts, *Dissenters*, 50-55; Burrage, *Early English dissenters*, vol. 2, 292-296.

After printing these thoughts in Middelburg in 1616, Jacob returned to London to gather a congregation and formed a visible church. The "Jessey-Memorandum" provides a brief account of the early years that led up to this moment:

> Of Mr. Jacob, the chief beginner of this Church and his Works . . . Henry Jacob . . . having with others, often and many ways, sought for Reformation, and showed the necessity thereof in regard to the Church of England's so far remoteness from the Apostolical Churches . . . [did request in 1609 that the King grant] permission to enjoy the Government of Christ in lieu of human Institutions and [for] abolishing that of the Antichristian Prelacy . . . [in 1616 the church] was gathered . . . hereupon the said Henry Jacob with . . . divers other well informed Saints having appointed a day to seek the face of the Lord in fasting and prayer, wherein that particular of their union together as a Church was mainly commended to the Lord. In the ending of the day they were united. Thus, those who minded this present union and so joining together joined both hands each with [an]other Brother and stood ringwise. Their intent being declared, H. Jacob and each of the rest made some confession or profession of their faith and repentance. . . . Then they covenanted together to walk in all of Gods ways as he had revealed or should make known to them. . . . After this Henry Jacob was chosen and ordained pastor to that church and many saints were joined to him.

But such a harmonious beginning was not to last. As it was with the General Baptists, Jacob's congregation suffered from differences amongst the believers. The "Jessey Memorandum" records that "in the time of his service, much trouble attended that State and people, within and without," perhaps referring to tensions within and outside the congregation. What eventually happened to Jacob is not certain. The "Jessey Memorandum" records that "about eight years H. Jacob was pastor of the said church and when upon his opportunity to go to

Virginia, to which he had been engaged before by their consent, he was remitted from his said office, and dismissed [by the] Congregation to go thither, wherein after [blank] years he ended his days." Jacob evidently left the Old World in the hopes of establishing a true church in the new, and died by 1624.[7]

The group that Jacob left behind "remained a year or two edifying one another in the best manner they could according to their gifts received from above, and then at length John Lathrop, sometimes a preacher in Kent," and a graduate of Cambridge, "joined the said congregation; and was afterwards chosen and ordained a pastor to them." While "Mr. Lathrop was an Elder" the ambiguous nature of the congregation's relationship to the Church of England, inherent in their semi-Separatist status, began to cause difficulties. Around 1630 a controversy erupted within the congregation over "some being grieved against one that had his child then baptized in the" parish church. The controversy does not appear to have been over the baptism of the infant, but rather the fact that the baptism was done by the unreformed Church of England. Voices within the congregation began to call for full separation from the Church of England on account of it being a false church. As a result, a small group identified with John Duppa removed themselves from fellowship with Lathrop's congregation.

The incident reveals the tension between those who wanted to reject completely the Church of England and those who were more moderate in their Separatism. Such tensions continued to develop but were put on hold in 1632 when most of the congregation was imprisoned for over a year. The experience embittered some members and convinced others that the price of dissent was too high. Upon their release from jail, the congregation fell into disarray. The experience of imprisonment and persecution embittered many members to the extent that they maintained little interest in sustaining contact with the "common assemblies" of the parish churches. By 1633 a group within the congregation was allowed "dismission that

---

[7]Burrage, *Early English Dissenters*, vol. 1, 312-320, vol. 2, 292-295.

they might become an entire church." This new division had less than a dozen members but their numbers soon doubled as another group from within the Jacob-Lathrop circle joined them. The resulting congregation was led by Samuel Eaton, who "with some others" received a "further baptism."

Lathrop himself decided, like Jacob, that his millennial dreams were best pursued in the New World. He explained to the congregation that it was no longer possible for him to achieve what he had originally intended. "At last there being no hope that Mr. Lathrop should do them further service in the Church, he having many motives to go to New England . . . he earnestly desire[d] the Church would release him of that office which (to his grief) he could no way preform, and that he might have their consent to go to New England." The congregation was unsure of what to do, but "after serious consideration," granted that he could leave his office with their consent. Upon his release from prison in 1634 he led over two dozen members of his congregation to New England.[8]

It is not clear whether or not Samuel Eaton and his break away group embraced believer's baptism or merely rejected the baptism of the Church of England. While it is possible that Eaton's group rejected infant baptism altogether at this point (rather than simply rejecting the baptism of a false church), it is unlikely that they had come to this position in 1633. The evidence is sparse in any case, but its silence on this matter would imply that Eaton and his group underwent radical-Separatist rebaptism as a rejection of the Church of England, as opposed to believer's baptism as the foundation of a new church. If Eaton's group had at this early stage come to embrace believer's baptism, it is likely that such an idea would have been debated and mentioned in the surviving evidence.[9]

---

[8]Burrage, *Early English Dissenters*, vol. 2, 295-302.

[9]For this opinion, see Tolmie, *Triumph*, 23 and his Appendix A. If however, such a reconstruction is incorrect, and Eaton and his congregation did accept believer's baptism as the foundation for a church, then this would be the first recognizable English Calvinist Baptist church.

While the theology underpinning their actions remains uncertain, it is clear that Eaton and his group received some form of rebaptism in 1633. This event raises the question of who baptized Eaton. A contemporary poem by John Taylor provides a possibility:

> Also one Spilsbury rose up of late,/
> (Who doth, or did dwell over Aldersgate)
> His office was to weigh Hay by the Truffe,
> (Fit for the Pallat of Bucephalus)
> He in short time left his Hay-weighing trade,
>
> And afterwards he Irish stockings made:
> He rebaptized in Anabaptist fashion
> One Eaton (of the new-found separation)
> A zealous Button-maker, grave and wise,
> And gave him orders, others to baptize;
> Who was so apt to learne that in one day,
> Hee'd do't as well as Spilsbury weigh'd Hay . . .

While the poet's veracity is certainly open to question, it is likely that these lines reveal that Eaton was re-baptized by John Spilsbury. [10]

John Spilsbury also appears to have been the first to practice believer's baptism among the members of Jacob's circle. The "Kiffin Memorandum" notes that in 1638 six members of the Jacob circle "being convinced that Baptism was not for infants, but professed believers, joined with Mr. Jonathan Spilsbury." The action of these six members of the Jacob circle mark the first indisputable Calvinist congregation that practiced believer's baptism in London, although it is possible that some had independently come to this position previously. Thus by 1638 at the absolute latest—and probably

---

[10]John Taylor, A *Swarme of Sectaries* (London, 1641), 6-7.

sometime before, out of the whirling mix of radical religious ideas in London, a congregation of Calvinist Baptists emerged.[11]

Lathrop's departure in 1634 had again left the remaining London congregation without a pastor. As before, the congregation ministered to each other to the best of their abilities. Then, after being frustrated in his own efforts to go to America, in the summer of 1637 Henry Jessey, who had received his BA from Cambridge in 1623, accepted an invitation to join the congregation as their pastor. Once he accepted the Jacob-Lathrop congregation's call, he remained in their service until his death in 1663. Not a year after Jessey had joined them, the division of Baptists "being convinced that Baptism was not for infants, but professed believers" left the Jacob-Lathrop, now Jessey, congregation and "joined with Mr. Spilsbury." In 1640 yet another division occurred, only this time not over theological matters. The congregation had grown and for reasons of safety and convenience "the church became two by mutual consent, just half being with" the colorfully named Praise-God Barbone "and the other half with Mr. Jessey."[12]

---

[11]Burrage, *Early English Dissenters*, vol. 2 , 302, cf. ibid., 299 (the "Jessey Memorandum") which for 1638 reads "Others joined to them . . . these also being of the same judgement with Sam. Eaton and desiring to depart and not to be censured our interest in them was remitted with prayer made in their behalf June 8th 1638. They having first forsaken us and joined with Mr. Spilsbury." With regards to Spilsbury, two questions arise. First, the nature of Spilsbury's rebaptism and second, where did his congregation initially come from. In answer to the first, it is possible that Spilsbury first came to a position of radical-Separatist rebaptism. In his rejection of the Church of England, he came to the logical conclusion that he must also reject the baptism that he had received from that church. (The impulse to avoid Anabaptism was weaker among laymen, such as Spilsbury, than it was among clergymen who had been taught during their theological training to fear rebaptism due to its association with the Anabaptists of Münster). It is a possible conjecture that Spilsbury's rebaptism was not believer's baptism and that he only came to this position later. What is clear is that he had reached this position by 1638. With regards to the origins of Spilsbury's church before 1638, Tolmie convincingly postulates that Spilsbury's congregation may have been an off shoot of John Duppa's church, which was mentioned above as the strict Separatist church that had divided from the Jacob circle by the start of the 1630s (Tolmie, *Triumph*, 24-25).

[12][Edward Whiston], *The Life and Death of Mr. Henry Jessey, late Preacher of the Gospel of Christ in London* (London, 1671), 5, 7, 9, 11; Burrage, vol. 2, 302.

In an age divided over doctrinal differences, Jessey displayed tremendous liberalism. His latitudinarian perspective both resulted from and encouraged his connections with a wide range of religious and political leaders. Before their departure to New England, Jessey had developed a relationship with the Winthrop family, which he continued even after they left England. After coming to London he was associated with a myriad of influential men, such as William Kiffin, John Simpson and Walter Cradcock. Later he would join with John Owen and others in their work on a new translation of the Bible. Jessey tolerated and sympathized with a number of different religious positions and was always more concerned with finding truth in unity than in quarreling and division. He was unquestionably one of the most fascinating and influential personalities at the center of religious radicalism in the mid-seventeenth century. Jessey began his public career as a Puritan, and then an Independent Puritan, but before the end of his life he could be called a Particular Baptist, a Fifth Monarchist, a Seventh-Day Baptist, and an Independent Baptist.[13] In addition to his broad influence across a number of religious perspectives, Jessey was also a dynamic force in the politics of the period. B. R. White identified three primary reasons that Jessey was so active politically: "[F]irst, that the will of God, as he believed it to be revealed by the Bible, must lead to concrete acts of obedience now. Secondly, that God shortly intended to manifest Christ's millennial reign upon earth. Thirdly, that the imminence of that kingdom required political preparation by Christians now." Despite his religious and political activities, Jessey found a way to maintain a balance between his firm convictions and Christ's command for kindness.[14]

The issue of baptism continued to be a concern once the Jacob-Lathrop congregation had come under Jessey's pastorate. By 1644

---

[13][Whiston], *Life of Jessey*, 10, 43-49. For Jessey generally, see *Biographical Dictionary of British Radicals, Dictionary of National Biography* and B. R. White "Henry Jessey and the Great Rebellion," in *Reformation, Conformity and Dissent*, ed. R. B. Knox (London: Epworth Press, 1977) 132-153.

[14]B. R. White, "Henry Jessey: A Pastor in Politics," *Baptist Quarterly* 25 (1973-1974): 99.

"about 16 previous souls left" Jessey's church having become convinced that believer's baptism was the true mode of baptism. This event forced Jessey to reconsider his position on baptism for "near a year's time," before himself accepting Baptist beliefs. On 22 June 1645 Jessey took it upon himself to write a letter to the "Churches of Christ in New England." Jessey had numerous contacts among the Puritans in New England and had lately been quite disturbed to hear of the New Englanders' harsh treatment "of some for being Anabaptists." Always an advocate of tolerance, Jessey explained that such actions only hurt the cause of the "Gathered Churches called Independents," for people in England had begun to say that if "in New England they will not suffer others to live with them, that differ from them" in religious matters, then what reason was there "to expect that here" in England they should be any more tolerant. Aside from the poor press that such actions generated, however, Jessey maintained that such "persecution for conscience sake" was not godly and that it should be done away with in deference to a more tolerant stance. Along with the letter, Jessey enclosed some anti-paedobaptist literature that he had found particularly persuasive in the hopes that if the New Englanders were not convinced, then at least they would be more sympathetic.[15]

A week after writing his letter calling for lenience to the people of New England, Jessey was himself baptized by Hanserd Knollys. Knollys had been a member of Jessey's church, but had been among the "precious souls" that left over the issue of baptism. Jessey had always been a Calvinist and so it was natural that after his conversion to Calvinist Baptist principles, he should have a close relationship with Particular Baptist leaders such as William Kiffin and Paul Hobson. Such men, in addition to sharing his Calvinist Baptist principles, had also been connected with the Jacob-Lathrop-Jessey congregation and formed something of an extended family tree from the parent congregation. Jessey, however, always had closer associations with the

---

[15]Philip J. Anderson, "Letters of Henry Jessey and John Tombes to the Churches of New England, 1645," *Baptist Quarterly* 28 (1979): 30-40.

London Independents and continued to act as pastor for the remaining core of the Jacob-Lathrop congregation. Yet many of the congregation did not agree with Jessey's new position on baptism, "most of them for infant baptism." Not wanting to cause another division, Jessey allowed those who wished, to stay within the congregation, whether or not they had undergone believer's baptism. The church covenant, and not believer's baptism, united Jessey's mixed congregation of re-baptized and non-re-baptized Christians. Over time most members accepted believer's baptism and were re-baptized, but Jessey never made baptism a bar to church communion, and thus even after the Restoration his congregation remained an open communion Baptist church.[16]

Like many of his brethren, eschatology was a central part of Jessey's worldview. He anxiously expected Christ's return and happily looked forward to that time. While he did not care for their intolerance or their violent rhetoric, Jessey supported the theological convictions behind the Fifth Monarchist movement, and along with Christopher Feake and John Simpson, lectured in the early 1650s at Allhallows the Great, "to pray for a new representative, and to preach somewhat against the old." Many of Jessey's congregation were also Fifth Monarchy supporters and signed the movement's manifestos. His searching of the prophecies and laws of the Bible also led him to advocate—along with other Fifth Monarchists—that England's laws be revised along Judaic lines. Around the time that some Fifth Monarchists began to be divided over the dating of the Sabbath (i.e. Saturday or Sunday), Jessey gathered together a small group to observe the Saturday Sabbath in private. His biography records that:

> As for what he held (in his latter days) concerning the seventh day Sabbath, to be kept by Christians evangelically; (without Jewish services or ceremonies) he managed his judgement and practice therein with great caution; that there might be no offence or breaches among professors; for at first

---

[16]Whiston, *Life of Jessey*, 83-87.

for some considerable time, (near two years) he kept his
opinion much to himself, and then afterwards (when he
communicated it to others) he observed the day in his own
chamber, with only 4 or 5 more of the same mind, and on the
first day of the week he preached, and met publicly and
privately as before. . . . Some (with whom he was intimately
acquainted near 20 years, . . .) Report that although their
judgement differed from his, both in point of Baptism and
Sabbath; He did not once urge it on them.[17]

Jessey's desire to keep peace among his congregation explains his
efforts to keep his Saturday observance quiet, for if it had been widely
known it may have caused further divisions. Related to Jessey's
interest in the Old Testament and the Jewish Sabbath was the central
role he played in the discussion over the readmission of the Jews to
England. Edward I had expelled the Jews from England in 1290, but
in the 1650s their readmission became a topic of debate and discussion. While earlier interpretations of Revelation had cast Jews in a
negative light, even suggesting that a Jew would be the Antichrist, by
the seventeenth century the perspective had changed and the Jews'
role in prophecy was viewed positively. Many religious figures shared
Jessey's belief that the "calling of the Jews" was a necessary precursor
to the return of Christ. They also believed that once the Jews were
readmitted to England, it would be hard for them to resist conversion
to the pure form of worship that Protestants had recovered. A
conference on Jewish readmission was called at Whitehall in 1655
and Jessey was one of the divines invited to attend. His published
account of the proceedings is one of the best sources for the debate
and clearly demonstrates his pro-readmission stance. Such a stance
was logical given Jessey's tolerant views, apocalyptic expectation for
the conversion of the Jews, and Sabbatarian sympathies.[18]

---

[17]Whiston, *The Life of Jessey*, 67-69, 87-88.

[18]Henry Jessey, *The Exceeding Riches of Grace Advanced by the Spirit of Grace*, 2nd ed.
(London, 1647), introduction; Bernard S. Capp, *The Fifth Monarchy Men: A Study in
Seventeenth-Century English Millenariansim* (London: Faber and Faber, 1972), 59; Whiston,

Jessey's wide-ranging religious beliefs and numerous sympathies make him difficult to classify. This is to be expected in an age before denominational labels had taken on their modern meanings. Nevertheless, the best way to characterize Jessey and other open communion Baptists like him is as an Independent Baptist. While Independent Baptists believed in a gathered church and often published in defense of Baptist principles, they did not make believer's baptism a necessary precondition for church membership.

Among the literature that Henry Jessey had sent to New England in his efforts to help the Baptists were the writings of John Tombes. Tombes was another independent Baptist and his writings may have been crucial in convincing Jessey of the validity of believer's baptism. Tombes's had graduated from and taught at Oxford and was one of the most educated Baptists of his time. Along with Jessey's copy of Tombes's *Examen*, Tombes's enclosed a letter to the New England churches that echoed Jessey's plea for toleration.[19]

The Broadmead congregation in Bristol can also be considered an Independent Baptist church. The most famous Independent Baptist

---

Life of Jessey, 67-69, 83-84, 87-88; Nuttall, *Visible Saints*, 143; Henry Jessey, *A Narrative of the Late Proceeds At White-Hall Concerning the Jews* (London, 1656). For the debate over Jewish readmission, see David S. Katz, *Philo-Semitism and the Readmission of the Jews to England 1603-1655* (Oxford: Oxford University Press, 1982), especially chapter 6 for Jessey's role. William Kiffin was also invited to attend the Whitehall conference on readmission. Interestingly, Katz implies he may have been invited to represent the merchant interest in the lucrative possibility of Jewish readmission (David S. Katz, *The Jews in The History of England 1485-1850* (Oxford: Oxford University Press, 1994), 119). Edward Whalley, while not involved in the Whitehall conference, expressed his wonderment that "so great variety of opinion should be amongst such men, as I hear are called to consult about" the matter. "It seems to me, that there are both politique and divine reasons that strongly make for their readmission . . . Doubtless to say no more, they will bring in much wealth . . . and where we both pray for their conversion, and know it shall be, I know not why we should deny the means" (John Thurloe, *A collection of the State Papers*, ed. Thomas Birch (London, 1742), vol. 4, 308). Ultimately, as a result of the discussions, Jews began to return to England.

[19]W. T. Whitley, "Baptists and Bartholomew's Day," *Transactions of the Baptist Historical Society* 1 (1908), 36; Anderson, "Letters of Jessey and Tombes," 33-40. As Watts points out, the letters of Jessey and Tombes later in the 1650s offer a glimpse of Independent Baptist organization, *Dissenters*, 161, but it is important to bear in mind White's insight that when such churches did organize, they usually did so with Independent (congregationalist) churches as opposed to other Independent Baptist Churches, *English Baptists*, 74.

congregation was that of John Bunyan in Bedford. These Independent Baptists influenced the General and Particular Baptists in a number of ways. They often had wider theological contacts and thus infused the Baptist movements with a variety of ideas. They also forced the General and Particular Baptists to make a decision concerning open versus closed communion. The majority chose closed communion, which provided these movements with a unique sense of identity.

The early gathered congregations of Baptists that sprang from the Jacob-Lathrop-Jessey circle were a manifestation of the eschatological sentiment on the radical fringes of English religious life at the beginning of the seventeenth century. They represented an effort to re-establish the apostolic church under the direct authority of King Jesus. Such gathered churches presented an alternative society for believers. J. F. McGregor viewed each of these early Baptist congregations as "a voluntary association of free and equal members, united in opposition to the doctrine, practices, and moral discipline of the national church and, by implication, of the social system whose values that church expressed." By appealing directly to the authority of Christ and by-passing all temporal authority, the gathered church was able to criticize the failures of the world freely, knowing that all they had to fear were earthly punishments—which were seen as almost mandatory for the saints.[20]

William Kiffin, who had joined Samuel Eaton's congregation in 1638, described the literal entry of the gathered churches into the Kingdom of Christ as one of "such truths as do immediately strike at Antichrist, and his false power. As namely this great truth, Christ the king of his Church; and that Christ hath given this Power to his Church, not to a Hierarchy, neither to a National Presbytery, but to a company of Saints in a Congregational way." William Kiffin wrote these words in his introduction to Thomas Goodwin's *A Glimpse of Sions Glory* (1641). In his introduction, Kiffin also expressed his eagerness for the yoke of Antichrist to "be broken off. . . . Nay the day

---

[20] J. F. McGregor and B. Reay, eds., *Radical Religion in the English Revolution* (Oxford: Oxford University Press, 1984), 39; Nuttall, *Visible Saints*, 163-165.

is now dawning, wherein Sion's Peace and Comforts shall be fulfilled, Jesus Christ set up, the sole and great King." Kiffin believed that there was more day left to dawn as the darkness of Antichrist rapidly dispersed before the brightness of Christ as the direct head of each gathered congregation. Kiffin explained that Goodwin's text needed to be read because

> these truths strike directly at the Antichrist, and therefore [are] kept and quelled down as errors. And so by reason of this obscurity (we being half blind) such bright truths seem strange to us, and go under many aspersions and calumnies . . . and truly we have been so accustomed to the yoke, that we seem to beat down freedom, with casting up a thousand surmises, dreaming of strange consequences.[21]

It was previously believed that the entire text of *Sions Glory* was written by Kiffin, or possibly Hanserd Knollys, but it is now believed that it was a copy of a sermon preached by Thomas Goodwin in Holland at the inauguration of a newly gathered church.[22] The text

---

[21]William Kiffin, *Remarkable Passages in the Life of William Kiffin*. ed., W. Orme (London, 1823), 14; Burrage, *Early English Dissenters*, vol. 2, 302; William Kiffin, epistle, *A Glimpse of Sions Glory* (London, 1641).

[22]Kiffin is given as the author of this text by numerous authorities, such as Charles Ripley Gillett, ed., *McAlpin Collection* (New York: Union Theological Seminary, 1927-30); J. Smith, *Anti-Quakeriana* (London, 1873; reprinted New York: Kraus Reprint Co., 1968); W. T. Whitley, *A Baptist Bibliography* (London: The Kingsgate Press, 1916-22). Hanserd Knollys is listed as the treatise's author by the British Museum (E 175 (5)) and in the Emmanuel College Cambridge library catalog, among others. Two recent studies have supported Goodwin's authorship, John Wilson, "A Glimpse of Sions Glory," *Church History* 31 (1962): 66-73 and A. R. Dallison "The Authorship of 'A Glimpse of Syons Glory,' " in Peter Toon ed., *Puritans, The Millennium and the Future of Israel: Puritan Eschatology 1600 to 1660* (London: James Clarke & Co., 1970). Paul Christianson, *Reformers and Babylon* (Toronto: University of Toronto Press, 1978) has produced an interesting argument in favor of Jeremiah Burrough's authorship (see his Appendix II). While this argument would be further supported by reference to page 14 of Kiffin's *Remarkable Passages*, Christianson's argument can be set aside on account of the unusual circumstances surrounding the production and origin of the text, in which case Wilson's argument seems to be the most convincing. However, while it appears that Kiffin himself did not write the text and that the author of the text was not the same as the author of the epistle, Wilson's exclusion of Kiffin

of the sermon itself demonstrates the apocalyptic excitement surrounding the gathering of churches. "This is the work that is in hand" and "as soon as ever this is done, that Antichrist is down, Babylon fallen, then comes in Jesus Christ reigning in glory." Christ's glory would be manifest in an earthly, not a mere heavenly, kingdom. The saints acted as God's tools in bringing this kingdom about and furthered the divine cause by entering into gathered congregations. Goodwin explained that there was a direct connection between the millennium and the gathered church and if "the Kingdom of Christ had been kept in Congregation, in that way that we and some other Churches are in," then it would have been "impossible for that Antichrist should have got" control of the church. Goodwin claimed that the signs showed that the millennium was very near, therefore the work of reconstituting God's church was particularly urgent.[23]

After his release from "the White Lyon Prison," where attempts had been made on his life, William Kiffin quickly took advantage of the lull in censorship by publishing Goodwin's text. In so doing, Kiffin became one of the first to publish this type of apocalyptic work in England. Along with John Archer's *The Personall Raigne of Christ Upon Earth* (1641), the text is one of the most important apocalyptic works published in English in the early 1640s. Kiffin probably resonated with Goodwin's insistence that the poor and meaner sort of people were to be in the vanguard of the millennium. Kiffin himself had been an "apprentice to a mean calling" and was worse off than most in his position. His family had died in the plague of 1625 when he was "but nine years of age . . . being left in the hands of such

---

as a possible author because he does not mention the work in his memoirs is misguided. Kiffin does not mention a single one of his many publications in his memoirs. While Wilson does not disprove Kiffin's authorship, his article supports the idea that the text was written by Goodwin (or at least preached by Goodwin and probably circulated in common books) and brought to publication by Kiffin with his epistle added. Wilson's argument also helps to explain why there is a copy of the text in the Library of Emmanuel College, Cambridge (326.5.9/3), that bears the words "By T.G." on the title page. (On these points, I am grateful to B. S. Capp for our discussion of the authorship of *Sions Glory* and for the assistance of P. J. Spreadbury, librarian at Emmanuel College, Cambridge).

[23]Goodwin, *Sions Glory*, 2, 7, 32.

friends as remained alive, I was by them taken care of; although they sought their own advantage; by possessing themselves of what was left of me, of which, as they afterwards failed in business, I never enjoyed but very little."[24]

During the time of Kiffin's painful poverty, he was an apprentice with and close friend of John Lilburne, the future Leveller leader. Kiffin developed a deep admiration for Lilburne and became familiar with his writings. In 1641, Kiffin decided to republish Lilburne's *Christian Mans Triall*, in light of the "more fuller vision" that was now dawning. Kiffin saw Lilburne's text as a further blow against Antichrist, and he hoped that its publication would help in part to shine light into some of the dark corners that remained. Kiffin's introductory epistle gave full expression to his criticisms of society. Despite the imprisonments and hardships he had suffered, he was not afraid to voice his discontent. His epistle declared that Lilburne's actions and writings revealed the true nature of "the malignant malice of the prelacy and that faction . . . who think by their hellish ways, to raze down Sion and the truth of God to the ground, and therefore they labor by the imprisonments and tortures of some to dash the rest out of heart."

But Kiffin refused to lose heart. Despite the cruelties of the magistrate and the prelates, Kiffin's introductory epistle demonstrated his optimism that "even in these our times, . . . Lord Jesus may be set up as Lord and King."[25] Lilburne's text was an outline of the spiritual battle that was at hand. In the struggle against Antichrist, the saints had an active duty to resist the evils of the present powers. He denounced all "lukewarmness" and divided the world into to an eschatological battlefield for the warring forces of Christ and Antichrist. The entire second half of Lilburne's book demonstrated a fixation with questions of eschatology. Kiffin's laudatory introduc-

---

[24]Goodwin, *Sions Glory*, 5, 26-28, 31; Kiffin, *Remarkable Passages*, 2, 16. Kiffin also discussed the poverty of his early years in connection with medical bills that he could not pay (20).

[25]John Lilburne, *The Christian Mans Triall* (London, 1641), from the epistle to the reader by William Kiffin.

tion of the text, as well as his publication of Goodwin's text, reveal that Kiffin agreed with these apocalyptic thinkers and appreciated their writings. His epistles to both books show how much Kiffin himself was influenced by apocalypticism and how anxious he was for the Kingdom of Christ to be established.[26]

Kiffin's actions, however, were not appreciated by the authorities, who soon regretted that they had so recently released him from jail. Before long, Kiffin found himself back in prison—which only gave him more time for writing. When he emerged from jail he appears to have decided like many other dissenters that he could not find God amidst the persecution of the Beast that prevailed in England. Like Lathrop and Jacob before him, Kiffin sought passage to the New World in the hopes of starting over. But God did not "open a way" for Kiffin to travel beyond the seas. Since the "providence of God" had prevented him from going, Kiffin realized that it was God's will that he seek Christ's Kingdom in England. Thus providence led him to join himself to the congregation that had been led by Samuel Eaton. Kiffin soon became one of the most important Baptist leaders of the century.[27]

---

[26]Lilburne, *The Christian Mans Triall*, 28. For more on the extent of Lilburne's apocalyptic thinking, see Christianson, *Reformers and Babylon*, chpt. 4. For Lilburne's later apparent abandonment of apocalyptic thinking in favor of more "secular" politics, see Iwan Russell-Jones, "The Relationship Between Theology and Politics in the Writings of John Lilburne, Richard Overton and William Walwyn," D.Phil. Dissertation, Oxford University, 1987, 155-156, 239.

[27]Kiffin, *Remarkable Passages*, 13-15.

5

DEFINITION AND DEVELOPMENT:
THE PARTICULAR BAPTIST
CONFESSIONS OF 1644 AND 1646

Soon after Kiffin joined the Particular Baptists, he emerged as a dynamic leader. His deep faith, quick mind and spiritual boldness assured him a central place in the movement's development. In the words of Thomas Edwards, William Kiffin became "the Metropolitan of that Fraternity" of Baptists. A demonstration of just how influential a leader he would be was given in 1644, when as contemporaries recognized, Kiffin was a moving force behind a meeting of seven Particular Baptist churches in London. The representatives were assembled for the purpose of issuing a confession of faith. The resulting confession marked the Particular Baptists' first public appearance as a self-conscious movement. As a result it signified a major step in the movement's development and self-definition.[1]

Such confessions were not an innovation on the part of the Particular Baptists. John Smyth had drawn up a confession of faith when he applied for membership with the Waterlanders. Thomas Helwys wrote one in 1611. Apparently in 1615, the future Leveller leader, Richard Overton, composed a confession of faith as well. In

---

[1]Daniel Featley, *The Dippers Dipt, or, the Anabaptists duck'ed and plung'd over Head and Eares* (London, 1645), 4. In describing the Baptist leaders, Thomas Edwards wrote that "another of these fellows, who counts himself inferior to none of the rest (of his seduced Brethren) one whose name is Will: Kiffin, sometimes servant to a Brewer (whose name is John Lilburne) . . . this mans man is now become a pretended Preachers . . . For a . . . manifestation of him [Kiffin, see] a pamphlet called, *The Confession of Faith of the Seven Anabaptisticall Churches*, there he is in underwritten first, as Metropolitan of that Fraternity," Edwards, *Gangraena*, (1st part, 2nd ed., 87-88.

1643 John Spilsbury had published a confession of faith along with his *Treatise Concerning the Lawfull Subiect of Baptisme*. Predating all of these Baptist confessions of faith was the Separatist confession of 1596. From this last confession the Particular Baptists drew much of their inspiration. Indeed, the Particular Baptist confession is so similar to the Separatist confession, that over half of it almost seems to have been taken word for word.

This adaption of the Separatist confession, however, was in line with Particular Baptist objectives. Unlike the confessions of faith of Smyth, Helwys and Overton, the Particular Baptist confession was intended for a wide public audience. In general, four primary reasons can be discerned for the publication of their confession in 1644. First, they desired to define themselves in contrast to the Continental Anabaptists. Second, they wanted to define themselves in contrast to the English General Baptists. Third, they were trying to define themselves for themselves, in the hopes of providing unity among believers as well as gaining additional converts. Finally, they published the confession in an effort to convince the established authority that they were not a threat. Although the confession was signed by seven churches, a number possibly chosen in echo of the seven churches of the Book of Revelation and as the symbol of Christian unity, the various Baptist congregations were not as united as they appeared. Like the other Baptist movements, the Particular Baptists were to experience internal divisions, especially in answer to the question of *apocalypse how?*[2]

Prior to the confession of 1644, numerous publications appeared criticizing the Baptists. Calvinist Baptists were becoming visible in both old and New England, much to the alarm of Puritan ministers. A series of pamphlets appeared denouncing this new sect and going to great lengths to associate the Particular Baptists with the Anabaptists of the Radical Reformation. The Baptists were particularly troubled in 1642 by the publication of *A Warning for England*, and *A*

---

[2]Burrage, *Early English Dissenters*, vol. 2, 178-181, 187-200, 216-219; Lumpkin, *Confessions*, 81-123.

Short History of the Anabaptists of High and Low Germany. The latter clearly aimed to associate all English Baptists with the anarchism of Münster. In 1644 the publication of *A Confutation of the Anabaptists and of All others who Affect Not Civill Government,* furthered Kiffin's belief that a public response was required to defend the Baptists against charges of Anabaptism.[3]

The 1644 confession differentiated the Particular Baptists from the Anabaptists primarily by presenting the Particular Baptists as good Protestants with few radical views. They took special care to avoid suggestions of communism, disobedience or polygamy—which, to the seventeenth-century mind were telltale characteristics of Anabaptism. The way in which the Baptists referred to themselves demonstrated their desire to be rid of the shadow of Münster. The confession was entitled "The Confession of Faith of those Churches which are commonly (though falsely) called Anabaptists." Their preface to the confession explained that they aimed to dispel the fantastic stories that were being spread about them and that they hoped that a statement of their orthodoxy would convince the public that they were not Anabaptists, "denying original sin, declaiming Magistracy, denying to assist them either in person or purse in any of their lawful Commands," and "doing acts unseemly in" baptism, "not to be named amongst Christians."

One of the main reasons that the Anabaptists were so feared by contemporaries was that they allegedly denied the legitimacy of all magistrates. Particular Baptists wanted to make clear that this was not true in their case, and went out of their way in concluding their confession by testifying that they were "bound to yield in subjection and obedience" to the rightful authorities of England. They defined these authorities as the "King and Parliament freely chosen by the Kingdom, and . . . all those civil laws which have been enacted by them," an interesting statement given that as the king and Parliament

---

[3]*A Warning for England* was published anonymously, but later acknowledged by Daniel Featly. *A Confutation* was likely written by Thomas Bakewell and *A Short History* was anonymous.

had been at war with each other since 1642. Before concluding, the confession stated that "tributes, customs, and all such lawful duties, ought willingly to be by us paid and performed, our lands, goods, and bodies, to submit to the magistrate" who is "in every way to be acknowledged, reverenced, and obeyed." In this way, Particular Baptists' identity was shaped in contrast to who they did not want to be, namely Anabaptists.[4]

Likewise, they needed to make clear that they were not General Baptists either. The sudden growth of the General Baptists, and the highly visible actions of General Baptist evangelists like Lambe and Oates, caused many people to confuse the General with the Particular Baptists. Others were not confused but aimed to malign the General and Particular Baptists together, blaming the shortcomings of either group equally on both. The Particular Baptists intended their confession to be a firm wall between themselves and the General Baptists. Again, they used the confession's preface to make this intent clear, saying they wished to allay the accusations that the Particular Baptists believed in "free-will" and the possibility of "falling away from grace." This last accusation they countered directly in Article XXIII in saying that "those that have this precious faith wrought in them by the Spirit, can never finally nor totally fall away."

In framing the articles, they intended to make their Calvinism as clear as it could be. They explained that the blood of Christ was meant to "reconcile His elect only"and that the aim of God's church was the "preservation and salvation of the elect." Article XXI reiterated the point: "That Christ by his death did bring forth salvation and reconciliation only for the elect." Additionally, faith was defined as the "gift of God wrought in the hearts of the elect." Statements like these in the confession were designed to show that the Particular Baptists were clearly a part of the Calvinist consensus, and although they had some similarities with the General Baptists,

---

[4]Lumpkin, *Confessions*, Articles XLIX, LII (first), 154-155, 169-170.

they were a distinct and separate group. They were neither Anabaptists nor General Baptists.[5]

The Particular Baptists hoped that once they had cleared themselves from association with Anabaptists and General Baptists, that some sympathetic people would "seriously . . . consider" the truth of their movement and possibly join. In this sense, the confession of faith was an evangelistic tool, partly designed to explain to the potential convert in the clearest possible language what being a Baptist meant in terms of a life of faith. Additionally, the Particular Baptists were trying to define for themselves what their movement was and what it aspired to be. The Particular Baptist confession shows the signers' desire for a federation of independent autonomous churches, defined by a common doctrine, and able to aid one another in their search for the truth. They wrote that

> although the particular congregation be distinct and several bodies, every one a compact and knit city in itself; yet are they all to walk by one and the same rule, and by all means convenient to have the counsel and help one of another in needful affairs of the church, as members of one body in the common faith under Christ their only Head.

Obviously, the most defining aspect of this "one and the same rule," was the doctrine that "Baptism is an ordinance of the New Testament, given by Christ, to be dispensed only upon persons professing faith." This is of course what they had in common with the other Baptist movements, although each movement emphasized this point to a different degree. Additionally, Particular Baptists asserted that the rule of "knowledge, faith, and obedience, concerning the worship and service of God, and all other Christian duties" was to be found only in "the word of God contained in the Canonical Scriptures." Moreover, "in this written word God has plainly revealed

---

[5]Lumpkin, *Confessions*, Articles, XXIII, XVII, XIX, XXI, XXII, V, 154-155, 158, 160-163.

whatsoever He has thought needful for us to know, believe, and acknowledge, touching the nature and office of Christ."[6]

The confession also set out the Particular Baptist belief that Christ was the head of the church and the congregation. At this point the Baptists came closest to a single sentence summary of their beliefs and future direction. The article at the center of the confession declared that:

1644

> Christ has here on earth a spiritual Kingdom, which is the Church, which He hath purchased and redeemed to Himself, as a particular inheritance: which Church, as it is visible to us, is a company of visible saints, called and separated from the world, by the word and the Spirit of God, to the visible profession of the faith of the Gospel, being baptized into the faith, and joined to the Lord, and each other, by mutual agreement, in the practice and enjoyment of the ordinances, commanded by Christ their head and King.

They also expressed their millenarian views in saying that "this Kingdom shall be then fully perfected when he shall the second time come in glory to reign among His saints . . . when He shall put down all rule and authority under His feet, that the glory of the Father may be full and perfectly manifested in his Son, and the glory of the Father and the Son in all his members." It was the duty and fate of the elect to be in constant conflict "against Satan, the World, the Flesh, and the temptations of them." Satan had "clouded and overwhelmed" the truth of God for a time, but was now being turned back. The battle against Satan was an important aspect of the Baptists' life. Article XXXI declared "that all believers in the time of this life, are in a continual warfare, combat, and opposition against sin, self, the world, and the Devil, and liable to all manner of afflictions, tribulations, and

---

[6]Lumpkin, *Confessions*, Articles XLVII, XXXIX, VII, VII, 155, 158, 167-169.

persecutions, and so shall continue until Christ comes in His Kingdom."[7]

Despite such radical language, the final reason for the confession's publication was for the purpose of accommodating with society. The confession aimed to minimize whenever possible the differences between the Particular Baptists and other religious groups who held power. They hoped that by minimizing their similarities and emphasizing their differences with other Baptists movements, that they could find greater acceptance. Part of the reasoning for this move was explained in Article L as aiming "to incline the magistrates hearts so far to tender our consciences, as that we might be protected by them." Baptists had seen their goal of liberty of conscience as part of an apocalyptic struggle between the forces of Christ and Antichrist. This struggle had demanded that the saints suffer and face persecution at the hands of Antichrist, but they were comforted by the knowledge that Christ's ultimate victory was near.

With the publishing of the confession of 1644, things had begun to change. The new liberal atmosphere provided by the Long Parliament allowed the Particular Baptists to recognize that they need not always oppose the present powers. It was possible that the authorities were not Antichrist. The confession, however, was crafted to give the illusion that the Baptists were prepared to jettison their critiques of society in exchange for liberty of conscience. Partly in an effort to define themselves in contrast to the Anabaptists, the Particular Baptists included in their confession of faith articles that called for obedience on the part of all Baptists: "We are to make humble supplication and prayer for Kings, and all that are in authority."[8]

The confession reveals the Baptists at a crossroads. There is a tension in the document between a radical call for further Reformation and an accommodationist effort to shed the title of "Anabap-

---

[7]Lumpkin, *Confessions*, Articles XXIX, XLII, XXXIII, XX, XL, XXX, XXXI, 162, 164-165, 167-168. With regards to Article XX, cf. Article 16 of the 1596 Separatist Confession (Lumpkin, 87).

[8]Lumpkin, *Confessions*, Article L, XLVII, 169

tists." The radical nature of the confession is apparent in a number of the articles. They saw Christ's current Kingdom on earth as a company of visible saints, but they clearly looked forward to when that "Kingdom shall be . . . fully perfected when he shall the second time come in glory to reign amongst his Saints." At the same time, the conservative goal of accommodating with society was also present in the confession. Recognizing that persecution was comparatively light and that they "had some breathing time," the Baptists sought to declare their obedience to "the supreme magistracy of this Kingdom," and to make a plea for religious liberty.

These two elements were in tension with each other; the best way to build God's Kingdom was not clear. The crossroads presented by the confession reveals a turning point for the Particular Baptists. It marked the beginning of their movement from a more oppositional to a relatively more accommodationist sect. The catalyst that prompted this movement was the new tolerant atmosphere of the revolution's early stages. The confession was indeed a radical document, but it was also published for the conservative purpose of accommodating to society. In the Baptists' life-long struggle to decide whether God could best be served within as opposed to outside the purviews of society, the confession marked the first step in favor of the former.[9]

During the time the confession was issued, Particular Baptists were experiencing an organizational crisis. Constant schism, theological bickering, and differences over ecclesiology plagued the nascent sect. While some members continued to push for a position of higher tension with society, other elements increasingly urged moderation, recognizing that further alienation from society would only hurt their agenda. These differences were set aside in order to issue the 1644 confession and they were not settled with its publication.

---

[9]Lumpkin, *Confessions*, Article XX, L, 162, 170. It is interesting to note that Thomas Bakewell maintains that Spilsbury told him that this kingship of Christ was not meant in a metaphorical sense, nor did it only apply to an "invisible" church, but a real visible gathered church (Thomas Bakewell, *An Answer or Confvtation of Divers Errors Broached and Maintained By the Seven Churches of Anabaptists*, (London, 1646), 5).

While none of the representatives who signed the confession had
received any formal theological training, there were clearly theological
leaders. William Kiffin, Samuel Richardson and John Spilsbury—some
of the signatories who had the longest history of nonconfor-
mity—were the most prominent. They were now emerging as a circle
of leaders among Particular Baptists and they later aimed to consoli-
date the acceptance already gained by accommodating with society.

The inter-congregational network necessary to assemble the seven
churches marked the start of an organizational system that would
stabilize the movement. The London Baptists had begun to oversee
an organizational system that by the time of the Protectorate
encompassed England, Scotland, Wales, and Ireland. Through the use
of delegates, letters, published confessions, and inter-congregational
financial support, this London-centered network provided the
foundation from which the later association system would develop.
This system could resolve theological and financial problems that
arose as the movement grew. These developments were instrumental
not only in the survival of the sect, but also in terms of its self-
definition and identity. The connections between the various
churches helped members to see themselves as part of a larger
movement with a defined set of doctrines and practices.[10]

This newly emerging orientation, while essential for Particular
Baptist survival, did not appeal to some of the signatories of the
confession. While the Kiffin-Richardson-Spilsbury circle sought
greater accommodation with society, other Baptist signatories

---

[10]See B. R. White, "The Organization of the Particular Baptists, 1644-1660," *Journal of
Ecclesiastical History* 17 (1966): 209-226. The signers of the 1644 confession were: William
Kiffin, Thomas Patient; John Spilsbury, George Tipping, Samuel Richardson; Thomas
Skippard (Sheppard?), Thomas Munday; Thomas Gunne, John Mabbatt; John Web (Webb),
Thomas Killcop; Paul Hobson, Thomas Goare (Gower); Joseph Phelpes, Edward Heath.
When the confession was reissued in 1646, it was again thought appropriate to have seven
churches. There were some slight changes however in the persons present. The signers in
1646 were Thomas Gunne, John Mabbatt, John Spilsbury, Samuel Richardson, Paul Hobson,
Thomas Goare, Benjamin Cockes (Cox), Thomas Kilikop (Killcop), Thomas Munden,
George Tipping, William Kiffin, Thomas Patient, Hanserd Knollys, Thomas Holms, Denis
le Barbier, and Christoph le Burer.

remained aloof. Nevertheless, those who remained outside this circle were still important to Baptist development and frequently associated with Kiffin, Spilsbury, and others who were more eager to accommodate with society. Such men were frequently fervent evangelists, many joined the Parliamentary army, and a large number were associated with the Levellers. Thomas Gower was a close friend of Paul Hobson's and the two men signed the 1644 confession together as representatives from the same church. Gower moved freely in radical circles and later in his life he was implicated in the Yorkshire Plot.[11]

A similar example of the kind of direct action embraced by some Particular Baptist leaders can be seen in John Webb, a member of Killcop's congregation. Webb had joined the army shortly after signing the confession of 1644. A military career suited his aggressive attitude, and he used the military as an opportunity for and a means of witnessing. The type of disturbances Webb caused in the name of his faith were noted by Thomas Edwards:

> John Webb, a Lieutenant, guarded with his soldiers, as Mr. Skinner was preaching in his [Skinner's] church, started up and with a loud voice publically interrupted him, called him a fool three times, Popish Priest, tub-preacher, bidding him often to come down out of his tub, saying, he taught lies to the people . . . in this manner he proceeded, . . . till one of the clock, and then in a rage went out of the Church, calling Mr. Skinner [a?] black frog of the Revelation.

Similar stories are recorded for a number of Particular Baptists. The Baptists also frequently used the opportunities provided by the army to plant churches throughout the British Isles; various congregations sprang up in the garrisons' wake. As officers like Webb traveled across England, the Baptist faith was spread to the far corners of the realm. Like other early Baptists, John Webb had a long history of dissent and was imprisoned while Archbishop Laud was in power on

---

[11]Gower and Hobson's plotting is discussed in Part III.

account of his criticisms of the Church of England. Thomas Sheppard also had a long history of dissent and trouble with the authorities. Along with Samuel Eaton, he was among those who separated from the Jacob-Lathrop church in 1633. Like Webb, Sheppard probably found his way into the army after signing the confession from the same church as Thomas Munday, who also had a deep past in dissenting circles around the Jacob-Lathrop-Jessey congregation.[12]

The new Baptist churches represented at the signing of the confession of 1644 were not cut off from the parent Jacob-Lathrop-Jessey congregation. Although they were striving to establish an independent identity, they were still in close contact with these fellow dissenters and the actions of both groups mutually influenced each other. After the publication of the 1644 confession, further tension developed within the Jacob-Lathrop-Jessey congregation over the issue of infant baptism. A large number of Jessey's congregation, including Jessey himself, concluded by 1644 that baptism was for believers only. The 1644 confession convinced some members of Jessey's congregation that the London Particular Baptists were not radical Anabaptists, but true Christians. The result was that a group separated from Jessey's congregation and under the leadership of Hanserd Knollys formed their own Particular Baptist congregation. Interestingly, they did not join themselves to a pre-existing Particular Baptist congregation. This was probably the result of Knollys's demonstrated abilities and their joint decision with the London Baptists that a group under Knollys's leadership should be formed. By the summer of 1645, Jessey himself had been re-baptized by Knollys. A large portion of Jessey's congregation disagreed with his decision to

---

[12]Additionally, "Webb said, that he himself was a minister of Jesus Christ, and cared not for the Ordinance of Parliament, or Synod, for what were they to him." Edwards, *Third Part of Gangraena*, 251-252. Perhaps this was also the Webb who Edwards reports claimed to be under "a New Light" and a "New truth." He is referred to as "a great Ring-leader of the seduced sect of Anabaptists." Edwards, *Gangraena*, (1st part, 2nd ed.), 86; Burrage, *Early English Dissenters*, vol. 1, 204, 326, vol. 2, 302-303. Sheppard may have been the trooper Shepherd from Ireton's regiment who was examined by the Commons in April 1647, see Tolmie, *Triumph*, 209, n. 36.

undergo another baptism and Jessey's group became a mixed congregation, an Independent Baptist church.[13]

Unlike the other Particular Baptist leaders, Hanserd Knollys had been educated at Cambridge, where he "heard all the godly Ministers" he could, and "got acquaintance with gracious Christians, then called Puritans." He was ordained a deacon and priest in the Church of England in 1629, but realizing that such office was from man and not God, he "renounced that Ordination, and silenced myself, resolving not to preach anymore until I had a clear call and commission from Christ to preach the Gospel." That call soon came and Knollys emerged as a tremendously popular preacher. A contemporary claimed that his sermons drew over a thousand people. After he left the Church of England, he reportedly came to see their ministry as "Antichristian." Knollys had traveled to New England in 1638, but even there he met with hardships and persecution. By 1641 he had returned to England to attend to his ailing father and soon joined Henry Jessey's congregation. Once he had become convinced of the validity of believer's baptism, he formed a Particular Baptist congregation. Along with Kiffin and Thomas Collier, he was one of the few Particular Baptist leaders to live from the Revolution of the 1640s to the Revolution of the 1680s and provided a link between the first two generations of English Particular Baptists.[14]

Knollys was also the most thorough and systematic millenarian thinker among the Particular Baptists. He is the only Baptist of his time to undertake an exposition of the entire book of Revelation.

---

[13]Burrage, *Early English Dissenters*, vol. 2, 304-305.

[14]Hanserd Knollys, *The Life and Death of that old Disciple of Jesus . . . Hanserd Knollys* (London, 1692), 3-4, 9. This text was edited, introduced, and published by William Kiffin, who along with Vavasor Powell prayed over Knollys during the sickness which began his demise; Edwards, *First and Second Part of Gangraena* (3rd ed.), 39- 40; idem, *Third Part of Gengraena*, 241. While a number of Baptists traveled to New England, it should not be thought that the journey by that time was an easy one. In addition to its expense, Knollys described how trying it was by saying that on the journey "my little child died with convulsion fits, our beer and water stank, our bisket was green, yellow and blue, moulded and rotten, and our cheese also, so that we suffered much hardship, being 12 weeks in our passage; but God was gracious to us, and lead us safe through those great deeps" (*Life*, 17).

While his millenarianism was apparent from his earliest years as a Baptist, it was later in his life, when age and infirmity limited his preaching abilities, that he turned to prodigious study of the apocalyptic texts. His knowledge of Greek and Hebrew, combined with his familiarity with ecclesiastical histories, made his commentaries very forceful. Like so many others, he saw Revelation as a roadmap for church history as well as a promise of a future millennium. He was concerned with the proper identification of the symbols and the visions. He saw the "great city, which spiritually is called Sodom, and Egypt," from Revelation 11:8 as London, and synchronized the two olive trees with the two candles and two witnesses, seeing them as the true ministers of God's word. The seven candle sticks were the same as the seven churches, that is the true congregational churches of Christ.

While he often maintained that it was not his place to determine the exact time of the Second Coming, near the end of his life he became convinced that the 1260 years (Rev. 11:3, reckoning a day for a year) "did begin about 428, [so] they will end about 1688, which a short time will manifest more certainly." He insisted that those who made an honest effort to determine the proximity of Christ's reappearance "may know that it is near, even at the door."

Late in the reign of Charles II, when Catholicism again influenced the court and there were rumors of numerous Catholic conspiracies, Knollys issued several apocalyptic expositions to warn people of the true nature of Catholicism, lest they fall back into Babylon. In these tracts Knollys identified "Papal-Rome" with "mystical-Babylon," the pope as the Beast, Catholicism as the Whore and Catholic priests as the false Prophets of Revelation. The historical and millenarian perspective on Revelation, which the Baptists had inherited, was clearly revealed throughout Knollys's writings. He expected "that the Lord Jesus Christ will come personally, visibly, and suddenly; That he will set up his Kingdom and will Reign, raise the Dead and Judge." During the 1640s and 1650s, his millenarianism brought him into contact with numerous radicals and subversives. He was on good terms with many of the Fifth Monarchists and some fourteen members of his congregation later signed the anti-Protectorate Fifth Monarchist *Declaration of Several of the Churches of Christ* in 1654. Knollys himself, however, believed that the power of Christ to usher in the Kingdom was "the power of the word, not the power of the sword." As a result, he was not involved with the militant millenarian schemes of his time.[15]

Hanserd Knollys was without question the most important Baptist convert after the publication of the 1644 confession. The "Kiffin-Manuscript" recorded both the motivation and the results of the confession, saying that the Baptists "being much spoken against as unsound in doctrine as if they were Arminians, and also against Magistrates etc. they joined together in a confession of their faith in fifty two articles which gave great satisfaction to many that had been prejudiced" against them. While Knollys's career demonstrates that some people were indeed relieved of their prejudices by the confession, others were not. While some admitted that they had been misguided in their conceptions of the Baptists, many critics argued that the confession did not represent the majority of Baptist opinion. Some saw it as a trick, "a little ratsbane in a great quantity of sugar." Baptists were disappointed that the confession had not achieved its intended goals.[16]

Particular Baptists were especially disturbed in the mid-1640s by a new spate of pamphlets denouncing the Anabaptists. A telling example was the *Anabaptists Catechisme: With all their Practices, Meetings and Exercises,* which appeared in London the year after the confession. This was an effort on the part of Independents to differentiate themselves from the Anabaptists. When the Anabaptist

---

[15]Hanserd Knollys, *An Exposition of the Whole Book of the Revelation* (London, 1689); idem, *An Exposition of the Eleventh Chapter of Revelation* (London, 1679), 10-13, 24-25; idem, *The World That Now is; and the World that is to Come: or The First and Second Coming of Jesus Christ* (London, 1681), sig. a2, 13; idem, *Mystical Babylon Unvailed* (London, 1679), 3, 7, 16, 24, passim.

[16]Burrage, *Early English Dissenters,* vol. 2, 304; Featley, *Dippers Dipt,* 220.

of the text was asked "Are all Independents of your opinion?" the response was "no, none but only Anabaptists." The Independent in the fictitious dialogue told the Anabaptist that "we deny to be Independents, though they call us so, because you and other factious people are so; common people not knowing the difference; we do . . . [abhor the] false doctrine which you do daily broach among you. There is more difference between us and you, than between you and Papists."

The pamphlet revived the old accusations of obscenity and promiscuity associated with Anabaptists. It was claimed that the Baptists lied to the public and kept secret the true activities of their meetings, "least the world render us more odious than they do already." The Anabaptists allegedly had to swear "not publicly to discover the failings of our brethren and sisters," before they could be baptized.

Another accusation commonly leveled against the Anabaptists was that they professed "that all goods, husband, wife, and all things whatsoever any Congregation have is in common to all," and that "no man is to lye with his brothers wife, whilst her husband is in presences, except he be fast asleep, or dead drunk." When the Anabaptist was asked "who are your preachers, and what are they?" the response was that "there are divers: viz. Mr. Patient, an honest Glover; and Mr. Griffin [Griffith], a reverend Taylor; and Mr. Knowles [Knollys], a learned scholar; Mr. Spilsbery [Spilsbury], a renowned Cobbler; Mr. Barber, a Button-maker, and diverse others, most gallant teachers, well grounded in their opinions."[17]

If Particular Baptists were not enraged enough at being mentioned by name in the "Anabaptists Catechisme," they considered it intolerable to be listed alongside well-known General Baptist leaders such as Griffith and Barber. In the same year that *The Anabaptists Catechisme* appeared, Daniel Featley published his sensational *The Dippers dipt. Or, The Anabaptists duck't and plunged Over Head and Ears.* This text proved immensely popular and almost immediately

---

[17]*The Anabaptists Catechisme* (London, 1645), 1, 3, 5-7, 10, 13.

went through three editions. The text was a combination of sensationalism and reasoned argument and thus had to be treated with more seriousness than purely scandalous publications like *The Anabaptists Catechisme*. Samuel Richardson, who would emerge as the principal Particular Baptist apologist, quickly responded to Featley's book with his *Some Briefe Considerations on Doctor Featley his Book* (1645).

Richardson strongly denied the Particular Baptists' association with the Anabaptists and pointed out that Featley was greatly misguided in attributing the panoply of European Anabaptist errors to the English Baptists. To make matters worse, Featley was also incorrect in his description of many of the Anabaptist errors. In addition to refuting a number of Featley's charges, Richardson also tried to discredit Featley himself, explaining that he was guilty of far greater errors and delusions than were the Baptists. Richardson also asked, even "if it be an error to be baptized again, whether the punishment . . . some have suffered, be not too great?" He reiterated the Baptist plea for liberty of conscience and associated those who persecuted, punished, and imprisoned with the forces of evil. In addition to his numerous charges against Baptists, Featley had also articulated a series of criticisms aimed directly at the 1644 confession. These charges were taken very seriously by the London leaders who were trying earnestly to accommodate.[18]

Recognizing that they were still being associated with the Anabaptists and the General Baptists and concerned by renewed criticism, Particular Baptist leaders gathered again in 1646 to revise and reissue the confession. They had the same objectives in mind as they had two years earlier. The first adjustment they made was to change almost all of the language that Featley had objected to in *The*

---

[18]Samuel Richardson, *Some Briefe Considerations on Doctor Featley his book, intituled, The Dipper Dipt, Wherein in Some measure is Discovered his Many great and False accusations of divers persons, Commonly Called Anabaptists, with an Answer to them, and some brief Reasons for their Practice . . .* (London, 1645), 4, passim.

Dippers dipt.[19] To make clear that they were not Anabaptists, the articles on the magistrate were condensed and two new articles included. The first new article permitted Baptists to hold public office and swear oaths, directly denying two well-known characteristics of the Continental Anabaptists. The second new article detailed the Baptists' belief in the nature of the final resurrection when "everyone shall give an account of himself to God." Despite this new article on the final judgment, the majority of revisions resulted in a softening of the millenarian suggestions of the 1644 edition. The article "Touching his Kingdom" and discussing the "conflicts against Satan, the World, the Flesh and the temptations of them" was substantially shortened. This article, with its descriptions of Christ's goodness being "clouded and overwhelmed for a time" and Satan's "ruling in the world," was condensed in the hope of winning favor with more conservative Protestants. Additionally, the article that discussed the unity of Christ and that all true believers were "co-heirs and joint heirs with [Christ] of the inheritance of all the promises of this life, and that which is to come," was significantly shortened.[20]

---

[19]Daniel Featley's critique of the confession consisted of six criticisms, the first five of which resulted in changes to the confession. Featley's criticism that the Baptists' use of Revelation, Corinthians and Ephesians in Article XXXI of the 1644 confession implied that only believers had any real ownership of property—something that sounded like the communism of Münster—resulted in an additional clause in 1646 saying that "Outward and temporal things are lawfully enjoyed by a civil right by them who have no faith." Featley also criticized the phrase "they that preach the Gospel, should live on the Gospel and not by constraint to be compelled from the people by forced Law" in Article XXXVIII. The clause was left out of the 1646 edition and the entire article removed from the 1651 edition. In reference to Article XXXIX, Featley maintained that it would not be heretical if the word "only" was omitted from the sentence "that Baptism is an Ordinance of the New Testament, given by Christ, to be dispensed only upon persons professing faith . . ." It was removed. The specific words used in Article XL were also revised according to Featley's criticism. As a result of Featley's mocking of the phrase "preaching Disciple" in Article XLI, the word "preaching" was omitted from all later editions. Featley's sixth objection was to the language of Article XLV, concerning the qualifications for prophecy, to which the Baptists did not directly respond (Featley, *Dippers Dipt*, 219-227; Lumpkin, *Confessions*, 140-170, especially 165-167).

[20]Lumpkin, *Confessions*, Article XIX, XXVII, LII, 148, 161-162, 164.

While the millenarian suggestions were softened, the Calvinism of the new edition was significantly strengthened. Again, this was part of the Particular Baptists' effort to define themselves in contrast to the General Baptists. The first confession had tried to make the Particular Baptists' Calvinist orthodoxy clear, it was now hoped that small technical revision would further that cause. Reprobation and the nature of the elect were emphasized. Additionally, after the appearance of the 1646 confession, Benjamin Cox wrote An Appendix to a Confession of Faith (1646), which was meant to accompany and clarify the new edition of the confession. Cox was a former clergyman and his Cambridge theological training was evident in his strong Calvinist writing. Cox had joined the Particular Baptists in the interval between the first and second confessions and of all the pieces of Baptists theology that he penned, his Appendix was perhaps the most important. This piece further emphasized the Particular Baptists' Calvinism, focusing on Christ's death for the elect only and the eternal punishment of the lost. Cox also explained an additional point in his Appendix. Now, only baptized believers should be allowed to the "use of the supper." Those who observed this doctrine came to accept only baptized believers as members of their congregations and became known as "closed communion" Baptists. This was in contrast to "open communion" churches, like those of Henry Jessey and John Bunyan. In this way the Appendix was helping to define the Particular Baptists in contrast not only to the General Baptists, but also against the Independent Baptists. William Kiffin would become a campion of this cause, while John Bunyan would write in defense of open communion.[21]

---

[21]Benjamin Cox, An Appendix to a Confession of Faith, or a more Full Declaration of the Faith and Judgement of Baptized Believers . . . Published for the Further Clearing of Truth, and discovery of Their Mistakes who have Imagined a Dissent in Fundamentals where there is none (London, 1646), 1-8, passim; White, English Baptists, 73-74; William Kiffin, A Sober Discourse of Right o Church-Communion. Wherein is proved by Scripture, the example of the primitive times, and the Practice of All that Have Professed the Christian Religion: that No Unbaptized Person may be regularly admitted to the Lords Supper (London, 1681); idem, epistle to [Some seri]ous reflections on that part of [Mr]. Bunion's [Con]fession of faith: [t]ouching [church] communion with [unbapti]zed persons (London, 1673); John Bunyan, A Confession

In addition to this newly highlighted Calvinism, the 1646 confession also contained a new conclusion that explained that the Baptists "desire to give unto Christ that which is his, and unto all lawful Authority that which is their due . . . so it may prove us to be conscionable, quiet, and harmless people, (no way dangerous or troublesome to human Society)." At the same time that Baptists insisted on their harmlessness, they reiterated their readiness to "die a thousand deaths, rather than to do any thing against the least tittle of the truth of God, or against the light of our own consciences." The 1646 confession ends with "Come, Lord Jesus, come quickly." This echo of the end of Revelation, augmented by a desperate adverb, reveals the continued importance of the apocalypse for the Baptists, despite their increased effort at accommodation.[22]

The conclusion to the 1646 confession demonstrates the Baptists' internal tension. The day after George Thomason obtained a copy of the newly revised confession, Samuel Richardson was standing outside the door of the House of Commons distributing copies to members as they entered the chamber. He hoped that this revised edition would win sympathy from the authorities. Other Baptists were not as eager. While the revised confession had a more conciliatory tone towards the world, many Baptists were still more interested in transforming society than appeasing it. Men such as Thomas Killcop and Paul Hobson, while intimate friends with more conservative Baptists such as Kiffin and Spilsbury, were not as devoted as their companions to pacifying the Baptists. The actions of such men provides some insight into the other half of the Baptists' transformation.[23]

---

of My Faith (London, 1672); idem, Differences in Judgment About Water-Baptism, No Bar to Communion (London, 1673).

   [22]Lumpkin, Confessions, 149. Changes to subsequent editions of the confession, reissued in 1651 and 1652, show that the current concern for the Baptists was the threat posed by the Quakers. Most of the significant changes in these later editions re-emphasized the Baptists' biblicism in response to the threat of George Fox's "inner light."

   [23]Journals of the House of Commons, vol. 4, 420-421. Richardson was certainly disappointed. Instead of being embraced by the House, he was detained and reprimanded, as was the confession's publisher. The House further ordered that "the Sergeant at Arms do immediately send some of his servants to seize and suppress the confession.

Thomas Killcop was associated with the Jacob-Lathrop-Jessey congregation by 1640, and later emerged as a central leader of the Particular Baptists in London. In 1642, he published the first Particular Baptist treatise on believer's baptism.[24] Six years later, Killcop was compelled to publish a tract attacking one of his fellow Baptist leaders. In 1647, Killcop's Baptist counterpart, Samuel Richardson, published a work entitled *Justification by Christ Alone*.[25] Killcop responded with his *Ancient and Durable Gospel*. In Killcop's mind, Richardson's eschatology was wrong. Using the millenarian perspective of Robert Maton, Killcop critiqued Richardson's misunderstanding of justification. He explained that "justification is by Christ alone, I grant, and that he shall take away and utterly destroy the sins of his people . . . I affirm; but that he hath done this already, I deny; for they are not spotless, till Christ's appearing." With Christ's appearing the Jews would be restored to the Holy Land and the Kingdom of God would be established on earth. The dead would then be raised and made pure.

Killcop insisted that his fellow Baptist leader had misunderstood the idea of redemption through Christ. Redemption had not occurred at the past moment of Christ's crucifixion, but would occur in the near future with Christ's return. Killcop explained that "the things purchased are not effected, nor by us fully enjoyed, till Christ's Second Coming, at which time the saints that sleep shall arise, and scattered Israel shall be gathered."

As a result of his millenarianism, Killcop also maintained that "Christ's disciples' authority for the practice of his commands is unlimited." While Killcop's ideas were never as widely accepted among the Baptists as Richardson's were, his argument demonstrates

---

[24]Thomas Killcop, *A short Treatise of Baptisme Wherein is Declared that only Christs Disciples or Beleevers are to be Baptised. And that the baptising of infants hath no footing in the Word of God, but is a mere tradition, received from our forefathers* (London, 1642). This text appeared around the same time as Barber's *A Small Treatise Of Baptisme* (London, 1642).

[25]The introduction to this text by Richardson was written by William Kiffin, showing the continued common friendship and theology between Richardson and Kiffin.

the way in which Baptists were defining themselves internally during the 1640s. They were not afraid to publish against each other, even though they had been fellow signatories of both the 1644 and 1646 confession.[26]

Paul Hobson was another Baptist leader opposed to accommodation. He spent much of the 1640s and 1650s serving in the Parliamentary forces. After the Restoration he was frequently in and out of jail for his alleged involvement in plots. While he preferred evangelizing to debating small points of doctrine, he also wrote some important works of theology. In 1645 he wrote *The Fallacy of Infants Baptisme Discovered*. The following year he published his *Practicall Divinity* and in 1647 he published the text of his famous sermon, *A Garden Inclosed*. While he was most influential as a preacher, these publications along with other tracts by Hobson helped to shape the Particular Baptist movement. Not only did they further define and defend Particular Baptist positions, but they also added a flavor of ecstatic spiritualism to Baptist theology. While his books were well received, he preferred preaching to publishing. Thomas Edwards blamed Hobson for disturbing congregations and, like John Webb, keeping ministers "out of their own pulpits by force of arms, . . . coming up into the ministers pulpits with their swords by their sides, and against the mind of ministers and people." Before 1646 he was busy evangelizing in Essex and later in Suffolk. He had joined the army by 1644 and was a captain in Fairfax's foot regiment, where he distinguished himself as a renowned lay preacher. He opposed the Protectorate,

---

[26]Thomas Killcop, *Ancient and Durable Gospel . . . By Way of Answer to a Book Intituled: Justification by Christ Alone: A Good Title, Were the Book but Sutable* (London, 1648), i, 2, 20,30-31, 105-108, Robert Maton, *Israel's Redemption or The Propheticall History of Our Saviours Kingdome on Earth* (London, 1642). Maton was an important theologian who whose writings on eschatology obvious influenced the Baptists. Killcop's work was heavily reliant on Maton and he ended his *Ancient and Durable Gospel* in saying, "I commend to thy further view the writings of Robert Maton," (108); Thomas Killcop, *The Unlimited Authority of Christs Disciples Cleared, or The Present Church and Ministry Vindicated* (London, 1651), 1-3. For more on the thought of Robert Maton, see Mark R. Bell, "The Revolutionary Roots of Anglo-American Millenarianism: Robert Maton's *Istrael's Redemption* and *Christ's Personall Reign on Earth*," *Journal of Millennial Studies* 2 (2000): 1-8.

strongly resented tithes, was frequently accused of plotting against the state, and was finally banished to exile in the Carolinas the year before his death.[27]

Hobson's preference for preaching over theorizing was not due to a lack of theological acumen. Instead, it was driven by apocalyptic urgency. Edwards noted: "Where ever he came he would preach publicly in the Churches, where he could get Pulpits, and privately to soldiers." As the new times were dawning, small points of doctrine were less important. Witnessing to the times at hand was his urgent mandate. He firmly believed that he was living at the start of an age of purification, when "congregations picked out of congregations" would continue to reach increased stages of bliss and proximity to Christ, until "there will be a people who kiss and embrace one another in spirit, and shall live in loving and enjoying one another far more than ever yet our eyes have seen."

Although he looked anxiously forward to the second advent, he also believed that Christ's Kingdom could be immediately entered by the saints in the present through a mystical union with Christ, for "no man can live in the bosom of Christ, and in the glory of Christ," and not be "made one with Christ. Saints, they are not only made perfect hereafter . . . but they are admitted and have some entrance to heaven here."[28]

Like many Baptists, such deep inner enthusiasm provided the courage and motivation to try outwardly to transform the world. Men such as Killcop and Hobson illustrate that even in the mid-1640s different Baptist leaders had different conceptions of the Kingdom and how to bring about its advent. Nevertheless, the accommodationist tendency among the Particular Baptists would accelerate as society became more accepting of them. Soon the Baptists began to

---

[27]Edwards, *Gangraena, Second Part of Gangraena,* 173, *Third Part of Gangraena,* 45-46. A thorough study of Hobson appears in Richard Greaves, *Saints and Rebels: Seven Nonconformists in Stuart England* (Macon: Mercer University Press, 1985), chpt. 5.

[28]Edwards, *Gangraena,* (1st part, 2nd ed.), 121-122; Paul Hobson, *Practicall Divinity: or a Helpe Through the Blessing of God to Lead men more To Look Within Themselves* (London, 1646), 86, 92.

disassociate themselves from more radical elements in society in order to win greater acceptance. The first major demonstration of such actions came in the late 1640s when the Baptists broke off their alliance with the politically radical Levellers.

6

UNEASY ALLIANCES:
BAPTISTS AND LEVELLERS

Paul Hobson was just one of many Baptists to find his way into the Parliamentary forces during the Civil Wars of the 1640s. Numerous Baptists joined the army, both as soldiers and as chaplains. The opportunity for advancement, regardless of religious belief, was an attractive aspect of military service. In a telling letter dated 1644 to Major General Crawford concerning his Baptist Lieutenant-Colonel Warner, Oliver Cromwell wrote, "Sir, the State, in choosing men to serve them, takes no notice of their opinions, if they be willing to faithfully serve . . . that satisfies."[1] Cromwell had an equally pithy rejoinder when he heard the complaint that one Baptist Lieutenant preached better than he fought: "Truly I think that he that prays and preaches best will fight best."[2]

The Baptists proved to be good preachers as well as good fighters in both of the Civil Wars.[3] Those who did not join the ranks often

---

[1]Wilbur Cortez Abbott, ed., *The Writings and Speeches of Oliver Cromwell* (Cambridge, Massachusetts: Harvard University Press, 1937), vol. 1, 277-278. Cromwell stressed that it was important "to bear with men of different minds from yourself" and to "take heed of being sharp . . . against those to whom you can object little but that they square not with you in every opinion concerning matters of religion." Evidently, Crawford was not very sympathetic towards Baptists, and had to be further reprimanded by Cromwell after Crawford had arrested one of Cromwell's lieutenants, the Baptist Robert Packer, for lay preaching. See David Masson, ed., *The Quarrel Between the Earl of Manchester and Oliver Cromwell: An Episode of the English Civil War* (Westminster: Camden Society, 1875), 59. Packer was later "allied with the London Fifth Monarchy preachers" (*Biographical Dictionary of British Radicals*, vol. 3, 1).

[2]Abbott, *The Writings and Speeches of Oliver Cromwell*, vol. 2, 378.

[3]Unlike the pacifist Anabaptists, the English Baptists had few reservations about war. This was certainly true for the Particular Baptist movement. Late in the 1650s some General Baptists appear to have become concerned about the question of Christians serving in the army, see White, *English Baptists*, 53.

served as influential chaplains in the army, such as Thomas Collier, "a rare man," greatly concerned with eschatological questions and extremely popular among the people, who flocked "from the towns . . . to hear him" preach.[4] The army provided a vehicle for the dissemination of Baptist ideas, and as Richard Baxter observed in despair, soon there were "swarms of Anabaptists in our armies."[5]

Soldiers were not the only converts. As Baptists were stationed in various regions throughout the British Isles, they formed Baptist churches among the inhabitants near their station. The result was that the army proved to be the most effective means of evangelizing in Britain, and it was only after their activities had abated that planned missionary efforts were required to continue the rapid spread of Baptist ideas. Of course, such coordinated missionary efforts would require further organization on the part of the Baptist leaders after the wars.

Many Baptists viewed the Civil Wars in an eschatological context as a fight between the forces of good and evil. They were not unique in this belief. Numerous Puritan ministers also understood the conflict between the king and Parliament as a battle between popery and godliness. While such Puritans shared Baptists' belief that the army was a divine tool for bringing about the Kingdom, they did not share the Baptists' hope that it would establish religious liberty. This hope was, however, shared by the Levellers.[6]

---

[4]Edwards, *Second Part of Gangraena*, 148. Numerous Baptists held important positions in the army, including, Lieutenant Robert Barrow, Captain Richard Beaumont, Lieutenant Edmund Chillenden, etc. Other important Baptist army chaplains were the General Baptists Jeremiah Ives and Thomas Lambe and the Particular Baptists Thomas Blackwood and Edward Harrison. For additional Baptist chaplains, see Anne Laurence, *Parliamentary Army Chaplains 1642-1651* (Woodbridge, Suffolk: Boydell Press, 1990) and the D.Phil. dissertation on which it is based, "Parliamentary Army Chaplains 1642-1651," Oxford University, 1981). The Seventh-Day Baptist leader, Edward Stennett, was also reportedly an army chaplain (see *Biographical Dictionary of British Radicals*) although he does not appear in Laurence's work.

[5]A. S .P Woodhouse, *Puritanism and Liberty* (London: J. M. Dent and Sons Limited, 1938), 388.

[6]The Levellers were not affiliated with any one single church or sect, although they received support from many sectaries.

The opponents of this movement gave them their name, implying that they wanted "to level all men's estates, and subvert all govern-ment."[7] Originating around 1645, the movement came to advocate various radical reforms, including a widening of the franchise, the opening of enclosed lands, the abolition of monarchy, and the equality of men under the law, as well as a social contract as the foundation for government. It is possible that the bases for the Leveller's egalitarian policies derived in part from General Baptist theology, particularly the idea of universal equality and accountability before God. The Levellers also shared the Baptist desire for religious liberty and the removal of tithes. Numerous personal affinities also brought the Baptist movements and the Levellers together. While common goals, mutual enemies, and shared experiences in the army allowed the Baptists and Levellers to cooperate in the mid-1640s, their alliance was always unstable. Their agendas frequently over-lapped, but they were never identical. As a result, the Baptists eventually abandoned the Levellers.[8]

In 1645, however, the breakdown of this alliance would have been hard to predict. At that time Baptist congregations were the natural allies of the Levellers. The three most prominent Leveller leaders, John Lilburne, William Walwyn, and Richard Overton, were already personally close to the congregations, which played a vital role in the organization of the Levellers' program. In the early days of the movement, John Lilburne, the main leader of the Levellers, "received the support of the Baptists led by his old friend William Kiffin," who had been his fellow apprentice. Lilburne was also well known to the various congregations in London. He was seen as a fellow sufferer for the sake of conscience. As Kiffin's epistle to Lilburne's *Christian Mans*

---

[7] Don Wolfe, ed., *Leveller Manifestoes* (New York: Nelson and Sons, 1944), 238.

[8] A similar story is true for the Levellers' relationship with other gathered churches, namely the Independents (i.e. Congregationalists). On this point and generally for the relationship between the London sectaries and the Levellers, see Tolmie, *Triumph*, and Iwan Russell-Jones, "The Relationship Between Theology and Politics in the Writings of John Lilburne, Richard Overton and William Walwyn." D.Phil. Dissertation, Oxford University, 1987.

Triall demonstrated, many saw Lilburne as a champion for their cause. Indeed, Particular Baptist leader Richard Lawrence even called Lilburne one of the "champions of these times." During one of Lilburne's numerous stints in prison, Hanserd Knollys, who was allegedly commanding large audiences, prayed "Lord, bring thy servant Lilburne out of prison, and honor him, for he hath honored thee."[9]

William Walwyn, another Leveller leader, also had a history of associating with Baptists. Amid the negative press that the Baptists were receiving in 1644, Walwyn published *The Compassionate Samaritane*, which defended the "Brownists and Anabaptists." He was "no separatist," but he could testify to "the innocency of their intentions and honesty of their lives." That same year he was associated with Paul Hobson, although the two may have known each other previously. His friends among the Particular Baptists were evidently familiar with *Compassionate Samaritane* and they echoed it in their confession later that year. Walwyn had also defended the Baptists personally when a committee of examinations targeted Baptists in order to control lay preaching. He remembered that this committee was "of a most persecuting disposition, and dealt most forwardly with divers conscientious people; with whom, and in whose behalf, I continually appeared; as for Mr. Kiffin, Mr. Patience [Patient], and many others, I cannot now remember." In other words, by the mid-1640s, Walwyn had a long history not only of sympathizing with the Baptists, but also of defending them publicly, both in print and in person.[10]

The third central Leveller leader, Richard Overton, had particularly close relations with the General Baptists. It appears certain that at some point in his life he was a member of the General Baptists, but the official status of his membership in the sect during the 1640s is

---

[9]William Haller, ed., *The Leveller Tracts 1647-1653* (New York: Columbia University Press, 1944), 6; Richard Lawrence, *The Antichristian Presbyter* (London, 1647), 5; Edwards, *Gangraena* (1st part, 2nd ed.), 40, 65-79;

[10]*Biographical Dictionary of British Radicals*, vol. 2, 95; David Wooton, ed., *Divine Right and Democracy* (New York: Penguin, 1986), 248-249; Haller, *The Leveller Tracts*, 354.

unclear. There exists in the Mennonite archives in Amsterdam an enigmatic document labeled by Champlin Burrage as "an undated Latin Confession of Faith by Richard Overton, probably written in 1615." This dating is in some dispute, and it has even been suggested that the document was signed as late as the 1640s.[11]

Overton's writings do not help clarify the nature of his relationship with the General Baptists, but he clearly had deep sympathies and close relations with the movement. He appears numerous times with various General Baptists and seems to have had both their trust and their support. Overton soon emerged as the finest polemicist for the Leveller cause, and through his writings, personal connections, and leadership, he recruited numerous General Baptists into the Leveller movement.

Thomas Edwards recorded how Overton took part in General Baptist disputation at Spitalfields "about the immortality of the soul" and specifically about the proposition that "God made man, and every part of man of the dust of the earth; and therefore man and every part of man must return to dust again." The General Baptist leader Thomas Lambe was another active participant in the debate. Lambe's congregation served as a hub for Overton's Leveller activities. It was evidently a place where the latest Leveller petitions could be sent and read for signatures. General Baptists also played a central role in the distribution of Leveller literature. Numerous visible General Baptist leaders connected to Lambe's congregation, such as Samuel Oates and Jeremiah Ives, were apprehended while carrying Leveller manifestos. Another General Baptist, Samuel Fulcher, was detained

---

[11]Richard Overton is often identified as a General Baptists and may have been a member of a General Baptist congregation in the 1640s, see for example W. Haller, *Liberty and Reformation in the Puritan Revolution* (New York: Columbia University Press, 1955), 175-178. Burrage, *Early English Dissenters*, vol. 2, 216-218. For the debate over the dating of this document, see Russell-Jones, "The Relationship Between Theology and Politics," 87-90 and Marie Gimelfarb-Brack, *Liberte, Egalite, Fraternite, Justice! la vie et l'oeuvre de Richard Overton, Niveleur* (Berne: P. Lang, 1979), where it is argued that Overton became a General Baptist in 1642. This argument, based on an apparent change in Overton's literary style and production, is not very convincing, see also Gimelfarb-Brack's article on Overton in *Biographical Dictionary of British Radicals*.

for selling a pamphlet titled *The Last Warning to all . . . of London*. The General Baptists also assisted Overton in the production of Leveller materials. By the mid-1640s Nicholas Tew of Lambe's congregation helped Overton run a secret press in Coleman Street, which brought Overton into contact with William Larner—the Baptist bookseller and publisher responsible for the production of both of the works that bore Kiffin's name in 1641. Tew and Overton's press ultimately brought them into contact with John Lilburne himself. The General Baptist influence among the lower ranks of the army meant their continued support of the Levellers was crucial for the Levellers' success. [12]

Edward Barber, the General Baptist frequently associated with the laying on of hands, was also a Leveller supporter. His stance against religious persecution was clear from the beginning of the 1640s when he petitioned the king to alleviate persecution, maintaining that compulsion would, at best, only make men hypocrites. Barber had been imprisoned for his rejection of infant baptism and had also been persecuted for his rejection of tithes, which he saw as a denial of the personal reign of Christ. From his first imprisonment in the early 1640s until his death, Barber continued to work for religious liberty and the abolition of tithes. In 1649 he published *An Answer to the Essex Watchmen's Watchword*, which in addition to reiterating many of his previous arguments against tithes and religious compulsion, also supported the Levellers' *Agreement of the People*. Barber explained that the Leveller program not only provided Englishmen their just natural

---

[12]Edwards, *Second Part of Gangraena*, 17-18. Prior to this debate, Overton had anonymously published his *Mans Mortalitie*, which made clear that he held the mortalist view that the human soul sleeps with the body until the Resurrection. While Overton's development of this idea came from a reading of ancient philosophers and church fathers, it is likely that the limited but not insignificant acceptance that it gained within General Baptist circles was due primarily to their belief in a literal resurrection and a literal interpretation of creation, as evidenced in phrase "God made . . . man of the dust . . . and therefore man . . . must return to the dust again." W. Haller, *The Rise of Puritanism* (New York: Columbia University Press, 1938), 396; Tolmie, *Triumph*, 151-152.

rights, but it also allowed for the free working of King Jesus to set up his government among the saints.[13]

Another leader and occasional millenarian, Edmund Chillenden, provides an example of General Baptist involvement in the Leveller movement. Although he was never a fully committed Leveller himself, Chillenden was once a close friend of John Lilburne and had deep sympathies for the Levellers. His position and his popularity meant that he had access to information from both army officers and lower ranking soldiers. In March 1647 he sent the army a copy of the Leveller petition that had been presented to the Commons. Along with this petition he sent a warning to agitators that the Parliament sought to divide the soldiers against each other. He kept the Baptists informed of Leveller developments and communicated Baptist input to Levellers in the army. Agitators also sent him to gather information in London regarding the disbanding of the army. Chillenden's contacts between London, the Baptist congregations, the agitators, and officers allowed him to act as an informant for the Leveller movement. Activities like those of the General Baptist Edmund Chillenden were also undertaken by Particular Baptists such as William Allen. Like Chillenden, Allen served as bridge between the congregations and the agitators.[14]

Such deep involvement between the Levellers and the Baptists is readily understood. The Leveller program offered the Baptists the best possibility of realizing their goal of religious liberty. Additionally, the Levellers wanted to abolish the tithe system, which was seen by the Baptists as a vestige of a popish church hierarchy. The Levellers, however, went one step beyond the Baptists in accepting the division of church and state as more than just a temporary expediency until

---

[13] Edward Barber, *To the Kings Most Excellent Majesty* (London, 1641); idem, *An Answer to the Essex Watchmen's Watchword* (London, 1649); *Biographical Dictionary of British Radicals*, vol. 1, 35.

[14]Capp. *Fifth Monarchy*, 91, 245; C. H. Firth, ed. *The Clarke Papers* (London: Camden Society, 1891), vol. 1, 430; Woodhouse, *Puritanism and Liberty*, 400-401; H. Cary, *Memorials of the Great Civil War* (London: Colburn, 1842), vol. 1, 201-205; Tolmie, *Triumph*, 160.

the coming of King Jesus. Rather, the Levellers rejected any form of godly rule; they advanced the "secular" state as legitimate in its own right based on rationality as opposed to divine grace. In the end, this difference proved to be too great a gap for the Baptist movements to bridge. As Iwan Russell-Jones concluded, "Thus, while the Levellers' political platform developed as an attempt to translate into reality the separation of church and state that was at the heart of Separatist ecclesiology, it failed because of the opposition of the very people whose ideas it was intended to reflect and embody." The Levellers were the Baptists' best hope for actualizing their long sought after goals. As it turned out, the support of the Baptist movements was the Levellers' best hope for winning the support necessary to realize their agenda.[15]

The months following the close of the first Civil War were a crucial time for the Baptists. They recognized that Parliament's victory over King Charles's forces offered an opportunity to advance their agenda, but they were uncertain as to how to proceed. From the beginning of the Civil War many Puritans had pushed for the establishment of a comprehensive Presbyterian system. Now that the war was over, many felt it was high-time that such a system was implemented.

When Baptists like William Allen, Paul Hobson, and Henry Denne, left the army, only to find themselves faced with the possibility of a conservative Presbyterian settlement, they quickly rejoined the ranks. At the same time that these Baptists were re-enlisting in the army, many Presbyterians were leaving in frustration over the regiments' refusal to disband. The Presbyterians recognized that their

---

[15]Russell-Jones, "The Relationship Between Theology and Politics," iii; Woodhouse in *Puritanism and Liberty* observed that "two significant types of opinion emerged among the sectaries. The one is recognizable as predominantly democratic in tendency, and ultimately secular in aim, though it maintains its emphasis on liberty of conscience and at times adopts the language of religious enthusiasm. This is the opinion of . . . Lilburne, Overton . . . and others. . . . The second type of opinion is at bottom neither democratic in tendency nor secular in aim. It emphasizes not the rights of the people, but the privileges of the Saints, and it looks forward to the millennium . . . when the Saints shall inherit the earth and rule it with, or on behalf of, Christ" (18).

center of power was in London, while the Baptists concluded that theirs remained in the army. Consequently, many Baptists were given the opportunity for rapid advancement through the ranks in order to fill the offices vacated by the Presbyterians. Paul Hobson became a major while his fellow Baptists John Turner and Nathaniel Strange were promoted to lieutenant. Soon Baptists John Gardiner and Benjamin Groome became captains and by 1649 Paul Hobson had risen all the way to Lieutenant-Colonel. Numerous other Baptists experienced a similar ascent. These Baptists knew that if a Presbyterian system were established, their religious liberty would be curtailed. The fear of conservative victory helped to hold together the alliance between the Levellers and the sectaries.[16]

At this stage, the uneasy alliance between the Baptists and the Levellers depended on two things: common goals and common opposition to the Presbyterians. For Baptists, both of these conditions stemmed from their eschatology. The eschatological outlook that Baptists had developed naturally led them to identify the Presbyterians with the forces of Antichrist. Since John Smyth the various Baptist movements had identified hierarchical religion as a mark of the Beast. Thomas Edwards reported that John Webb, a leader of the "Anabaptists . . . loves not the Scottish Nation, but terms them the Babylonish Beast, and the Presbyteriall Government the Priests Monopoly." In other words, the Baptists perceived their struggle against the Presbyterians as a continuation of their fight against the forces of Antichrist.[17]

In the same way, the Baptists could not conceive of the Leveller reforms in terms of a society based on something similar to a social contract conception of government based on rights. Instead they saw such reforms in a millenarian light. The apocalyptic nature of Baptist opposition to the Presbyterians and their support for the Levellers' reforms was demonstrated in two Baptist publications appearing in 1647.

---

[16]Tolmie, *Triumph*, 158.
[17]Edwards, *Gangraena* (1st part, 2nd ed.), 86-87.

The first of these two texts was penned by Richard Lawrence, a Particular Baptist who had risen to the military rank of Marshal-General of the Horse in 1645. Lawrence wanted to delineate the full ramifications of a Presbyterian settlement, not because he had petty feuds with individual Presbyterians, but rather because he recognized the apocalyptic implications of such a settlement. As a result, he published *The Antichristan Presbyter: or Antichrist Transformed; Assuming the New Shape of a Reformed Presbyter, as his Last and Subtlest Disguise to Deceive the Nations* (1647). Lawrence placed on the title page a quotation from Revelation 13 that described how Antichrist would deceive the people. The quotation concisely summarized the thrust of his text: Antichrist, he argued, was a crafty deceiver and the saints must not be too confident that he had been banished from England. Indeed, Lawrence recognized that Antichrist was now working through the Presbyterians in a last-ditch effort to ruin England. If Presbyterians succeeded in settling themselves in the old bishops' seats, then Antichrist would triumph and all the blood spilled in the war against the king would have been for naught.

Lawrence warned Englishmen that "old Antichrist" had taken on a "new shape." In order to demonstrate how Antichrist could "shift" form, Lawrence gave a brief account of England's long battle against the forces of evil. This historical/patriotic perspective on the eschato-logical battle was common in England at the time. Lawrence acknowledged that the forces of Antichrist had caused so much bloodshed throughout the Reformation until the "reign of Queen Elizabeth." With Elizabeth's ascension the saints believed that Antichrist would quickly be completely "cast out of Church and State." Such complacency was just what Antichrist had wanted, for now he shifted from being just the forces of popery to taking a Protestant shape. While still expected to take the form of Catholic powers like Rome and Spain and to work through agents such as the Jesuits and "men for the Gun-powder Plot," Antichrist had begun to creep in all around Charles I. Soon the Antichristian plague had spread throughout the nation to such an extent that amputation was required. Lawrence demonstrated how the workings of Antichrist could be seen in numerous events in recent history, such as "ship-money" and "a Book of Common-prayer to be imposed upon the Church of Scotland." For those who insisted that Antichrist was still to be identified as the pope, Lawrence replied "I shall refer you to . . . Mr. Prynne, Dr. Bastwick, Mr. Burton, and Lieu-Col. Lilburne: I wish them to remember the loss of their eares, their branding in the face, their pillory, their whipping-cart, their exile and imprisonment. Ask them if Antichrist cannot persecute as well in the shape of a Protestant as a Papist."

Now that the war was over, Lawrence feared that the same laxity that had allowed Antichrist to come in under Charles I would allow Antichrist to reemerge under the victorious Parliament. He warned that now, because Antichrist's old disguises

> of papists, malignants, cavaliers, etc. are grown odious [and recognizable] to the people . . . this cunning High Priest of theirs, Antichrist, teaches them to call themselves Presbyterians. . . . Thus friends, if you have not resolved to say it is dark when the Sun shines, if ever your parsons tell you so, you may see this Spirit of Malignance and Antichrist in all parts of this Kingdom, in the shape or likeness of Presbyters.

Lawrence argued that the Presbyterians would not be any less brutal and oppressive than previous Antichristian regimes. They were certain to introduce ordinances "against Heresies and Blasphemy, etc." For Antichrist wanted blood and violence, and if the Presbyterians should come to power there would be no peace but only further bloodshed.

Typical of the Baptist conviction that they were in the late stages of the eschatological battle, Lawrence also claimed that Antichrist's latest form was his "last and subtlest disguise to deceive the nations." He implied that once this challenge was overcome, the Kingdom would follow. He warned the saints not to be fooled: this was still the same Antichrist that they had been fighting all along, only now "Antichrist is crept in amongst us in the shape of a Presbyter."

Lawrence's work is an example of the type of eschatological thinking behind many Baptists' resistance to the Presbyterians.[18]

If Lawrence's work demonstrates the eschatological underpinning of the Baptist resistance to the Presbyterians, Thomas Collier's sermon delivered at Putney a few months later illustrates the millenarian foundation for Baptists' support of the Levellers' agenda. Collier was a great Baptist leader and a fervent evangelist who spent most of his life in the western sections of England establishing Baptist churches. He published the sermon that he preached to the soldiers at Putney on September 29, 1647 under the title A *Discovery of the New Creation*.

Christopher Hill saw Collier's sermon as advancing most of the major points of the Leveller program. For Collier and his auditors, a new day had truly burst forth in England. The soldiers' success, the religious freedom, the new light in many of the saints, and the Levellers' proposed reforms all blended without distinction in a beam of radiance reflecting the New Jerusalem.[19]

Collier explained that in "this new creation there is not only New heavens, but a New Earth." This New Earth would see radical reforms in a variety of areas. The New Earth was beginning and Collier wanted to explain what was to be done. "This is the great work . . . that God calls for at your hands, whom he hath raised up for that end." At the foundation of the New Earth would be "the execution of righteousness, justice and mercy, without respect of persons. It is to undo every yoke." Both spiritual and temporal oppression were to be eradicated. The New Earth would be without

> spiritual oppressions in matters of conscience. . . . You know that a long time man hath assumed this power to himself, to rule over the consciences of their brethren: a great oppression and that which cannot be borne in souls who live in light, and

---

[18]Richard Lawrence, *The Antichristian Presbyter* (London, 1647), 1-3, 5, 8-9, 15, 17.
[19]Christopher Hill, *World Turned Upside Down* (London: Penguin Books, 1972), 59.

that from which God will deliver his people, and punish all that oppressed them.

In addition to the spiritual oppressions upon the saints, Collier also gave a list of "temporal oppressions" that were to be undone. These included the "tyrannical and oppressing laws, and courts of justice; hence it comes to pass many times that to seek a remedy proves destructive—the cure proves worse than the disease." There was also the oppression of having laws written in an "unknown tongue" and the call for laws to be publically promulgated in English. There was also the persistent "oppression . . . of tithes," as well as the complaints of the soldiers and the "provisions for the soldiers' pay." Collier concluded this section of his sermon by saying that "whatsoever bears but the face of oppression in it, let it be removed. . . . It is the great design of God at present to exalt righteousness, and certainly God calls for it at your hands."

While these proposed reforms were consistent with the Levellers' agenda, they only represented half of Collier's vision. Alongside the New Earth was the New Heaven. Before there could be a New Earth, Christ was to establish a "glorious Kingdom in the Saints . . . this is the new creation, . . . the Kingdom of heaven that is in the Saints. . . . God himself is the Saints' Kingdom. . . . Where God is manifesting himself, there is his and the Saints' Kingdom." Reforms were to come about not through new laws based on rationality and natural rights, but by "the abundance of light" that accompanies Christ's coming. The unity and equality the Levellers envisioned was only conceivable to the Baptists in terms of a "godly rule," which missed the point of the Levellers' program. Collier explained that it was

> only the glorious light of this new creation that will put an end to these divisions amongst Christians. It is not magisterial power, . . . but that one Spirit of light and truth that must bring the Saints into this unity. . . . And the truth is that nothing else will be able to put an end to these divisions but this spiritual dispensation, this new creation of God . . . and

this is and shall be the glory of this heaven, unity and peace amongst Saints.[20]

For Collier and many other Baptists, the promise of future political transformation was closely connected with the millennium. The Levellers' reforms would be fully realized as part of the eschatological transformation occurring in England, not as part of a "secular" order free from "godly rule." Eschatology lay at the heart of the Baptist-Leveller alliance against the Presbyterians and of Baptist support for Leveller reforms. This had three implications. First, as the threat of a Presbyterian settlement faded, Baptists were less inclined to support the Levellers. Second, as Baptists realized that the Levellers' proposals were not grounded in the same concerns as theirs, Baptists' affinity for the movement subsided. Finally, as Baptists such as Richardson began to change the direction of their eschatology from criticizing the establishment to endorsing it, those aspects of the Leveller agenda that Baptists had supported became less attractive.

The same month that Collier delivered his Putney apocalypse sermon, Kiffin was visiting the captive King Charles at Hampton Court, seeking a settlement favorable to the Particular Baptists. He emerged with the intent of raising support among the Baptists for Oliver Cromwell's initiative of a personal treaty with the king. Apparently, Kiffin and Baptist leaders of a similar mind believed that supporting a personal treaty would provide for religious liberty and at the same time clear them of any accusations of being anarchists. The Levellers deeply resented this effort to win support for Cromwell's policies. Looking back, Lilburne remembered the Baptist leader Samuel Richardson as

> a preacher amongst those unnatural, un-English-like men, that would now destroy the innocent . . . [who] first promot[ed] in England (as Cromwell's beagles to do his

---

[20]Thomas Collier, *A Discovery of a New Creation* (London, 1647), 3-40, also in Woodhouse, *Puritanism and Liberty*, 390-396.

pleasure) . . . the first petition for a personal treaty almost two years ago, and [who] commonly style themselves the preachers to the seven churches of Anabaptists.[21]

Signs of Baptist disenchantment with the Leveller movement continued to appear in 1647. That year a pamphlet appeared entitled, *A Declaration by Severall Congregationall Societies in, and about the City of London; as well of those Commonly Called Anabaptists, as others. In way of vindication of themselves.* The text fervently disowned both the alleged Anabaptist practices of polygamy and communism, as well as the Leveller proposals for "carnal liberty." The text explained that the only form of liberty that should be sought was religious liberty. The document denounced a "secular" constitutional government in preference to magistrates who "fear the Lord," because the authors believed somewhat naively that such magistrates would be more inclined to "protect godly men . . . than other men will be."

This anonymous document written on behalf of those "people fearing God," further denounced the Leveller program as harmful to society. "[F]or all to be equal" in earthly power was thought to be detrimental to "human society, and the promotion of the good of Commonwealths, cities, armies or families." Under such circumstances, the authors asked, "what can be expected but disorders, confusions, jealousies, factions, yea Civil Wars themselves?" The implication was that radical firebrands and not King Charles's policies had been responsible for the recent conflict. Most important, the *Declaration*, demonstrated that its authors believed disassociating themselves from the Levellers was related to disassociating themselves from the radical anarchism of the Anabaptists.

The public expression of such beliefs should have been a warning to the Levellers, but they failed to comprehend that common goals were not enough to hold the alliance together. They assumed that this scurrilous declaration was the work of a few of their Independent enemies, and like most Londoners, they dismissed it. By this time the

---

[21]Haller, *Leveller Tracts*, 209.

rapid advancement of many Baptists in the army had rendered the needs and concerns of the lower ranks less relevant. As the Baptists climbed into new offices, they were less inclined to listen to the Levellers' insistence that the common soldier deserved a greater voice. Near the end of 1647, when the Levellers tried to win the support of the army, Paul Hobson, recently risen in the ranks, supported a *Remonstrance Sent from Colonell Lilburnes Regiment,* which declared the officers' support for Fairfax and declined to support the Levellers. Other Baptists followed his example.[22]

The real writers of the *Declaration by Severall Congregationall Societies* only became apparent in 1651 when the group admitted their authorship in a publication entitled *A Declaration of Divers Elders and Brethren.* With hindsight, however, it is easy to determine the identity of the authors. Persistently eager to avoid the label of "Anabaptists," Hanserd Knollys, William Kiffin, and a number of other Baptists and future Fifth Monarchists made up the majority of signatories. This new declaration still had an apocalyptic tone, but it insisted that it was "but by degrees" that "we attain to further knowledge of the Mystery of Christ and of Antichrist." So many Englishmen had "been drunk with the Babylonish cup," that "the dregs and darkness hence, are not quite dispelled from us." They claimed that the "same common enemies . . . the flesh, the Devil, and the World" had still to be defeated. "The time is coming, and we hope is near at hand. . . . Then they shall have such external Visible Union and Communion that shall Convince the World . . . that the Father hath loved them . . . and therefore it shall certainly be effected."

The apocalyptic language, however, wavered in its direction. The authors admitted that recently "many of them have been judged

---

[22]*A Declaration by Severall Congregationall Societies in, and about the City of London. In way of vindication of themselves* (London, 1647), 3-9; *Remonstrance Sent From Colonell Lilburnes Regiment . . . to Thomas Fairfax . . . Wherein They Declare their Resolutions, to Stand and Fall with him* (London, 1647), the officers' remonstrance, in addition to pledging loyalty, also urged that both Parliament and the army would get on with "that great work that lies upon them," (4); Greaves, *Saints and Rebels,* 139-140. For more on the Levellers and Baptists, see Tolmie, *Treiumph.* The following discussion largely follows Tolmie's "The Particular Baptists reject the Levellers," *Triumph,* 181-184.

worthy of offices and places of trust and preferment." While they had risen and achieved favor with the world, they maintained that it was not in self-interest that obedience should now be offered to the government. They insisted that for the sake of the nation, the good of the churches, and the advancement of their cause, it was best that the "members of churches" honor and submit to the present powers. Now, on the doorstep of a world beyond Babylon, the Baptists hesitated.[23]

When the second Civil War began in 1648, however, the publication of the *Declaration of Divers Elders and Brethren* was still far in the future. A few months after fighting had resumed, Parliament passed a strict blasphemy ordinance calling for the imprisonment of all those who denied infant baptism. Again, a united front among the radicals and congregations seemed necessary. But the Independents were rising and the Levellers were no longer as advantageous an ally. On 6 December 1648, Colonel Thomas Pride stood at the door to the House of Commons, arresting or barring entrance to over 140 Presbyterian members. Those who remained in the "Rump" Parliament were decidedly Independents and they soon set about the trial and execution of the king.

Once the victory of Independency seemed secured, the Particular Baptists rejected the Levellers. The conservative Baptist leaders were now confident that they could pursue their goals without the Levellers. On the last Sunday of March 1649, Levellers came to the gatherings of the Particular Baptists in London hoping to have the congregations support for their latest petition, *The Second Part of England's New Chaines Discovered*. The Leveller agents came to the Baptist meetings and expounded upon the "dangerous condition of the Commonwealth" hoping that "those then present might subscribe" their names to the petition. Evidently, Kiffin's congregation was not persuaded, for three days later one of its members, Daniel

---

[23]A *Declaration of Divers Elders and Brethren* (London, 1651), 1-8. Many of the signatories of this document would later decide their obedience had been too promptly professed and would rebound in the opposite direction, fiercely criticizing the government.

Axtell, arrested the Leveller leader Richard Overton. Lilburne and Walwyn soon joined Overton in the Tower. Before the week was over, Richardson went to see them and asked that they abandon their critiques of the government. The Leveller leaders were surprised by Richardson's apparent betrayal and they refused to mitigate their criticisms.[24]

If Lilburne, Overton, and Walwyn were surprised at Richardson's request that they compromise their radical program, they were even more stunned by the Particular Baptists' actions the next day. That Sunday, Particular Baptist leaders presented to their congregations their own petition, denouncing the one read by the Levellers the previous Sunday. Again, the petition demonstrated the Particular Baptists effort to define themselves in contrast to Anabaptists. They noted "how through the injustice of historians, or the headiness of some unruly men formerly in Germany called Anabaptists, our righteous profession heretofore hath been and now may be made odious, as if it were the fountain and source of all disobedience."

But now, in addition to defining their movement in contrast to Anabaptists, they also defined themselves in stark contrast to the Levellers. They condemned the Levellers' petition and agenda. The petition also assured authorities that "our meetings are not at all to intermeddle with the orderings or altering civil government," despite the well-known fact that Baptist congregations served as a network for the Levellers.

After it was circulated to the various Particular Baptists, this brief petition was presented to Parliament on April 2 and William Kiffin was allowed to address the House. It is difficult to imagine the great relief that Kiffin felt when the Speaker returned the House's answer: "That for yourselves and other Christians walking answerable to such professions as in this petition you make, they do assure you of liberty

---

[24]*The Humble Petition and Representation of Several Churches of God in London, Commonly (though Falsly) called Anabaptists* (London, 1649), 4, 7. Axtell's brutal behavior shocked the Levellers, who once considered him a friend, Haller, *Leveller Tracts*, 209-210, 213-214, 228. Tolmie suggest that such behavior may have arisen "from the doctrinal rivalry of the two kinds of" Baptists, *Triumph*, 189.

and protection." Half a decade before Kiffin had assembled seven London churches in an effort to disassociate the Particular Baptists from the Anabaptists and General Baptists and gain acceptance from society. After years of slander, it now appeared that such long sought after liberty was secured. For the moment, Kiffin could rest.[25]

The Leveller leaders' tremendous feeling of betrayal demonstrates the degree to which the Baptists and Levellers were intertwined. After Kiffin had presented his petition to Parliament, Lilburne was at a complete loss to explain what had made "the preachers in the Anabaptist congregations so mad at us." Since he had fought for "their liberties" as much as anyone's "and never put a provocation upon them that I know of," he could not understand why they had turned on him. He knew that it was not a coincidence that Kiffin had carried the Baptists' petition to Parliament. He recognized that his former fellow apprentice was the moving force behind such actions. A member of Kiffin's congregation had even told Lilburne that Kiffin "was put upon doing of what he did by some Parliament men, who he perceived were . . . desirous to be rid of us . . . so they might come off handsomely without too much loss of credit to themselves." In other words, to Lilburne's mind, the Baptists sought to secure liberty for themselves by scuttling the Levellers.

Lilburne also speculated that Kiffin, Spilsbury, Richardson, and others deceived their congregations by later removing lines from the petition that were favorable to the Levellers, and then submitted the altered petition with the original signatures "to the Parliament in the name of their congregations." Thus, Lilburne claimed, "they have delivered it a lie and a falsehood, and are a pack of fawning daubing knaves for so doing." William Walwyn, who had been one of the earliest defenders of the Baptists, considered the petition "an ill requital for our faithful adherence unto them in the worst of times, and by whose endeavors under God they attained that freedom that

---

[25]*The Humble Petition and Representation of Several Churches of God in London, Commonly (though Falsly) called Anabaptists* (London, 1649), 4-8. It is perhaps ironic, that appearing on the title-page of the British Library's copy of this petition, in addition to Thomason's annotation of "April 3rd" are the hand written words "London- Anabaptists."

they now enjoy." Richard Overton was certain that "the generality of the people dissented from their petition against us." He explained that "they had scarce ten in some congregations to sign it, in some not above two or three, in some none." Overall, he said, the petition did not represent the opinion of the majority of the Baptists, only that of some leaders who were themselves too timid to continue to stand up to Parliament. Perhaps they were too frightened; it is also possible that they were too confident of their own abilities to succeed without their old allies.[26]

Regardless of whether the petition represented the majority of the Baptists' opinions, Kiffin made it abundantly clear that it represented his own when on April 23, 1649, his name appeared on the pamphlet *Walwins Wiles*. This represented a full-scale attack on the Leveller program in general, and Walwyn in particular. "For although in words they profess, yet in works they deny, and destroy the interest of England." The Levellers, that "Satanical faction," were now accused of atheism, anarchism, impropriety, and communism—many of the accusations previously reserved for those often, though falsely, called Anabaptists. The epistle to the army that preceded the text continued this line of thought, dividing the world into an eschatological dualism: "[T]he great contention between Christ and the Devil, and the seed of either, is to destroy each others' work in the world; and although the issue thereof shall be the mortal crushing of the head of one; yet shall the heel of the other be bruised thereby." This epistle was probably written by Kiffin, and it was here that his disapproval for the Levellers came into full view. He denounced their effort to win the support of the army as the work of "the Antichristian whore," and encouraged the soldiers to obey their superiors, who were "men commissioned by God."[27]

---

[26]Haller, *Leveller Tracts*, 213, 228-230, 374; William Walwyn, *The Foundation of Slaunder Discovered* (London, 1649), 19.

[27]The authorship of the text is debated. The Wing catalog notes "The main responsibility has been variously given to Kiffin and to Price." Judging from Kiffin's other writings, the text would seem to be Price's, but the dedicatory epistle appears to be Kiffin's. In either case, Kiffin's prominent signature above the other signers denotes his agreement

This epistle demonstrates the way Kiffin's eschatology was changing. Eschatology still shaped the Baptists' outlook and their explanation of their actions, but now the millennium had changed. When in 1641 Kiffin wrote an epistle in defense of Lilburne, he railed at the government, "the malignant malice of" all those who used authority to command obedience. He hoped that "even in these our times" the world would be transformed and he vowed that "all the saints . . . [will] never give up crying to God and men, till it be razed down to the ground, so that the Lord Jesus Christ may be set up as Lord and King." In 1641 Kiffin saw Antichrist's power as manifested in the "barbarous and tyrannical dealings" of those who used authority to enforce obedience. By 1649, he viewed Antichrist as working through those who tried to stir up contention. Eight years earlier, the Beast had operated through those who were trying to impose order.[28]

This type of language, once employed by Kiffin to defend Lilburne, was now used to attack him fiercely. Kiffin explained that the equality advocated by Levellers was an impossibility, for "where all men are alike rulers, none will be ruled." While Kiffin had previously seen oppression and persecution as a mark of the Beast, he now maintained that some oppression was necessary since even "the best of Government cannot secure each individual from oppression." He also urged the soldiers not to be so eager for their wages and to be content to receive "your rewards from the immediate hand of God alone . . . at that great pay day." The apocalyptic language that had previously been employed as a critique of the status quo, now defended it. As many Baptists became more adjusted to the world, their desire for its demise had faded. The transformation of society was no longer as urgent. It had been easier to wish God's destruction upon a world that

---

with the text even if he was not necessarily the primary author. *Walwins Wiles: or The Manifestators Manifested viz. Liev. Col. John Lilburn, Mr Will. Walwin, Mr Richard Overton, and Mr Tho. Prince. Discovering themselves to be Englands New Chains and Irelands Back Friends* (London, 1649), sig. a-a2, 13, 31-32. The text also claimed that the Leveller leaders "strike hands with the Devil and his party, Atheists and Papists, and profane malignants"(32).

[28]William Kiffin, epistle, *Christian Mans Triall*, sig. a-a2.

one scorned rather than accepted. Thus Baptists' eschatological perspective began to validate the current society instead of opposing it. With the publication of *Walwins Wiles*, Kiffin made clear that, in the words of Christopher Hill, "stability was what 'responsible' men wanted now."[29]

About a month after obtaining *Walwins Wiles*, the book collector George Thomason picked up another Baptist text critical of the Levellers. On May 24, 1649 he acquired *The Levellers Designe Discovered*. This time the Levellers' critic was not a Particular Baptist like Kiffin, but the influential General Baptist leader Henry Denne, whose pronounced apocalyptic beliefs had recently led him to demand that the king be brought to justice. In May 1649, tired of waiting for "that great pay day," he helped lead an army mutiny at Salisbury. After being apprehended he was court-martialed, and along with three other leaders condemned to death.

For some unknown reason, Denne was pardoned at the last moment while his three companions were executed by a firing squad. While it is not known why Denne was released, the fact that he published *The Levellers Designe Discovered* within days of his pardon suggests that he was spared on the condition that he write against the Levellers. This he did, distancing himself from the Levellers' agenda and, like Kiffin, urging unity and obedience among the soldiers. He wrote: "Justly did the Lord disown us, to teach all men that he is a God of order, and not of confusion, to teach us that he needs not our disobedience to superiors, or any evil action, to consummate this determination." And to those who objected that there were still "oppressions and . . . grievances of the people" to be addressed, Denne responded that it was best now to wait and be thankful for what had been achieved without pressing for further changes. Denne said in this regard he was thankful that his mutiny had failed: "I do admire

---

[29]*Walwins Wiles*, sig. a3; Hill, *Experience of Defeat: Milton and Some Contemporaries* (London: Faber and Faber, 1984), 55.

the great providence of God, who withheld them from turning things upside down."[30]

This new denunciation by a leading General Baptist sounded the death knell of the Levellers' relationship with the Baptist movements. Kiffin and Denne showed the Leveller leaders that they could not depend on the very congregations so important for their support and organization. Fellow travelers thus parted ways. The Leveller movement, already significantly frustrated during 1647, was stranded. They quickly faded, while the Baptists survived.

---

[30]Samuel Gardiner, *History of the Commonwealth and Protectorate 1649-1656*, new edition (London: Longmans, Green and Co., 1903), vol. 1, 53-54; Henry Denne, *The Levellers Designe Discovered* (London, 1649), 6, 8.

7

RESPONSIBLE MEN AND RESISTANT SAINTS:
THE EMERGENCE OF BAPTIST LEADERSHIP AND ORGANIZATION

The break with the Levellers marked the beginning of a new phase of development for the Baptist movements. This phase would be increasingly characterized by the establishment of inter-congregational organization and the leadership of individuals. Heading these new organizational structures were individuals who assumed responsibility for their proto-denominations. These changes occurred more slowly and less deliberately for the General Baptists, but they affected both the General and the Particular Baptists profoundly. After the rejection of the Levellers, these leaders laid the groundwork for the formation of modern denominations.

The Levellers had provided the General Baptists with a connection to the political activities of the time. With the collapse of the Leveller movement, the General Baptists were slowly forced back into the isolation that they had experienced in the 1620s. At the same time, the General Baptist leaders worked to improve their inter-congregational organization. The foundation for this organization was the lose federation of General Baptist churches from the 1620s. The opportunity and impetus for evangelizing in the 1640s meant that this system was further improved to facilitate planned missionary efforts. The first two decades of General Baptist organization in Britain furthered a General Baptist identity that allowed the members of the various congregations to see themselves as part of a larger movement.

By the 1650s a sophisticated General Baptist network appeared, claiming to represent the General Baptists. It engaged in public polemics as well as inter-congregational communication and assistance.

The extent of this inter-congregational organization became apparent with the 1651 publication of *The Faith and Practise of Thirty Congregations* and other such documents. The thirty churches that were represented traveled from an area twenty miles wide and one hundred miles long, stretching from Lincolnshire to Oxford and from Leicestershire to Rutland. While this is the first surviving confession representing the views of more than one General Baptist church, it suggests that large scale inter-congregational meetings may have taken place previously. Certainly, in order to bring so many churches together from such a large area demanded some form of advanced network. The existence of such a network and the publication of confessions like that the *Faith and Practice* brought the General Baptists churches closer together, both in theology and in cooperation.

As the Confession stated, the support of the poor brethren was not the responsibility solely of the single congregation, but of the body of churches together and "if the poor fearing God cannot conveniently have a competent maintenance" supplied by the local congregation, then "send or give intelligence to the other Churches or saints of God." They also agreed that "if any controversy should so fall out, that the case cannot easily be determined by that society" then other churches in fellowship with them should be called into "for their assistance therein." In addition to these practical provisions, theological statements were also approved. Jesus Christ was proclaimed as "not only King or Governor, but also the Apostle or Prophet of the Truth professed, or the true profession of the Saints." Perhaps most importantly they stated that "all actions performed by man towards God, ought to flow from a principle of Love." General Baptists apparently did not feel that it was appropriate to have an article of their faith calling for submission to governmental power, as had the Particular Baptist confessions of 1644 and 1646. Instead, out of an awareness of these Particular Baptist statements and in an effort to clear themselves of association with anarchy, they penned a postscript to their declaration: "[W]e do own a Magistratical power for the governing of this our English Nation, to be determined in a just Parliamentary way; and that we ought to pray for good governors, and good Government." Like the Particular Baptists, these General Baptists were in the process of determining their relation to each other, to God, and to the state.[1]

Such inter-congregational meetings often stemmed from common congregational founders. In the 1640s active General Baptist evangelists like Lambe and Oates had traveled extensively in England planting congregations. Once these groups were formed, the founding evangelist frequently returned to help the fledgling congregations. When they could not visit they wrote letters encouraging new congregations to support and visit each other. Thus the beginnings of numerous congregations were endowed with a natural proclivity towards inter-congregational communication and identification. Already by 1651, congregations from Bedfordshire, Huntingdonshire, Lincolnshire, Northamptonshire, Oxfordshire, Rutland, and War-wickshire were close enough to unite and issue the *Faith and Practice of Thirty Congregations*. The year after this confession, a further demonstration of General Baptist joint-action came when various General Baptist congregations came together to issue a warning to Oliver Cromwell. They explained that the many "burdens and grievances" against which General Baptists had long protested still remained. If these were not removed, then a true "thorough reforma-tion" remained unattainable. The petition, signed on behalf of various churches throughout Leicestershire, Northamptonshire, Shropshire, and Straffordshire, also personally cautioned Cromwell against "seeking high or great things for yourself."[2]

---

[1]Whitley, *British Baptists*, 89; Lumpkin, *Confessions*, Articles 23, 36, 65 (cf. 57) and 70, 173-174, 179-180, 184-186, 188.

[2]John Nicholls, *Original Letters and Papers of State Addressed to Oliver Cromwell* (London: William Bawyer, 1743), 80-81; Whitley, *British Baptists*, 89; Ruth Butterfield, "The Royal Commission of King Jesus," *Baptist Quarterly* 35 (1993): 56-67.

Meetings like the one that issued the *Faith and Practice* or the letter to Cromwell on behalf of the General Baptists were probably occasional meetings based on shared origins and beliefs and called out of political or theological necessity. Nevertheless, by the late 1640s or the early 1650s large scale joint meetings occurred on a regular basis among General Baptist congregations. The joint meetings held in the East Midlands in the 1650s are possibly some of the earliest regular meetings. By 1652 the regular inter-congregational meetings of General Baptists in Kent were well established. Furthermore, as early as 1653, regular inter-congregational meetings were also being held in the Cambridge area.

The General Baptist Arthur Hindes was the host for the series of these "general meetings," which took place in Cambridge from 1653 to 1655. These general meetings consisted of the "elders and brethren assembled" together for the discussion of various matters ranging from the commissioning of evangelists to mutual congregational support. In 1655 another Cambridge general meeting determined that "for the better attaining to, and retaining of, unity and order in the churches, . . . we should unite ourselves together into a strong combination, to meet often together . . . at such times and places as should be thought most convenient."

Later that year, a follow-up meeting at Cambridge declared that it was unlawful "for any member of the congregation to be married unto one without the congregation." As General Baptist congregations began to prohibit mixed marriages (marriages between General Baptists and non-believers), they also began to emphasize closed communion, resulting in a renewed emphasis on the uniqueness of General Baptist identity.

Additionally, the representatives at Cambridge issued an official rebuke towards those members who had fallen away and joined the Quakers. While these inter-congregational meetings were increasingly concerned with the threat posed by the Quakers, they did not succeed in preventing substantial numbers from defecting to the Friends. A subsequent meeting held in 1656 resolved that congregation members were no longer allowed to move from place to place without a letter from their congregation. They also decided that every General Baptist should "sit down with some congregation to give an account of his actions," and that a register should be made of each church. Such decisions reflect the way in which the General Baptists were maturing. The associational meetings helped to initiate and define a number of practices that the congregations would not have adopted in isolation.[3]

At the same time that these association, or "general meetings" were occurring in Cambridge, similar meetings were taking place among General Baptist congregations throughout England. General Baptist leader John Griffith reported that a major meeting took place in Kent in July 1652 to determine the General Baptists' position on whether or not a believer could fall away from grace. The congregations in Kent soon developed a hierarchical system of messengers and elders who represented the various churches at periodic meetings. Like other General Baptist meetings, they sought to establish guidelines for the congregations and resolve disputes. Since General Baptist churches existed outside of the state system, they received little support and found it necessary to aid one another. Frequently, their general meetings discussed and made arrangements for assistance to poor members and struggling congregations. Additionally, they debated theological questions and determined punishments for members who had failed to walk according to the truth. Church discipline, the laying on of hands, closed communion, and mixed marriage were frequent topics discussed at these inter-congregational meetings. Later in the 1650s the inter-congregational meetings in Kent wrestled with such questions as the lawfulness of military service and the appropriate day for Christian worship (i.e. Saturday or Sunday).[4]

---

[3]Underhill, *Records of the Churches of Christ*, 126, 144; White, *English Baptists*, 47-49; Butterfield, "The Royal Commission of King Jesus," 65-67, 71-75.

[4]John Griffith, *A Treatise Touching falling from Grace. Or thirteen arguments Tending to Prove that Believers cannot fall from grace, as they were laid down at a conference at Yalding in Kent* (London, 1653), preface; White, *English Baptists*, 48-49; Butterfield, "The Royal Commission of King Jesus," passim.

In addition to the numerous regional hierarchical structures, the General Baptists also sought to establish some form of national organization that could speak for the General Baptists of England as a whole. In 1654, 1656, 1660 and 1663 nationwide meetings of General Baptists were called. The first such meeting sought to make the General Baptists' views "touching the civil power of this nation" known and to disassociate themselves from the Fifth Monarchist movement. The second nationwide meeting addressed theological and ecclesiastical problems within the church, especially the issue of church discipline. The third nationwide meeting was called in 1660 when the Restoration appeared imminent. They brought forth a confession of faith, which at their fourth nationwide meeting in 1663 received the approval of a wide number of General Baptist churches and later became regarded as the "Standard" confession of the General Baptists.

By that time, it was clear that after the rejection of the Levellers, the General Baptists had built an impressive inter-congregational network. In the eyes of historian B. R. White, the story of General Baptists' early organizational development "reads like an attempt to impose some order on a spreading, growing community threatened by the chaos that followed local independence and local initiative at a time when for many people . . . the world had been turned upside down." This attempt was successful. Such organization was established and helped to stabilize the movement. Without the inter-congregational network begun in 1620s and elaborated in the decades following, the development of a General Baptist identity would have been arrested and the movement would have had little chance of survival.[5]

While the rejection of the Levellers by the Baptist movements meant that the General Baptists were again isolated, the Particular Baptists were for the first time briefly incorporated. Unlike the General Baptists, the Particular Baptists' rejection of the Levellers provided the movement with greater social acceptance. After the

---

[5]White, *English Baptists*, 47-52; Lumpkin, *Confessions*, 221-223.

Leveller movement faded, Particular Baptist leadership emerged into full view. Again, in contrast to the General Baptists, who had strong leaders scattered throughout the country, Particular Baptist leadership was centered in London. This London-centered leadership was tremendously influential for the development of Particular Baptists throughout England, and was dominant until the end of the century.

Powerful leaders are often an essential feature for the survival of a nascent sect for two reasons. First, their leadership, charisma, and intelligence are required for the establishment of an organizational structure that will insure survival. Second, they are needed to win favor with influential elites in society in order to protect their sect from abuse. Some observers have commented on the Baptists' lack of such figures in their earliest stages. With regards to the Particular Baptists, one of the foremost Baptist historians, W. T. Whitley, noted that during the mid-seventeenth-century, "there was no outstanding leader, in action any more than in thought . . . in an age that saw George Fox serve the kingdom of God . . . Baptists had no one . . . eminent."[6]

While it is true that the Baptists lacked a George Fox, a William Penn, or a John Wesley, this discussion has argued that there were, in fact, two types of Particular Baptist leaders during the formative years of the movement. The first type continued to be engaged in actions such as evangelizing, radical politics, and military service aimed at transforming society. On the other end of the spectrum was a more clearly defined leadership circle. It was concerned with apologetics and was generally more conservative in tone and action. The eschatology of the members of this circle can be seen endorsing society rather than opposing it. This circle centered primarily on the veteran leaders William Kiffin, Samuel Richardson, and John Spilsbury. Such divisions are more heuristic than historical, and most Baptists do not easily fit into such categories.

This discussion's focus on London is for good reason, as London,

---

[6]Whitley, *British Baptists*, 96.

in addition to providing the origins, soon became the center of the Particular Baptist movement. Not only was there a concentration of leaders in the city representing various interpretations of the Baptist message, but these London Particular Baptists, starting with the 1644 confession, were the first to organize and develop an inter-congregational identity. Their organization took place not only among themselves, as in the case of the meeting of the seven churches in 1644, but they also organized to facilitate missionary endeavors. The London churches maintained a close relationship with the churches resulting from these evangelical efforts. They saw it as their responsibility to provide for the newer congregations, both spiritually and financially. In a demonstration of both their inter-congregational cohesion and their involvement with the churches beyond the city, the London churches decided that a central fund for the "maintenance of the a Gospel ministry abroad and in the countries [i.e. counties] and for the relief of those which . . . are not able to maintain" should be established. The London churches wrote to the smaller churches, explaining that since in "the apostolic times the churches did hold an association together in their contributions," it was appropriate for such a fund to be maintained and it was suggested that the churches contribute whatever they could. The churches were asked to send their responses to this proposal to "the messengers at London meeting weekly at brother Spilsbury's house."

While this fund does not appear to have been successful, it will be remembered that Spilsbury was one of the earliest known Particular Baptists, and as the churches' request implies, he was at the center of an association of London Particular Baptists. Along with Kiffin, Spilsbury had been a moving force in the publication of the first inter-congregational statement of theological beliefs, the 1644 confession. Along with Kiffin, he would continue to define Particular Baptist theology.[7]

---

[7]B. R. White, *Association Records of the Particular Baptists of England, Wales, and Ireland to 1660* (London: Baptist Historical Society), vol. 3, 174-175.

In addition to their theological acumen, the London Baptists also had the most worldly influence, whether it was the financial assets and courtly connections of William Kiffin, or the military status of Paul Hobson. Thus when later associations of Baptists began to organize they looked to London for leadership and guidance. The messengers at Abingdon decided that since "there is the same relation betwixt the particular churches each towards each other as there is betwixt members of one church," as "the churches of Christ do all make up one body or church in general under Christ their head," therefore "we conclude that every church ought to manifest its care over other churches as fellow members of the same body of Christ." In June 1653 this Abingdon Association wrote to "the church of Christ of which our brethren John Spilsbury and William Kiffin are members and to the rest of the churches in and near London" to report the conclusions of their association meeting. They explained "these things we represent to you, not only because we desire to conceal nothing of this nature from you, but also that we may manifest both our due esteem of you and also our desire to partake of the benefit of the gifts which God hath given you for counsel and advice and brotherly assistance." Like the other known associations, the Abingdon Association was closely tied to London.[8]

Therefore, in terms of theology, organization, and practice, London set the tone and was the center of the Particular Baptist movement in England. The more conservative leaders dominated the London Particular Baptists during the Interregnum and pushed radicalism to the perimeters, both geographically and theologically. Geographically, enthusiastic Baptists had to go to the west of England or to Ireland to escape the constriction of the Kiffin circle. Theologically, intensely apocalyptic Baptists were forced into the folds of the Fifth Monarchists or the Seventh-Day Baptists.

It is difficult to answer why long-time dissenters such as William Kiffin, Samuel Richardson and John Spilsbury came to accept the world that they had previously rejected. Dramatic alterations had

---

[8]White, *Association Records*, vol. 3, 126,131.

occurred since these men first became Separatists and many changes that they had only dreamt of had been realized. But the world they had envisioned in their youth was not yet achieved. As their youthful enthusiasms faded and these experienced Separatists matured, they likely became more practical in their outlook and objectives. Or perhaps, as political instability declined, the potential for regeneration appeared to dissipate. There are certainly a number of reasons for this change, many too subtle to be detected even if more biographical evidence existed. But surviving evidence does suggest at least one common factor involved: during the seventeenth century, a number of the leading Baptists eager for accommodation with society had gained considerable wealth. This increase in wealth was frequently accompanied by a change in social position, which gave many Baptists a greater incentive to accommodate with society.

A number of leading Baptists illustrate this pattern. William Kiffin's close friend and ally, Samuel Richardson, came to be considered "a substantial London tradesman and was certainly one of the shrewdest and most influential of the Baptist leaders in the capital." By 1647 Richardson was wealthy enough to purchase one thousand pounds' worth of soldiers' back pay. Not long afterwards he was frustrated when Royalist privateers captured a ship in which he held half interest. The Particular Baptist Edward Cresset, radical in his youth, also prospered under the Protectorate by holding numerous offices. For example, he was Registrar and then Master of the Charterhouse, entrusted with the sale of forest lands, investigating inventions, seeking out fraudulent debtors and managing the mint. Cresset also became one of Cromwell's "Triers" and in his maturity associated with William Kiffin. John Tomkins, a Particular Baptist leader in Abingdon, was successful enough to leave six thousand pounds sterling in his will. The Particular Baptist William Steele became the Recorder of London. Hanserd Knollys also prospered from his investments in international trade.[9]

Most spectacular of all was the rise of the man who first introduced Hanserd Knollys to the Dutch trade—William Kiffin himself. The difficult conditions surrounding his childhood, such as the death of his parents and abuse by his guardians, have been mentioned above. With a childhood spent in poverty, Kiffin's primary recollection of his youth was that he "never enjoyed but very little." Even in his early adulthood, he was "not a little troubled" by financial woes. Kiffin had his first taste of the money to be made in the Dutch trade in 1643, but he was convinced by his congregation not to pursue it fervently in deference to religion. He remembered that "I went over to Holland with some small commodities, which I found profit by. But on coming home again, I was greatly pressed by the people, with whom I was a member, to continue with them. This I did, omitting the opportunity of proceeding in that trade, and spending my time chiefly in studying the word of God." Finding himself at the end of his rope again in 1645, Kiffin resumed his trading, finding a member of his congregation to take some more of the mysterious "commodity" to Holland, from which they both profited greatly. It is interesting that Kiffin frequently declines to name his "commodities," especially in light of the accusations of smuggling and bringing in "prohibited goods" that surrounded his newly amassed fortune. His memoirs reveal that there was some justification for these allegations and Kiffin was probably violating the Merchant Adventurers' government monopoly, at a tremendous profit.[10]

Once he began to acquire substantial wealth, it was easy for a shrewd man like Kiffin to augment his worth quickly. By 1647 he had already been named a parliamentary tax assessor for Middlesex. Almost a decade later, Kiffin served as a Member of Parliament for Middlesex at the Parliament of 1656. Through exploiting numerous

---

[9]W. K. Jordan, *The Development of Religious Toleration in England* (Cambridge: Harvard University Press, 1938), 515; Bod. Rawl. Ms. A38, f.487; White, *Association Records*, vol. 3, 208; Underwood, *Baptists*, 78-79.

[10]Kiffin, *Remarkable Passages*, 2, 20, 22, 24-25.

opportunities, he was soon able to gain a large enough fortune to receive attention at Court, first under the Protectorate, and then continually after the Restoration. Kiffin's influence at Court was so considerable that General Baptists resorted to asking for his help in crucial situations.

On one occasion after the Restoration, when twelve General Baptists were to be executed for their faith, Thomas Monk asked Kiffin to intercede on the prisoners' behalf. Kiffin went immediately to Court, where he was promptly seen by King Charles II. After a brief discussion with the monarch, the convicted Baptists were spared. Such extraordinary influence was rare, but Kiffin had managed to become acquainted with a wide array of leaders and influential persons. He was probably one of the few individuals during the century of revolution who could say at different times of John Lilburne and Oliver Cromwell as he did of the Earl of Clarendon, that he "was very much my friend."

A particularly telling incident was when King Charles II, "much in want of money," called on Kiffin "requesting a loan of forty thousand pounds." Kiffin shrewdly suggested that instead of the full amount, he provide an immediate gift of ten thousand pounds. The king accepted and Kiffin later recounted "that by giving ten, he had saved thirty thousand."

In 1671, Kiffin became master of the Leathersellers' Company in London, demonstrating his incredible position within London's financial world. Kiffin's prominence continued to grow under James II, when he was appointed an alderman of the City of London. When William and Mary arrived in England after the Glorious Revolution of 1688, Kiffin presented them with an address of welcome on behalf of the Particular Baptists. He also made a personal contribution of five hundred pounds to their new government.

In many ways, Kiffin's new wealth had changed him. John Bunyan believed that Kiffin felt himself superior to Bunyan because of his affluence. Bunyan claimed that Kiffin disregarded him "because of my low descent among men, stigmatizing me for a person of that rank, that needed not be heeded." Frustrated, Bunyan asked "and why is my rank so mean, that the most gracious and godly among you may not duly and soberly consider what I have said?" Other Baptists expressed similar frustrations towards the new Baptist leadership.

Nevertheless, in light of his spectacular rise from a maligned orphan to an extremely affluent courtier, it is not surprising that Kiffin should modify his early radicalism. Indeed, what is surprising is that given this dramatic change in circumstance, how little Kiffin altered his views, and how committed he remained to a faith that frequently jeopardized himself and his family. It is safe to say that remaining a Baptist did not benefit Kiffin financially and that a conversion would have proven more lucrative. [11]

The increased prosperity of some of its leaders played a substantial part in the transformation of the Particular Baptists. Christopher Feake would later denounce the "gaping professors of those times" that sought to serve Mammon as well as God. A Fifth Monarchist Baptist, John Spittlehouse, attributed the transformation to the temptation of "vast treasures got by the sweat of other men's brows." Yet another Fifth Monarchist, John Tillinghast, noted that the faithful had grown too concerned with "profits, preferments and encouragements . . . in the world" and had grown too eager "to please and serve men rather than Christ." Quaker critics later explained that the Baptists' hearts had been "darkened" and their zeal quenched "and so much corrupted through places of honor." The truth in these accusations led Christopher Hill to comment that "if one's object is to attain worldly ends, then there is everything to be said for union among like-minded men and women. If the object is to save one's soul, it seems less obvious."[12]

---

[11]Kiffin, *Remarkable Passages*, 85-87, 160; *Dictionary of National Biography*; *Biographical Dictionary of British Radicals*, vol. 2, 155; Edward Rogers, *Some Account of the Life and Opinions of a Fifth Monarchy Man* (London: Longmans, 1867), passim; White, *English Baptists*, 106, 162; John Bunyan, *Differences in Judgment about Water-Baptism* (London, 1673) quoted in Christopher Hill, *A Turbulent, Seditious, and Factious People: John Bunyan and His Church* (Oxford: Oxford University Press, 1988), 140-141.

[12]Christopher Feake, sermon in British Museum Add. Ms. 39942 f. 13v, quoted in Capp, *Fifth Monarchy*, 93; John Spittlehouse, *The First Address to His Excellencie the Lord General* (London, 1653), 4, John Tillinghast, *Generation-Work*, Part III (London, 1655), sig. B4-4v.

Indeed, Kiffin would seek to appease each government that followed the execution of the king in order to win acceptance for the Baptists, yet his diary reveals his longings for the experiences of God he had in his "younger days" when the "vanities of this present evil world" had not saturated his heart. By the end of his life, he recognized the dangers that worldly wealth posed to spiritual purity and he admonished his children and grandchildren to "have a care of your hearts. . . . Oh! let not that which your father hath received as a mercy from God be so used, that at last it may prove a curse to you."[13]

---

quoted in Christopher Hill, *Experience of Defeat*, 56-57; Richard Hubberthorn, *An Answer to a Declaration* (London, 1659), 18; Hill, *Experience of Defeat*, 292;

[13]Kiffin, *Remarkable Passages*, 46.

8

FURTHER AFIELD:
PARTICULAR BAPTISTS BEYOND LONDON

After the rejection of the Levellers, many Particular Baptists who still believed in transforming the world or advocated a radical theology either had to leave London or leave the Baptists. Less vocal Baptists avoided the dilemma by simply keeping quiet. Their silence is a hindrance to the historian, who is left with only the pronounced calls for submission that emanated from Kiffin's circle to the Particular Baptists scattered throughout the British Isles. By 1650, thanks to active evangelists and military activities both Particular and General Baptists had managed to spread themselves far and wide.[1] A denominational identity was growing, especially for the Particular Baptists, who increasingly looked to London to resolve various problems. The London leaders played an active role and frequently visited the various Particular Baptist associations that had begun to appear in the early 1650s. The London leadership made an effort to locate all of the Particular Baptist congregations so that they could help them form associations and monitor their well-being.[2]

In 1649 the influential London church at Glazier's Hall dispatched John Miles to South Wales in the hopes that he would be

---

[1]The fact that the General and Particular Baptists had been able to spread out so extensively by 1650 was a crucial element in their survival. It meant that even if persecution (or defection to the Quakers) became intense in one area and Baptists were wiped out, other Baptist congregations would continue to exist in other areas.

[2]See Kiffin et al. cover letter dated "the 24th day of the 5th month 1653" reproduced in White, *Association Records*, vol. 2, 111-112 and Underhill, *Records of the Churches of Christ*, 339.

able to establish Particular Baptist churches there. Miles had great success and soon there were four churches in the region. After winning some converts away from an Independent Baptist church that was briefly associated with John Tombes, there were soon five Particular Baptist churches in South Wales. Far away from London and spread out over a large geographical area, these churches began holding joint meetings in 1650, and by 1654 had made plans to have regular inter-congregational assemblies. The development of these Welsh churches was closely watched by the London Baptists. Letters were sent between Wales and London and representatives from the congregations visited London, as John Miles did in 1652. Such communications, visits, and inter-congregational meetings formed a skeletal organization for the earliest Baptists beyond London. London continued to serve, however, as the hub that connected these nascent organizations, providing the vital function of giving some direction to an almost spontaneous process.[3]

Since London was so central to Particular Baptist development, it is revealing that the confession issued by the Midland Association in 1655 differs from the London Confessions. All of the editions of the London Confession that had appeared since its first publication in 1644 had made certain to set forth the Particular Baptists declared obedience to the civil authorities. The messengers who assembled at Warwick did not feel that such submission was an article of their faith. While they followed the London Confessions in a number of respects, and probably did not wholly disagree with their statements of obedience, it was not seen as appropriate to include such wording in their own sixteen article confession of faith. They did, however, declare that "Christ is the only true King, Priest, and Prophet of the Church." They also explained that those who profess their faith should receive baptism and that "this baptizing is not by sprinkling, but dipping of the persons in water, representing the death, burial and

---

[3]Glazier's Hall is usually associated with the names of the leaders Thomas Gunne and Thomas Mabbat. White, "The Organization of the Particular Baptists," 209-213; D. Densil Morgan, "John Myles (1621-83) and the Future of Ilston's Past, Welsh Baptists after three and a half centuries," *Baptist Quarterly* 38 (1999): 176-184.

resurrection of Christ." In their penultimate article they explained that "all these ordinances of Christ are enjoined in His Church, being to be observed till His Second Coming, which we all ought diligently to wait for."

Despite the discrepancies, the Midland Association was also closely connected with London and its formation may have resulted from the direct action of the London leaders. The suggestion of the London Baptists to Daniel King, a "preacher of the word near Coventry," to form an association might have been the foundation for the general meeting of messengers who issued the Midland Confession. King anxiously awaited the return of Christ and held that the recovery of believer's baptism was necessary for the establishment of the true church. In recovering God's ordinances, the stumbling blocks were "removed out of the way" and "some beams of light" were let in "for the further clearing up of the way." King set forth a number of his beliefs and a defense of Baptist practices in 1650 a book entitled *A Way to Sion Sought Out, and Found, for Believers to Walke in*. The dedicatory epistle contained the signature of a number of leading London Baptists, such as William Kiffin, John Spilsbury and Thomas Patient, revealing King's connection with the London leadership.[4]

These Particular Baptist associations, initially called "general meetings," were similar to the General Baptists' inter-congregational assemblies. They were gatherings of regional representatives from Baptist congregations assembled to resolve theological and ecclesiological questions, provide financial support to other congregations and members, plan evangelical missions, and receive information on the status of neighboring Baptist congregations. Aside from the organization in London, before the Restoration their were five Particular Baptist associations from which records have survived. In England there were the Western, the Midland, and the Abingdon Associations. There were two other associations of Particular Baptists outside

---

[4]Lumpkin, *Confessions*, Article IX, XIV, XV, on pages 196, 198, this Confession is also available in White, *Association Records*, vol. 1, 18-20, White relegates the phrase concerning Christ's Second Coming to a footnote on page 39; Daniel King, *A Way to Sion Sought Out* (London, 1650), epistle, passim.

of England, the one just mentioned in Wales, and another in Ireland. In the 1650s there were also Baptist churches in Scotland, but as for numerous other Particular Baptist churches throughout the British Isles, it is not known if they formed associations. It is highly probable that they did, either out of necessity or following the advice of London.

The surviving evidence from the Particular Baptist associations shows that the associations were wrestling with many of the same questions that General Baptists were encountering during the same period. The troublesome practice of the laying on of hands was frequently discussed at meetings, as was the issue of tithes and the importance of closed communion. The Baptists also had to work out their relationship with non-believers and other related issues. The records of these meetings provide a snapshot of a movement in transition. Sometimes from the work of a single evangelist, small congregations had grown up until they meshed with the larger Particular Baptist organization in their region. These regional structures were then connected to London, and thus interlinked with each other. This system of associations represented and reconfirmed the Particular Baptists' interdependency and it is unlikely that the movement would have survived and expanded without them.[5]

Thomas Collier, the chaplain who delivered the apocalyptic sermon at Putney, was the leading force in the Western Association of Particular Baptists. He was an extremely influential and talented evangelist and much of the Particular Baptists' success in western

---

[5]These records were collected and published by B. R. White in three volumes under the title of *Association Records of the Particular Baptists of England, Wales and Ireland* (London: Baptist Historical Society, 1971-1977). A letter from the Baptists at Leith to the church at Hexham in 1653 implied that there was a thriving congregation already present. The Leith letter also expressed the congregations hope that "King Jesus shall be lifted up as an ensign . . . We believe that all these things are fulfilling . . . [and that the Lord is pleased] in bringing down the kingdom and power of Antichrist, and in the enlarging, establishing, and erecting the kingdom of his son." They also urged the Hexham congregation to be zealous, for "now it is high time to awake out of sleep, for now is your salvation nearer . . . The night is far spent, the day is at hand" (Underhill, *Records of the Churches of Christ*, 326). The gifted preacher of Hexham, Thomas Tillam, was even invited to be a chaplain to the soldiers in Scotland (318)).

sections of England was due to his unflagging efforts. Collier demonstrates the malleability of Particular Baptist thought during its formative years. While Collier was certainly a Particular Baptist and won many adherents to their beliefs, he did not follow the London line. He provides an excellent reminder that Baptist beliefs were still busy being born and that a cohesive doctrine was not universal among believers. Collier is a forceful example of how different Baptists had differing ideas as to what the movement should become.

The apocalyptic sermon Collier delivered to the soldiers at Putney was not the first instance of his eschatological concern. Rather, eschatology had always been at the center of Collier's theology and his politics, if such a distinction can be made. He saw the baptism of infants as part of Antichrist's effort to defeat Christ and he published numerous works discussing the rule of the saints in the Kingdom. He supported the readmission of the Jews to England, in the hopes that they would be converted to Christianity and discussed their theological and eschatological significance in print.

Even after the rejection of the Levellers, Collier's theology remained focused on millenarianism. Related to his intense apocalypticism was Collier's continued criticism of the status quo and the government. He wanted greater religious liberty and denied the validity of any restraint on conscience. In his support of the radical agitation culminating in the execution of the king, Collier's conscience and eschatology compelled him to take an active role. He published A *Vindication of the Army-Remonstrance*, to inform England that "the day of our deliverance is at hand," for now "a glorious dispensation of righteousness and liberty" would be poured "forth, both within and without [God's] people." Collier's early millenarianism was characterized by the belief that as people perfected themselves individually within, the entire world would be reformed without. The dawning of the Kingdom was both an internal and external process, for "God will bring salvation to his people, and righteousness by them to the world." The godly revolution that had begun in the early 1640s and was peaking by the end of the decade confirmed Collier's belief. The reappearance of the visible church, greater religious freedom, and the tearing down of Antichrist's temple proved that a new day had dawned. "There is a dispensation of righteousness to be brought fourth in the world . . . for the punishment of evil doers, and for the praise of them who do well . . . for the work in hand is the creation of these New Heavens, and New Earth."

Collier's views combined spiritual with literal millenarianism. While his eschatology was mixed, his message was clear. Preparation for the coming Kingdom should be the saints, only concern. He advised: "Lay aside all private, selfish interests, let your end and acting be for the accomplishment of this great work in hand." As the sun began to set on such millennial expectations after the 1650s, Collier's eschatology still called him to action. In 1659 he published *The Decision & Clearing* urging the restored Rump to resist the calls for a religious settlement on the grounds that such action was against Christ's Kingdom. The day, while delayed, still "cometh."[6]

Collier's apocalypticism did not decline in the years after the execution of the king. His sermon to the soldiers at Putney and his *Vindication* demonstrate his early mixing of literal and spiritual millenarianism. The Kingdom of God was being built in his saints. He argued, "When Christ, the King of Saints ruleth in them, then they rule in judgement and righteousness, and bring forth righteousness to the Nation." At the same time, he believed "that great fall and ruin of Babylon, mentioned in Revelation 18:19, is not only intended in

---

[6]Thomas Collier, A *Vindication of the Army-Remonstrance* (London, 1648), sig. a2-a5; idem, *The Decision & Clearing of the Great Point now in Controversie about the Interest of Christ* (London, 1659), passim; G. F. Nuttall, "The Baptist Western Association 1653-1658," *Journal of Ecclesiastical History* 11 (1960): 213-218; Edwards, *Second Part of Gangraena*, 148; idem, *Third Part of Gangraena*, 27-30, 51-52; Thomas Collier, *Certaine Queries: or Points now in Controvercy Examined* . . . (London, 1645), 25-29, passim; idem, A *Brief Answer to Some of the Objections and Demurs Made Against the Coming in and Inhabiting of the Jews* (London, 1656); B. R. White, "Thomas Collier and Gangraena Edwards" *Baptist Quarterly* 24 (1972): 99-110. For an extended discussion of Thomas Collier's political activities and their context, see Richard Dale Land, "Doctrinal Controversies of English Particular Baptists (1644-1691) as Illustrated by the Career and Writings of Thomas Collier," D. Phil. dissertation, Oxford University, 1980, particularly chpt 2, where Land documents "Collier's involvement in the most radical of English political actions" and concludes that "it would be difficult to find anyone . . . in Particular Baptist life who . . . was as deeply involved as Collier" (116-117).

the mystery and spirit, but in the letter; God will give them blood to drink, for they are worthy, and they, to wit, his Saints shall follow Christ to that great day, or battle of the Lord."

As the years passed, however, Collier's eschatology became more literal. He went down the path that many of the Fifth Monarchists chose in the face of the apparent apostasy of the saints. In 1657, with the publication of *The Personal Appearing and Reign of Christs Kingdom Upon Earth,* Collier made clear that he was not a Fifth Monarchist. He published this tract to set forth "the great truth of this last generation or age of the World," which was that Christ was shortly to come and personally reign on the earth. Collier also published the tract to refute those Fifth Monarchists who claimed that the saints should institute their rule by the sword. He was responding specifically to the most learned of the Fifth Monarchists, John Tillinghast, and his 1654 book *Knowledge of the Times.* Collier rejected Tillinghast's text, saying that he would trust "no man or men" to carry out that work that was clearly reserved from Christ's hand alone. Thus, while Collier's eschatology did not require the saints actively to tear down the existing powers with the sword, it did demand that they prepare for Christ's personal rule on earth by witnessing against the Beast and remaining in a lowly suffering state.[7]

Collier was able to maintain both his high leadership position and his radical views because of his distance from London. Collier had enjoyed good relations with London in the mid-1640s, but they began to sour as Collier became more politically and theologically radical at the same time that London leaders were seeking greater accommodation. Unfortunately, his distance from London could not free him from the London leaders' interference. Tensions may have begun to escalate in the early 1650s, for by the middle of the decade Collier

---

[7]Thomas Collier, *Remonstrance,* sig. a3, a5; idem, *The Personal Appearing and Reign of Christs kingdom upon the Earth. Stated and Proved from the Scripture of Truth. And the State of the Saints till then . . . suffering, and not of Reigning and Conquering with a Materiall Sword as Some Imagine. With an Answer to Mr. Tillinghast's grounds for such practice . . . And some other Arguments and Objections answered tending to the same thing* (London, 1657), sig.a1-a2, 31, quoted in Land, "Doctrinal Controversies," 250.

and his Western Association of churches put forward the Somerset Confession of Faith, possibly in an effort to make peace with London. They affirmed most of the doctrines of the London Confessions and declared them to be orthodox.

Such statements of unity probably did little to reassure London, as there were small but significant differences in some points of theology. Additionally, Collier's intense apocalypticism was manifest in the preface as well as in Article XXXIX, which focused on Christ's Second Coming and declared that the time was close at hand. The Somerset Confession also contained an article on the calling of the Jews, explaining that as an article of faith the saints were to pray for and be constantly "expecting their [the Jews] calling, and so much the rather, because their conversion will be to us life from the dead." The Western Association agreed to this Confession and its subsequent publication. In doing so, the association both accepted the London Confessions of Faith and asserted their independence from them. Although the London Confessions were true statements of Particular Baptist beliefs, they were not the single standard for all Calvinist baptized believers. They were not authoritative statements for all Particular Baptists. Not only was each association free to make its own declaration of faith, but also the decisions of the association, much less London, were not binding on the individual churches. Thus the Somerset Confession reasserted the fundamental principal found in the earliest Baptist movements—congregational independence.[8]

Difficulties between the West Country and London deepened rather than diminished. By 1674 Collier's variance with the London leaders had become intolerable. That year he published *The Body of Divinity, or a Confession of Faith being the Substance of Christianity.* Since he viewed this work as his most articulate statement of beliefs, he claimed that it was the standard by which all of his previous

---

[8]*A Confession of Faith of Several Churches of Christ, in the County of Somerset, and of Some Churches in the Counties Neer and Adjacent* (London, 1656), passim; Lumpkin, *Confessions,* Articles XXXV, XXXIX, on pages 213-214. For Lumpkin's discussion of the differences between the Somerset and London Confessions in terms of the doctrine of election, see *Confessions,* 202.

actions and statements should be measured. To London it was heresy. Not only did he deny original sin and advance ideas of general atonement, but Collier's tract also contained a questionable account of the nature of Christ's person. Collier further explained his ideas in his 1676 publication of *An Additional Word to the Body of Divinity*.

Along with other leaders from London, Kiffin then traveled to the West Country to find Collier and try to persuade him to renounce his errors. They summoned him to a meeting and demanded that he see his mistakes or else they would publish against him and remove him from the Baptists. Kiffin strongly "admonished him as a Heretick." Collier refused to recant and had the support of his congregation and other churches in the area. The London leaders returned to the city frustrated. They then summoned Collier to London, possibly in the hopes that removing him from his supporters would prompt a change of heart. Collier refused to come, saying that he would likely never go to London again. The London church "then proceeded . . . to reject him as an a Heretick . . . and sent forth their long promised book" entitled *Vindicia Veritatis, or, A confutation . . . of the Heresies and Gross Errours Asserted By Thomas Collier*. The text was written by Nehemiah Coxe, but the introductory epistle was signed by Kiffin and others, denouncing Collier.[9]

This repudiation of Collier coincided with a renewed effort on the part of the Particular Baptist leaders to find greater acceptance. By that time, in the atmosphere of the second decade of the Restoration, the Baptists aimed to minimize their differences with other dissenters. The Restoration had forced all nonconformists into closer coopera-tion and the London leaders no longer saw their old enemy, the Presbyterians, as Antichrist. In an effort to put forward a united front

---

[9]W. T. Whitley, "Thomas Collier," *Transactions of the Baptist Historical Society* 1 (1908), 121-122; Thomas Collier, *The Body of Divinity* (London, 1674), 28-32, 109-121, passim; idem, *A Brief and True Narrative of the Unrighteous Dealings with Thomas Collier* (London, 1677?), 2-7 quoted from Land "Doctrinal Controversies," 269-270, 280, this *Narrative* was published for the purpose of convincing the local churches around Collier, many of which had begun to question his teachings, that the London church had dealt unfairly with him (*Narrative*, 11-12); Nehemiah Coxe, *Vindicia Veritatis, or a Confutation . . . the heresies and gross Errours asserted by Thomas Collier in his . . . body of divinity* (London, 1677), sig. a.1.

with the Presbyterians and Congregationalists, the London Particular Baptists adapted the Presbyterian Westminster Confession (1646) along with the Congregationalists' Savoy Confession (1658) (which was largely taken from the Westminster Confession as well) and used them as the basis for a new Baptist confession. This new Confession declared that it was "put forth by the Elders and Brethren of many Congregations of Christians (baptized upon Profession of Faith) in London and the Country." Whenever possible the wording of the Presbyterian and Congregationalist confessions was adopted in order to demonstrate "our hearty agreement with them in that wholesome protestant doctrine, which, with so clear evidence of Scripture they have asserted."

The preface also claimed that the new 1677 Baptist confession was in agreement with the Baptists' 1644 confession, but this was manifestly not the case. Among other changes, there were deviations in the doctrine of marriage, the use of the Scripture, and the issue of open versus closed communion. Again, in their efforts to win acceptance, the Baptists had adapted their beliefs. The new confession of 1677 would serve as the basis for the 1689 "Second London Confession," which further modified the Particular Baptists' views, dropping the appendix discussing open and closed communion that had been attached to the 1677 confession and inviting the Broadmead Independent Baptist church to join them in the signing. This "Second London Confession" of 1689 would prove to be the longest lasting Baptist confession, still employed by numerous Baptists today.[10]

Collier of course did not approve of the 1677 confession or the rebuking he received in *Vindicia Veritatis*. In 1677 Collier published *A Sober and Moderate Answer to Nehemiah Coxe's Invective*. Collier defended himself but called into question the behavior of the London leaders, who were "100 miles distant" from him. After restating his views, Collier spent the latter half of his work focusing on eschatology

---

[10]Lumpkin, *Confessions*, 236-237, 239; White, *English Baptists*, 11.

and speculating on the nature of punishment for the damned after the final resurrection.

Perhaps such speculation was meant as an admonition to the London Baptists, whom Collier clearly felt had lost the spirit of brotherly love. In 1678 Collier issued another confession of faith, both defending himself and objecting to the theology of the 1677 London confession. The latter half of Collier's 1678 confession demonstrated his continued concern with eschatology. Just before his death Collier composed a *Doctrinal Discourse of Self-Denial* (1691), which was published posthumously along with *A Short Confession*. Several churches signed this confession in support of Collier's views. These last two texts testify to Collier's unwillingness to be cowed into accepting beliefs that did not meet the test of Scripture or the test of his soul. Many Baptists supported him and considered him the primary Baptist theologian up until his death. Although he had chosen to go his own way, he had done so in good company.[11]

This discussion of Collier has taken us far from the Western Association to which he devoted much of his life, particularly during the 1650s. While later historians would judge him as unorthodox, Collier was committed to the Particular Baptist movement and spent most of his life working for that cause. His efforts in the Western Association were vital for the increased acceptance of Baptist beliefs. Most of our knowledge about the association that Collier founded in the West Country comes from letters signed by Collier and his radical companion Nathaniel Strange. Strange had been in the army and

---

[11]Thomas Collier, *A Sober and Moderate Answer* (London, 1677), sig, a2, 40-70, quoted in Land, "Doctrinal Controversies," 275, 277. It is interesting to note that the Independent Baptist church at Broadmead agreed that Thomas Collier was "holding forth some unsound doctrine," and when the London leaders were in the area to reprimand Collier, they were invited to attend the Broadmead church. (Edward B. Underhill, ed. *The Records of A Church of Christ, meeting in Broadmead, Bristol, 1640-1687* (London: Hanserd Knollys Society, 1847), 358). This might be a partial explanation for their inclusion in the conference that produced the Second London Confession. It may have been a necessary alliance on the part of London to isolate Collier and the believers that followed him.

later became a Fifth Monarchist. As late as the mid-1660s he was reportedly trying to stir up risings against the government.[12]

Thomas Glasse assisted both Strange and Collier in their work of spreading the Baptist message. Glasse shared their eschatology and like Strange was later a supporter of the Fifth Monarchists. In addition to men such as Strange and Glasse, Collier was also in very close contact with another dynamic Baptist leader, "the famous preacher Mr. Pendarves of Abingdon."[13] John Pendarves did not take up Fifth Monarchy views until the mid-1650s, but by then he apparently advocated violence as a legitimate means of achieving social change.[14] Although Pendarves played his most prominent role in the Abingdon Association, his name appears alongside Collier's on many of the documents of the Western Association. B. R. White, in his introduction to the collection of these documents, recognizes that they place "a continued emphasis upon the need for holy living, for evangelism, for the member congregations to realize their fellowship in one body and, sounding through them all, an undertone of expectancy, of millenarian excitement." As late as 1656, the association, in answer to the question "what is the saints' most proper and

---

[12]Nuttall, "The Baptist Western Association 1653-1658," 213-218, White, *Association Records*, vol. 2-3, passim; Capp, *Fifth Monarchy*, 264.

[13]Bod. Rawl. Ms. D 859 (f.162). Pendarves was responsible for the "further and more orderly ordaining [of] our dearly beloved brother Thomas Collier" (White, *Association Records*, vol. 2, 103). This occurred in 1654. Collier, who had been active as a Baptist evangelist for well over a decade by this time, evidently had not been "formerly ordained." This very event in itself reveals the greater rigidity and formality within the Particular Baptists after 1649. The idea of some form of succession was seen as Antichristian by the earliest English Baptists. Additionally, Collier's acceptance of this ordinance, where as he had previously advocated a life above ordinances and forms, is a sign of greater theological conservatism even among the more radical Particular Baptists. Land wisely attributes this greater formality to a response on the Baptists part to the Quaker threat (Land, "Doctrinal Controversies," 50-51).

[14]White claimed that Pendarves, while involved with the Fifth Monarchists, did not advocate the use of violence, B. R. White "John Pendarves, the Calvinist Baptists and the Fifth Monarchy," *Baptist Quarterly* 25 (1974): 251-271. He later revised himself in his entry for Pendarves in the *Biographical Dictionary of British Radicals*. For more on Pendarves and the Abingdon Baptist congregations, see Geoffrey F. Nuttall "Abingdon Revisited 1656-1675," *Baptist Quarterly* 36 (1995): 96-103.

special work at this day?" responded that "the coming of the Lord draweth nigh, we judge it doth much concern the saints." They should, however, "wait upon [the Lord] for the Spirit to be poured forth: for the bringing down of Babylon and the building of Zion." They were also instructed to pray for the conversion of the Jews and to study the prophetic texts. [15]

When John Pendarves died in 1656, his funeral provided the opportunity for a meeting of a large group of radicals. The authorities were informed that letters had been sent to various distant locations encouraging attendance at the funeral. This confirmed the government's suspicion that the occasion would be used to launch a rising. A substantial number attended the funeral and remained for an extended debate and discussion that took place for several days afterwards. It was reported that among other issues discussed, one "question being started there by one in prayer, 'whether God's people must be a bloody people.' " This questions was answered "in the affirmative . . . that they must be a bloody people" who actively engaged in violence. Another statement that the participants agreed with was that it was "worse to stay in Babylon," than to pursue the Kingdom of God without definite direction. "The call must be obeyed, thou as Abram did, you go you know not whither." The meeting was forcefully broken up by a large number of soldiers sent to prevent an uprising. As the soldiers began making arrests, some cried out "now Lord appear, now or never for confounding of these thine and our enemies." The common sentiment of the radicals in attendance at the funeral can be seen in their statement that "we are not for Cromwell's Kingdom, for Priests and Universities, but for the Kingdom of Christ." Similar sentiments were expressed in a pamphlet published near the time of Pendarves's death. The text, *The Banner of Truth Displayed: or, a Testimony for Christ, and Against Anti-Christ* (1656), recognized Cromwell as the little horn of the Beast of Revelation and maintained that "Munster" was no "monster," but rather an inspiration. It explained that the obligation of the saints was to prepare to "appear

---

[15]White, *Association Records*, vol. 2, 53, 65.

in a military posture for Christ, which we call the great combat between Christ and the . . . rulers of the world" and to "work . . . against Nations, Provinces, Universities, Corporations, Cities, Towns, Kings, [and] Rulers." Such comments would certainly not have pleased Kiffin. In fact, such sentiments were so contrary to the efforts of Kiffin and the conservative Particular Baptist leadership that they can be seen as a rejection of such efforts. While Kiffin was working towards greater accommodation, many Baptists were resisting, and some were preparing for direct opposition.[16]

Three years before his death and tumultuous funeral, John Pendarves told a fellow Baptist that Major-General Charles Fleetwood (Cromwell's son-in-law and Lord Deputy of Ireland from 1652 to 1655) had invited him to Ireland. Pendarves had responded that he would only be able to go if his congregation would release him, which never occurred. Fleetwood was an Independent (Congregationalist), but his presence at numerous Baptist meetings and his close association with their leadership caused him to be labeled as a Baptist by both contemporaries and later historians. Fleetwood probably wanted Pendarves to come to Ireland and join the number of Baptists already there under Fleetwood's patronage and protection. By that time, Cromwell had assumed direct legal control in England and was nervous about possible opposition. While religious groups like the Baptists and Independents had initially supported him, they had soon grown discontented. The affinity between Fleetwood and the radical Baptists of Ireland troubled Cromwell, who thought it best to send his son Henry to investigate the situation.

A letter from H. Warren to Ireland concerning the Baptists urged that "special care of my lord [Henry Cromwell should be taken], that

---

[16]W. Hughes, *Munster and Abingdon or the Open Rebellion There, and Unhappy Tumult here. (Bred in the same wombe)* . . . (Oxford, 1657), 72-75, 89-90, 93-94; *The Banner of Truth Displayed: or, A Testimony for Christ, and Against Anti-Christ. Being the substance of severall . . . who are waiting for the visible appearance of Christ's Kingdome, in and over the world; and Residing in and about the City of London* (London, 1656), 25-28, 48-49, 71; C. Burrage, "The Fifth Monarchy Insurrections," *The English Historical Review* 25 (1910): 724; Capp, *Fifth Monarchy*, 116.

none of them be alone with him. Remember Leyden. Though the same principle does not always produce the very same effect in circumstances, yet give it time . . . and in substance it will." In Warren's mind, the Baptists in Dublin were of the same character as the Anabaptists of Münster, and Henry Cromwell's treatment of the Baptists proved to be consistent with this perspective. With Henry's arrival, the activities of the Baptists came under constant surveillance. The Baptists had been in Ireland well before Henry Cromwell's subsequent appearance and interference in their affairs. The earliest Baptist arrived in Ireland with the New Model Army, which consisted of the remodeled Parliamentary forces. It was under Fleetwood's administration that intensely apocalyptic Baptists like Christopher Blackwood became influential among the soldiers stationed in Ireland. Blackwood had returned from New England in 1642 and became a Baptist after hearing the General Baptist Francis Cornwell preach.

While at first a General Baptist, Blackwood became a Particular Baptist before becoming active in the army, which took him to Ireland. Blackwood preached for a time at Kilkenny and founded the Particular Baptist church at Wexford before becoming a preacher at Dublin Cathedral, where he was referred to as "the oracle of the Anabaptists in Ireland." Daniel Axtell, a member of Kiffin's congregation later executed for his role in the King's trial, also arrived in Ireland, where he became a constant concern to Henry Cromwell.[17]

The Baptist congregations in Ireland were dependent on the army for their establishment and support, but in a relatively short time they

---

[17]John Atherton, *The pastor turn'd pope* (London, 1654), passim; Thurloe, *State Papers*, vol. 4, 90, 315; Louise F. Brown, *The Political Activities of the Baptists and Fifth Monarchy Men in England During the Interregnum* (Washington: American Historical Association, 1912) 155, 160, 165; Richard Greaves, *God's Other Children: Protestant Nonconformists and the Emergence of Denominational Churches in Ireland, 1660-1700* (Stanford: Stanford University Press, 1997), 25; White, *Association Records*, vol. 2, 120; *Biographical Dictionary of British Radicals*; Blackwood apparently arrived along with Fleetwood (Jordan, *Religious Toleration*, 462), Blackwood was an important advocate of religious liberty, and like many Baptists, he saw religious persecution as Antichristian (see Jordan, *Religious Toleration*, 462-467).

spread across much of the island.[18] One millenarian Baptist who ended up in Ireland was Adjutant-General William Allen, who already had an impressive radical resume by the time of his arrival. He was originally a felt-maker before he joined the army. During his time as a solider he was once captured and wounded twice. He was an Agitator and "prominent in bringing Charles I to trial." Allen's connection between the Baptists and the Levellers was mentioned above. His hatred for both monarchy and tyranny were sincere, and even after the Restoration appeared inevitable, he published a plea to the army in an effort to stop the return of the king. Like the men around him, he was also fiercely critical of Oliver Cromwell's Protectorate, although he confessed his deep admiration for Cromwell himself.

Cromwell's son, Henry, was a different matter, and Allen strongly resented his presence in Ireland. Fleetwood convinced Oliver Cromwell's Secretary of State, John Thurloe, that imprisoning Allen for his expressed opposition to Oliver Cromwell would likely inflame public opinion and have a greater negative effect than leaving him free. The result was that Allen had more liberty than Henry Cromwell would have preferred. As he became increasingly radical, Allen moved into Fifth Monarchist circles. In 1658, he traveled to Dorchester in an effort to convince the Particular Baptists who had not already joined the Fifth Monarchists to do so.[19]

---

[18]They had been active in Galway by 1652 and before the establishment of the Protectorate they had churches in Bandon, Carrickfergus, Clonmel, Cork, Dublin, Kerry, Kilkenny, Kinsale, Limerick and Waterford. Soon they were to have congregations in Belfast, Carlow, Enniscorthy, Belturbet, Maryborough and Gowran. By 1655, twelve of the military governors were Baptists and "with the exception of a few extreme Independents . . . practically the whole administration came to be in the hands of Baptists" (Brown, *Baptists and Fifth Monarchy*, 136). This statement is something of an exaggeration, but it certainly appeared that way to many contemporaries (see Greaves, *God's Other Children*, 26; W. T. Whitley, "The Plantation of Ireland and the Early Baptist Churches," *Baptists Quarterly* 1 (1922-1923): 279-280; White, *Association Records*, vol. 2, 119-120).

[19]*Biographic Dictionary of British Radicals*; Underwood, *Baptists*, 74; William Allen, *A Word to the Army* (London, 1660), passim; Brown, *Baptists and Fifth Monarchy*, 78; Greaves, *God's Other Children*, 27; White, *Association Records*, vol. 2, 97.

Through their military office and their popularity among the soldiers, Baptists such as Christopher Blackwood and William Allen were able to command influence in Ireland vastly disproportionate to the Baptists' small numbers. Even before men like Blackwood and Allen had arrived, Baptist leader Thomas Patient had made his presence felt in Ireland. After his own return from New England, Patient had been a leading Baptist in London. By 1650, however, he was no longer able to stay in London. He eventually arrived in Ireland, where he was responsible for churches from Waterford to Dublin. Soon after this, Patient created divisions within John Rogers's Dublin congregation. While Rogers was willing to show a large degree of lenience on Baptist issues, Patient was less flexible, insisting that believer's baptism was an ordinance necessary for church membership. Patient eventually won over the congregation and Rogers returned to London. Rogers's departure from Ireland was to have a serious impact on both the Baptists and the Protectorate, for Rogers quickly became one of the most vocal critics of Cromwell in London as well as one of the most visible Fifth Monarchist leaders.[20]

In 1653, several months before the establishment of the Protectorate, Patient, along with Christopher Blackwood and twenty-eight other prominent Baptists, sent a letter to the Baptist leaders in London. This intriguing document revealed not only the sustained eschatological hopes of the Irish Baptists in the months before the failure of the Barebones Parliament, but also the strained relationship between the Irish Baptists and the London Baptist leaders. The letter opened by expressing "grief of heart" over London's failure to respond to the Irish Baptists' requests for information: "You may remember, sometime since, our earnest request, which request was to you once and again, to have a perfect account from you . . . which desire, had it been answered, might have prevented our long sad silence." They offered to forget about the previous differences between the Baptists on the two islands, which they "earnestly desire may be mutually laid

---

[20]Thurloe, *State Papers*, vol. 4, 90; Rogers, *Some Account of the Life and Opinions of a Fifth Monarchy Man*, 29.

to heart by us all for to prevent the like occasion of complaining for the future."

Despite this offer of a truce, the authors could not help but bemoan "oh, how many packets have passed filled with worldly matters since we have heard one word from you. . . . Alas, alas, what means the dull, cold estranged frame of heart we bare each to other as is before mentioned?" The authors aimed at amending the past differences between the Baptists of Ireland and London so that they could focus on the important work at hand "in these latter days wherein our God is working terrible things in righteousness."[21]

The lack of communication between London and Ireland meant that the Irish Baptists had developed relatively free from the interference of the Kiffin circle. Consequently, the letter reflected a type of intense eschatological expectation that was no longer acceptable among the responsible men of London. It was an eschatology still looking for the imminent active transformation of the world and a complete purification of the status quo. The Irish Baptists realized that recently "God hath greatly reproved kings and mighty men" for the sake "of the commonwealth of Israel." They interpreted their rise in the army and to positions of influence in Ireland as a fulfillment of eschatological prophecies to "set his poor despised ones on high from the kings of the earth . . . Yea, God hath done great things for us."

Likewise, the decline in persecution was part of the Lord's "casting contempt upon princes and taking away the reproach of his people who were some years since brought low through oppressions, afflictions and sorrow." But this was by no means an excuse for complacency. It was not time to embrace society, but rather the moment had arrived to transform it. The Irish Baptists realized that the London Baptists' enthusiasm had grown cold and their letter was an attempt to wake London from its slumber "whilst our bridegroom

---

[21]White, *Association Records*, vol. 2, 112-113, 115. There are no extant copies of the original letter from Ireland to England. The copies of the letter that survive were made by the London leaders for distribution throughout England, Scotland and Wales in the hopes of gathering information about as many other congregations as possible. It is not known if any changes to the original Irish letter were made before the London leaders distributed it.

tarrieth" for "we have observed Satan, our subtle enemy . . . whose time we believe is short."

In preparation for the rapidly approaching return, it was necessary "to put on the whole armor of God that we may be able to stand in this day." They sternly warned against falling into further "carnal security . . . for surely the Lord is now at hand!" The letter described at great length "the great work now desired and endeavored." The Irish Baptists concluded, "lastly, friends, mightily cry unto our God, even the God and Father of our Lord Jesus Christ, give him no rest until he be entreated by us in the things within mentioned . . . larger promises and vast expenses." They signed their names after describing themselves as "your poor weak brethren yet fellow heirs, expecters of the consolation ready to be revealed at the appearing of our Lord Jesus Christ, who will now come, without sin, to our salvation."[22]

This reminder of the eschatological orientation that had previously underlain the Baptists' worldview was a wake-up call for the London Baptists. They confessed that they had been "sleeping and slumbering with those wise virgins mentioned by our Savior " and that they were guilty of "backslidings." Unfortunately, the new relationship between London and the Irish Baptists did not last long enough to see the end of the year. The letter from Ireland had been received in the summer of 1653, and by the following winter, the Baptists faced a new challenge in the form of yet another change of government.

When the saints of the Barebones Parliament packed up their Bibles and headed home, not only were expectations dashed, but a new form of government had to be erected. On 16 December 1653, Oliver Cromwell accepted the Instrument of Government, one of the earliest written constitutions in modern times and the only one in England's history. Cromwell went from being Lord General of the army to being Lord Protector of the Commonwealth. For many, the Protectorate looked uncomfortably similar to the monarchy that God had so recently called on them to overthrow. The saints were extremely dissatisfied. But for Kiffin and his circle, this was simply

---

[22]White, *Association Records*, vol. 2, 112-113, 115-118.

another government that had to be appeased in order to preserve the de facto toleration that they had gained.[23]

There was, however, a considerable outcry over the establishment of the Protectorate from many Baptists, even in London. But the Baptists in Ireland shouted the loudest. In response, Kiffin, Spilsbury, and Joseph Fansom (Sansom) sent a letter to the Baptists in Ireland, chastising their protests and demanding their immediate unqualified acquiescence to the present government. This was hardly the brotherly response Patient and the other Baptists in Ireland imagined when they sent their impassioned letter to London some months earlier. Yet, Kiffin and his companions were compelled to write a stern letter in the face of "rumors . . . that since this late alteration of government . . . there is raised up in many amongst you a spirit of great dissatisfaction and opposition against the present authority, insomuch we hear it is your resolution to make a public protest against it." There were fears on the part of the London leadership that such protests "might proceed to the shedding of blood."

They began their letter to the Irish Baptists by saying, "as there is nothing more occasions rejoicing in us than to hear of your increase in the knowledge . . . of God, expressed by a *humble and patient waiting for the Kingdom of our Lord Jesus Christ,* so there is nothing more grievous to us than to hear any thing done by you . . . which may occasion any blemish" upon the Baptists. The London letter went on to insist that the Irish Baptists refrain from any actions that might bring disregard on the "baptized churches." They had worked hard to reassure the government of their compliance and they hoped that the Irish Baptists would not undertake any actions that might cause them to be slandered as they were in the 1640s, when it was thought that "we deny authority, and would pull down all magistracy." The letter declared that the Protectorate was a legitimate government that had saved the country from the chaos posed by radical millenarians. It urged the Irish Baptists to abandon Fifth Monarchist sympathies, insisting that "we are clearly satisfied" that if "the principles held forth

---

[23]White, *Association Records,* vol. 2, 111.

by those . . . of the fifth monarchy" had been pursued, they "would have brought as great a dishonor to the name of God, and shame and contempt to the whole nation, as we think could have been imagined." The London letter then concluded: "This we can say, that we have not had any occasion of sorrow in this matter from any of the churches in this nation, with whom we have communion; they with one heart desiring to bless God for their liberty, and with all willingness to be subject to the present authority. And we trust to hear the same from you."[24]

In a letter dated 8 March 1654, Henry Cromwell wrote to Secretary Thurloe, that after a long journey and his arrival back in Dublin he had been making a general inquiry into the soldiers' opinions concerning the state of the government. He reported that

the army generally, both here and about the headquarters as also those in the other parts of the nation, are abundantly satisfied and well pleased with the present government in England; unless it be some few inconsiderable persons of the anabaptist judgment, who are . . . not very well contented; but I believe they will receive much satisfaction from a letter very lately come to their hands from Mr. Kiffin and Spilsbury, in which they have dealt very homely with those of that judgment here.

Indeed, Kiffin and Spilsbury had certainly hoped that their letter would achieve the intended affect of calming their brethren.[25]

Kiffin's nervousness over the new situation was apparent in the stretching of the truth at the end of his letter to Ireland—"that we have not had any occasion of sorrow in the matter from any of the churches in this nation"—for such harmony was certainly not the case. Tremendous tension developed among the Baptists over the issue of loyalty to the new government. Paul Hobson eventually

---

[24]J. Nickolls, *Original Letters and Papers of State*, 159-160.
[25]Thurloe, *State Papers*, vol. 2, 149.

articulated eight arguments in favor of excommunicating all those
loyal to the Protectorate. Major John Bramston, a Baptist, agreed with
these arguments and incorporated them into his admonitory letter to
one of the Baptist churches in London. He wrote the letter because
he had not heard from them anything "tending to the awakening of
Zion" for some time. He scolded the church for branding as unwanted
those who resisted the Protectorate.

> Have you forgot since you yourselves were called factious, and
> such as wear the disturbers and troublers of Israel . . . have
> you so soon forgotten your old resolutions which was that you
> would have no King but Jesus . . . oh is it not a sad thing that
> you, who have so much abhorred the Court pride and vanity,
> should now become fawners and flatterers there as some of
> you are . . . have not I heard and seen you deny to pray for
> saints that were in prison because they did not contend with
> the corrupt powers of the Earth? . . . the day of the Lord is
> coming, it is near at hand, and if judgment begin at the House
> of God, where shall the ungodly and sinners appear?

Numerous other Baptists objected to the Protectorate and agreed
with Hobson that those who accepted it should be excommunicated
from communion with the saints.[26]

Kiffin's circle took measures to limit this internal agitation.
Thomas Cooper, who was closely associated with Kiffin, Spilsbury,
and Richardson, went to Belfast to quiet the Baptists who were overly
vocal in their denunciations of the Protectorate. Letters were also
sent from London to Henry Cromwell in Ireland, reassuring him of
the Baptists' obedience. Samuel Richardson took to the pulpit to

---

[26]Greaves, *Saints and Rebels*, 147, Hobson had announced these as "8 diabolical reasons"
and they were reported by Thurloe's spies; *For the Church of Christ Assembled at the Glas
House in broad street, London, 25 of the 10 moneth* (London, 1654), British Museum, Birch
Collection, Add. MS., 4459, fol. 145-147, from Brown, *Baptists and Fifth Monarchy*, 73-74;
W. T. Whitley, "Rev. Paul Hobson, Fellow of Eaton," *Baptist Quarterly* 9 (1939): 308; Capp,
Fifth Monarchy, 126.

defend the new regime. In 1654 he also published *An Apology for the Present Government*. This articulate and impassioned defense of the new government's legitimacy reveals the criticism that were most resonant among the Baptist movements. Richardson tried to address the Baptists' prominent concerns, such as the objection that "this government in the hand of a single person is in effect a kingly government" and "the Army hath declared against Kingly Government, and in having power in one single person, and now they are for it; therefore they have broken all their Declarations and engagements."

At the heart of the criticisms Richardson was responding to were the ideas that the Baptists were morally obligated "to witness against this Government, " and that "this government hinders Christ from reigning." To this, Richardson responded that the London leaders still hoped for the return of Christ, but at present, it was best to wait. "We desire Christ may come, we trust we shall lovingly embrace him when he comes, we desire you to agree with us and to this government but til he come." Richardson also tried to manipulate apocalyptic language in order to endorse the status quo. He argued that if the Baptists objected that Cromwell's Protectorate was illegitimate because it was "a kingly government," then they must also denounce "Christ, for his government is kingly." Fortunately for Kiffin's cause, Richardson had more articulate arguments than this in defense of the Protectorate. One of his most compelling arguments was that those who ignorantly complained that Cromwell's government was persecuting the saints, "never knew what it was to be persecuted." He echoed Cromwell in defending the imprisonment of Christopher Feake, explaining that this Fifth Monarchist leader was in jail "not for religion, but for the safety of the Civil peace."

After harshly criticizing Feake, he applauded the arrest of another visible Fifth Monarchist, John Rogers. Richardson said that these preachers had "meddled with wordly matters" in their pulpits and as a result deserved imprisonment, as did others who followed their example. "It was well done to imprison them, to prevent further danger; and if they will not be peaceable . . . let them lie there till they will be quiet." The message was clear, if critical preachers would not be silent of their own volition, then they would be silenced by jail. Such statements would hardly have been imaginable by Baptist leaders a decade earlier. Richardson did acknowledge that the present government had some minor problems, namely "the business of tithes." But for the sake of peace and expediency, Richardson argued that the saints should overlook this issue rather than "to begin a new war."

In concluding his apology, Richardson reiterated what had become the party line for the Kiffin circle, by rhetorically asking "whether it be not better for us to be content with what we have, and hope, and wait for more, then by discontent to make ourselves worse in losing what we have? For if we should fall out among ourselves, and destroy one another, the King's party are like to possess all, then it will be worse" than at present. "I do from my heart believe, that it is best for this whole nation, to be content with this government, and quietly to sit down under it, and to thank God that things are no worse than they are."[27]

The Irish Baptists tried to obey London's request for obedience as much as their consciences would allow. But the policies of Henry Cromwell, who was transferring prominent Baptists to remote posts and slashing their salaries, combined with the dismissal of the Protectorate Parliament, proved too much for some Baptists in Ireland. In 1656 the leading Irish Baptists, William Allen, Daniel Axtell, Robert Barrow, and John Vernon, resigned their commissions in protest.[28] The results were very satisfying to Henry Cromwell; although it was claimed "that the godly are discouraged," he could see

---

[27]Brown, *Baptists and Fifth Monarchy*, 99, 163; Underwood, *Baptists*, 80; Samuel Richardson, *An Apology for the Present Government, and Governour* (London, 1654), 3-6, 13-15.

[28]Others, such as Richard Goodgroom, had also been removed by 1656 for their objection to the Protectorate. Little is known about Goodgroom, but he provides another example of a radical opponent of the Protectorate who was a Fifth Monarchist and a Seventh-Day Baptists. He was later arrested as one of the leaders of a seventh-day church, along with John Belcher and taken to the Tower (*Calendar of State Papers Domestic*, 1671, 356-357.

no abnormal signs of protest. Henry had hated these officers and the "venom they spit against me." As long as their removal did not cause a general mutiny among the ranks, he was glad to be rid of them. Henry wrote to Thurloe that "the Anabaptists and others, whose way and principles were inconsistent with settlement and our interest, do find themselves disabled from doing much harm. My inclination now is . . . not to crush them quite, least through despair they attempt things dangerous; and withal, least others take occasion to become insolent and violent, and so put us to new trouble." Henry had learned that it was poor policy to make martyrs out of millenarians.[29]

The Baptists in Scotland were less troublesome because they were less numerous and never attained the positions of influence that their brethren achieved in Ireland. Nevertheless, they seemed to have sided with Dublin's sympathies over London. Captain Langley, stationed near Edinburgh, was continually concerned about the activities of the Baptists in the locality. Near the end of the Protectorate he had become so concerned that he decided to write to Secretary Thurloe and inform him of the Baptists' discontent. "Fresh desires in the Anabaptists to begin a new propagation, and for that end they have presented many with new books . . . containing all their strongest arguments against paedobaptism, as they call it." Langley feared that this literature also had a subversive intent, and he was confirmed in his suspicion by the fact that "just at the time when it is whispered, that my lord protector is very dangerously ill, they should thus break out with these things, in which they have been silent for many years, nay resolved, they was not to meddle with that controversy any more." But now, as it appeared that the government was about to change hands, the Baptists in Scotland were eager to prepare the people for the coming of King Jesus. Events had put a "fresh light to their design, which hath always been in their eye, though hereto strangled in their hearts." However, Langely's fears did not material-ize; the Scottish Baptists, like their Irish counterparts were quieted.[30]

---

[29]Thurloe, *State Papers*, vol. 5, 670-672, 710.
[30]Thurloe, *State Papers*, vol. 7, 371-373.

The success of the London leaders in silencing the most vocal dissension beyond London did not mean that Kiffin and his companions were free from troubles. The issue of the Protectorate was deeply divisive and contention arose even in the London churches. Kiffin soon discovered that the eggs of another movement had been laid in numerous Baptist congregations. The heated controversy over the Protectorate would cause these cuckoos to hatch and for the Fifth Monarchists to emerge as their own movement, which subsequently threatened to undo all of Kiffin's hard work and swallow the Baptists whole.

Kiffin had come a long way since writing the introduction to Goodwin's text in 1641. Enjoying the liberty of the mid-1640s, he had helped to organize the confession of 1644, which was to provide a model for both future Particular Baptist apologetics and organization. He had managed to herd his proto-denomination away from the wolfish jaws of the Levellers, even if it had meant the denunciation of men close to the Baptist movement who considered themselves Kiffin's friends. After being cleared of the label of "Anabaptist" Kiffin and the London leadership set about improving an organizational network that would insure the Baptists' survival through the century and provide the bases for a denominational identity. When faced with the challenge of strident protest by fellow Baptists against the government, this network proved useful in quieting discontent. They quickly circulated letters, sent envoys, and published apologetics. While the leaders were busy building an organization, some believed that the Baptist movement had lost sight of its original goals. Additionally, many detested the Baptists' subservience to the regime and endorsement of the status quo. In the Particular Baptist leaders' race to jettison the challenging parts of their program, they had alienated those Baptists who were not ready to accommodate. After the rejection of the Levellers, these discontented Baptists would supply the members and leaders for two of the movements that began to grow alongside the mainstream Baptist movements. The one was the militant millenarianism of the Fifth Monarchists; the other was the passive eschatology of the Seventh-Day Sabbatarians.

PART III

"UNORTHODOX" BAPTISTS

As I beheld in visions by night, behold, one like the Son of Man came in the clouds of heaven, . . . And he gave him dominion, and honor, and a Kingdom that all people, nations, and languages should serve him, his dominion is an everlasting dominion, which shall never be taken away; and his Kingdom shall never be destroyed. . . . And the Kingdom, and dominion, and the greatness of the Kingdom under the whole heaven shall be given to the holy people.
—Daniel 7: 13-14, 27

Remember the Sabbath day, to keep it holy. Six days shalt thou labor, and do all thy work, but the seventh day is the Sabbath of the Lord thy God.
—Exodus 20: 9-10

9

FIFTH MONARCHISTS AND BAPTISTS

Before the 1650s, the Baptist movements had defined themselves in contrast to more conservative movements. They had appeared on the English religious landscape crying out against the corrupt forms of worship they saw all around them. But with the 1644 Confession, the Particular Baptists began to also define themselves in contrast to the more radical Anabaptists. This trend would continue in the 1650s. As groups like the Quakers found the inner light, the Baptists found enemies on both the left and the right.[1]

In closest proximity were two new movements that caused concern among the older Baptist movements—the Fifth Monarchists and the Seventh-Day Baptists. Both of these new movements had

---

[1]Space does not allow for a full treatment of the way that the Quakers prompted developments within the Baptist movements, although the evidence demonstrates that Quakers won many converts away from the Baptist benches during the 1650s. J. F. McGregor notes that "From 1654 the Quakers made considerable inroads into the ranks of the Baptists, both General and Particular. Ordinances were rejected as dead forms; believers' baptism as a carnal representation of the true baptism of the spirit . . . Quakerism consciously proclaimed itself a revival of the pure ideals of Separatist evangelism. The Baptists, it was claimed, had grown worldly and lax in comfortable toleration, corrupted by the privileges which they had received from the powers of the world" (McGregor, *Radical Religion*, 61). The Quakers also appealed to women Baptists. By 1654 the Western Association had officially declared that " a woman is not permitted at all to speak in the church" (White, *Association Records*, vol. 2, 55). Phyllis Mack's *Visionary Women* (Berkeley: University of California Press, 1992), describes how Quaker women enjoyed greater freedoms. See also the recent work by T. L. Underwood, *Primitivism, Radicalism and the Lamb's War: The Baptist-Quaker Conflict in Seventeenth-Century England* (Oxford: Oxford University Press, 1997). Other groups, such as the Ranters, while less of a threat, were also troublesome.

some antecedents in the 1640s, but were primarily post-regnum phenomena. The Fifth Monarchists and the Seventh-Day Baptists share three important characteristics. First, at base they were both eschatologically driven movements. Second, their eschatological impetus stemmed from rigid observance of specific biblical texts. Third, both sects drew many of their members and leaders from dissatisfied Baptists. The connection between these two new groups and the Baptists can be described as a result of the older Baptist movements' efforts to accommodate and the new movements' attempts to preserve or rekindle original enthusiasms. The Fifth Monarchy movement will be discussed in this chapter, followed by a discussion of the Seventh-Day Baptist movement. It is clear, however, that the two were largely contemporaneous and many individuals held both views simultaneously.

The Fifth Monarchists were the last manifestation of the most forceful millenarian radicalism unleashed by the Reformation. The movement took its name from members' belief that the fifth monarchy, the rule of Christ and his saints, was at hand. The seventh chapter of Daniel served as their primary proof text. From it they determined that the Assyrian, Persian, Greek and Roman empires were the first four monarchies, which preceded the reign of Christ in the fifth monarchy. Now that Rome was undone by the Revolution, the fifth monarchy was dawning and no authority save Christ's was legitimately constituted.

The Fifth Monarchists found some supporters among the Presbyterians, but their membership was primarily drawn from Baptists and Independents. The Fifth Monarchists are most often defined by their willingness to use violence to clear the way for King Jesus. Bernard S. Capp, the most prominent historian of the movement, comments that

the Fifth Monarchists were a political and religious sect expecting the imminent Kingdom of Christ on earth, a theocratic regime in which the saints would establish a godly discipline over the unregenerate masses and prepare for the

Second Coming. . . . the essence of their beliefs was a declared readiness to destroy by force the kingdoms of the world, to invert the social order, and thereafter to be the rulers of the earth.

Capp's work, however, itself demonstrates that the Fifth Monarchists were not always sure when violent force was called for and some members believed the only permissible weapons were spiritual in nature. It has been suggested that some people in the mid-seventeenth century believed in the coming of the fifth monarchy and employed Fifth Monarchist terminology without espousing military ambitions or endorsing the direct use of violence.[2]

While the Fifth Monarchy movement itself was the most pronounced manifestation of radical millenarianism in early modern England, it developed as a response to waning apocalypticism. When the general apocalypticism that pervaded English Protestantism in the 1640s crested with the execution of Charles I in 1649 and subsequently began to fade in the 1650s, those who clung to it formed a distinct movement, seeing themselves as a remnant of God's faithful in opposition to the world. Many saw the king's execution as the final preparation for the fifth monarchy of King Jesus.

In the year of Charles's execution a Baptist named James Toppe anxiously anticipated "Christ's monarchical and personal reign upon earth over all the kingdoms of the world." But while there were no barriers to Reformation after the king's death, there was also little progress. For the Fifth Monarchists, the calling of the Barebones Parliament seemed a step in the right direction. When this Parliament of the saints was dismissed, the eschatological enthusiasms flowing from the execution of the king turned into despair at the failure for the actual rule of the saints to be realized on earth. Thus the Fifth

---

[2]Additionally, it is questionable whether there were congregations comprised wholly of Fifth Monarchists. Capp, *Fifth Monarchy*, 14, 131; B.R. White, "John Pendarves, the Calvinist Baptists and the Fifth Monarchy," *Baptist Quarterly* 25 (1974): 251-271; Bryan W. Ball, *A Great Expectation: Eschatological Thought in English Protestantism to 1660* (Leiden: E. J. Brill, 1975), 181-192.

Monarchists were born of both the despair at the failure of the Barebones Parliament and the despair over the failure of Christ's return. The Fifth Monarchists were then a direct effort to revitalize the eschatological enthusiasm and social criticism that had been present at the gathering of congregations half a generation earlier.[3]

The understanding of the precise relationship between the Baptist movements and the Fifth Monarchists has changed in the last hundred years. Historians in the first half of the twentieth-century such as W. T. Whitley and L. F. Brown, saw a close connection between Baptists and Fifth Monarchists. In the latter half of the twentieth-century, historians such as B. S. Capp and B. R. White have downplayed the link between the movements.[4] This presentation supports the former interpretation by showing the significant degree of traffic between Fifth Monarchists and Baptists. Baptists—General, Particular, Independent and Seventh-Day—joined the Fifth Monarchists, just as Fifth Monarchists adopted Baptist principles. While a large part of the Fifth Monarchists' theoretical framework was provided by Independents who had been exposed to millenarianism during their theological studies, the Fifth Monarchists' beliefs were also a natural extension of the Baptists' biblicism and eschatological concern. This close connection means that the Fifth Monarchists must be seen as part of the context of the Baptist movements. The Fifth Monarchists both affected and were influenced by the other Baptist movements. Additionally, a probable majority of

---

[3]Toppe quoted in W. T. Whitley, "Seventh Day Baptists in England," *Baptists Quarterly* 12 (1946-1948): 252.

[4]While Bernard S. Capp's excellent book, *The Fifth Monarchy Men*, is certainly the best source available for the study of the Fifth Monarchists, his determination not to be a denominational historian resulted in a somewhat questionable presentation of the Baptists' role in the Fifth Monarchy movement. His failure to include Henry Jessey or Hanserd Knollys in his appendix of Fifth Monarchists, which does include eight members of an obscure conventicle in Hendon which was fined in 1665, is one example of questionable categorizing. For a guide to some of the pitfalls of Capp's work, see G. F. Nuttall, review of *The Fifth Monarchy Men*, by B.S. Capp, *Journal of Theological Studies* 24 (1973): 309-312 and B.R. White "John Pendarves." Likewise, denominational historians, such as B. R. White, are determined to clear their Baptist predecessors from the charge of radicalism.

Fifth Monarchists accepted believer's baptism.[5] Very few of the Fifth Monarchists lacked ties with the Baptists. Only the revolutionary Thomas Venner, the choleric John Rogers, and the "seldom effectual" Robert Overton can be counted among the foremost Fifth Monarchists who were free of Baptist association.

The sustained connection between the Baptist movements and Fifth Monarchists is further confirmed by looking at the congregations

---

[5]Unfortunately, so little is known about the Fifth Monarchists that this question, whether or not the majority favored believer's baptism, cannot be answered definitively. The problem is exacerbated by the number of Fifth Monarchists, even those who themselves underwent a re-baptism, who did not make believer's baptism a requirement for church fellowship. Like Jessey, they were better described as Independent Baptists. The result is that it is difficult to gauge their respective congregations' persuasion on this issue (although it was noted that in the 1650s a number of Fifth Monarchists "have already taken up that ordinance," of believer's baptism. Thurloe, *State Papers*, vol. 4, 727). Brown in *Baptists and Fifth Monarchy* presents the case that Baptists predominated the movement (203-204; see also Whitley, *Baptist Bibliography*, note to item 4-658). B. S. Capp, on the other hand, in his study of the movement simply states that "The Fifth Monarchists contained saints of both persuasions, but there was probably a majority in favor of infant baptism." The footnote for this assertion reads "L. F. Brown . . . was mistaken in thinking that the Baptists predominated" (180). No other evidence is given. My claim comes from the following logic: Most of Capp's description of the Fifth Monarchists relies on his extrapolation from the activities of a few leaders to the rest of the movement. Given the limited evidence, this is a legitimate technique, but it must also be permissible when examining the issue of believer's baptism. Even if an attempt were made to reach a conclusion based only on Capp's own list of Fifth Monarchists (from which men like Jessey are absent), there are between 35 and 43 individuals who appear to have Particular Baptist connections, primarily either as members of a Baptist congregation or because they were later licensed as Baptists. There are then 10 General Baptists. As will be discussed in the section on Seventh-Day Baptists, there are between 43-49 Seventh-Day Baptists listed in Capp's appendix. Finally, there are 6 leaders, Carew, Courtney, Langden, Pooley, Powell and Rudduck who were re-baptized in the 1650s. Thomas Harrison also underwent believer's baptism in 1658 (*Public Intelligencer* 8 February 1658; Whitley, *Baptist Bibliography*, 5-658). Therefore, out of the 242 people in Capp's appendix alone, there are some 100 to 108 individuals who seemingly adhered to believer's baptism, or about 45% of the names listed. Since some of the people listed in the appendix (like John Archer), were neither Baptists nor Fifth Monarchists, and since for the majority of entries there is little more than "Samand, Alexander de . . . Servant in London," it is difficult to discern their persuasion one way or another. Therefore, there seems to be good evidence to suggest that a majority, or very near a majority of the members and leaders of the Fifth Monarchy movement, accepted believer's baptism. While such a statistical exercise does not prove this point, it suggests the close relationship between the Baptists and the Fifth Monarchists. This close connection permits an examination of the Fifth Monarchists in the context of the Baptist movements.

and "pockets" of Fifth Monarchists. Outside of London, the various Fifth Monarchist gatherings consistently demonstrated a Baptist connection. Powell's work in Wales was frequently among gathered Baptist churches. In Abingdon, the Fifth Monarchists were centered on the church of John Pendarves, a well known Baptist leader. After Pendarves's death, the members of the congregation who stayed together took out a Baptist license in 1672. Nearby in Reading, the active Fifth Monarchists were noted in connection with John Sturgeon's activities. Sturgeon was a member of Chillenden's General Baptist congregation, and in 1656 he established a Baptist church in the area. The activities of Lieutenant-Colonel John Wigan helped to establish small congregations in Manchester and throughout Cheshire representing the only known Fifth Monarchist groups in those areas, although such groups are probably more accurately referred to as Fifth Monarchist-Baptist congregations, as Wigan had developed Baptist convictions before 1650.

As will be discussed below, the activities of Christopher Pooley and Thomas Tillam in the North Country resulted in several congregations that can be called Fifth Monarchist, but they were also distinctively Baptists, and usually Seventh-Day Baptists. Such groups were noted in Colchester, North Walsham, Nottingham, Norwich, and Wymondham. The Fifth Monarchist sited in Warwick was possibly Daniel King, the influential Baptist leader who was a member of the Midland Association of Particular Baptists. London demonstrates a similar pattern. The meetings at Worcester House and in the White Horse Yard, near Somerset, had Baptist connections. The Fifth Monarchists reported at Bell Lane were led by John Belcher, an excommunicated Particular Baptist who later led a Seventh-Day Baptist congregation for over thirty years. Fifth Monarchist "pockets" were found intermingled with Baptists in the congregations around Henry Jessey, Hanserd Knollys, Praise-God Barebones, Francis Raworth, and John Fenton. The Stone Chapel and Lothbury Square congregations, both viewed as Fifth Monarchist, were led by the General Baptists Edmund Chillenden and Peter Chamberlen, respectively. The notorious congregation at Allhallows the Great was under the leadership of John Simpson. While Simpson was already a Baptist in the 1640s, he was an Independent Baptist, never making believer's baptism a necessity for church membership. By 1653, however, nearly two hundred adult members of "the church meeting at Great Allhallows, London," had been baptized over the previous three years.[6]

Perhaps the idea of "pockets" is the best way to conceptualize the earliest Fifth Monarchists. They did not appear as their own coherent movement but existed at first within other congregations—primarily Baptist and Independent. Just as Baptist congregations today contain some members who place a greater emphasis on contact with the Holy Spirit, the Fifth Monarchists were congregational members who emphasized a radical literalist eschatology. The Fifth Monarchists' political activities as well as their theological positions stemmed from their eschatology. In the early 1650s the distinction between Fifth Monarchists and other members of gathered churches was amorphous. In some instances, conflict with other Baptists may have radicalized some believers and led them towards Fifth Monarchist views. Peter Chamberlen was an example of this phenomenon.

Peter Chamberlen was an ingenious and ambitious man who envisioned a transformed society. Throughout his life Chamberlen published progressive ideas concerning innovations in public health, trade, the elimination of poverty, phonetics, a central bank, law reform, Christian unification, and wind-powered carriages. His family kept the medical secret of obstetrical forceps. His possession of this device made him a world-famous physician and he served at the court of Charles and Henrietta Maria. Aside from his creative and medical endeavors, Chamberlen was also a very religious man who was moved by the urgency of his eschatology. His eschatological convictions had led him to join the General Baptists by 1648. Although he tried to

---

[6]Capp, *Fifth Monarchy*, 271-275; Public Record Office, SP 29/190/104; Brown, *Baptists and Fifth Monarchy*, 209; *A Declaration of Several of the Churches of Christ* (London, 1654), 17-19; T. Dowley, "John Wigan and the First Baptists of Manchester" *Baptist Quarterly* 25 (1973) 151-162; Underhill, *Records of the Churches of Christ*, 346; White, "Organization of the Particular Baptists," 223.

foster relationships with Baptists of differing opinions, his confidence and argumentativeness often hindered his efforts. Additionally, his commitment to recovering the truth led him to conclusions that many Baptists found unacceptable.[7]

In the early 1650s Chamberlen came into conflict with several leading London Baptists. In 1654 he opposed two members of his congregation, John More and Theodore Naudin, in an argument over the role of women Baptists in worship. The disagreement followed divisions within the congregation over the proper interpretation of apocalyptic symbols, including the White horse, the Angels and the Star. The controversy over women centered on Anne Harriman, who wanted to speak at congregation meetings. Naudin insisted that he could "not walk with such as give liberty to women to speak in churches." Harriman said she "could not walk where she [had] no liberty." While Chamberlen's argument fell short of an outright defense of a woman's right to speak in the congregation, he advocated that if women members felt called by the spirit to act as "prophetesses," then they should have the liberty to speak.[8]

---

[7]*Biographical Dictionary of British Radicals*, (s.v. Spittlehouse); *Dictionary of National Biography*; J. H. Aveling, *The Chamberlens and the Midwifery Forceps* (London: J. & A. Churchill, 1882), 30-125. Chamberlen's fame was allegedly so great that even the Czar of Russia requested the use of his skills (Aveling, *The Chamberlens*, 32-33, 89, 123). Chamberlen made sure to emphasize his royal connections. In one of his radical pamphlets, after first establishing that he was "a member of the Church of Christ," he made clear he was also "first and eldest physician to his majesty's person . . . above 62 years standing: Having been physician [to] three Kings and Queens . . ." (*England's Choice*, (London, 1682, 1), see also Aveling, *The Chamberlens*, 106. The insatiably curious can find more on Chamberlen in J. W. Thirtle's "A Sabbatarian Pioneer—Dr. Peter Chamberlen" *Transactions of the Baptist Historical Society* 2 (1910-1911): 1-30 (part I): 110-117 (part II).

[8]Bod. Rawl. MS. D828, f28-32, 32 reads "the conclusion is a woman (maid, wife, or widow) being a Prophetess (1 Cor. 11) may speak, prophesie, pray, with a veil. Others may not." See also Burrage, "A True and Short Declaration," *Transactions of the Baptist Historical Society* 2 (1911): 145-146; White, *English Baptists*, 147-148. Chamberlen appears to have spent some time searching the Scriptures to see what is "particulary set down that women ought to" do (Chamberlen, *A Discourse Between Cap. Kiffin, and Dr. Chamberlain, about Imposition of Hands* (London, 1654), 5), this interest was undoubtedly related to his profession as an obstetrician, Aveling, *The Chamberlens*, 49-60.

The same year, in addition to debating the role of women in the church, Chamberlen was also one of the main participants in a debate concerning the laying on of hands. Chamberlen had come to agree with the Barber-Griffith type of General Baptists in their observance of this practice. By the 1650s this issue was troubling both the General Baptists, and the Particular Baptists. William Kiffin recognized the danger this practice posed. Not only did it threaten to divide the Particular Baptists, but its adoption raised the possibility that the Particular Baptist movement would be associated with the General Baptists—an association Kiffin had worked hard to prevent. As a result, Kiffin emerged as the Particular Baptist spokesman against this practice and debated with the articulate Chamberlen on the issue.

Chamberlen told Kiffin that "it is necessary for me to beat you out of all those holds that would detain you from the truth." He also maintained that Kiffin's argument against the imposition of hands was a reiteration of the argument used a decade earlier to denounce Kiffin's cause of believer's baptism. In Chamberlen's view, Kiffin was resorting to the same Antichristian logic that the persecuting Presbyterians had used to defame the Baptists. Chamberlen's differences with other Baptists probably furthered his view that they were not wholly reformed. Seeing many Baptists as still wallowing in Babylon and ignorant to the imminence and importance of the cause of King Jesus, Chamberlen became a Fifth Monarchist supporter. In 1654, the same year as his debates with Naudin and Kiffin, Chamberlen's church became the only Baptist congregation unanimously to support the Fifth Monarchists' 1654 *Declaration of Several of the Churches of Christ* . His radical drift continued and he soon began to observe the Seventh-Day Sabbath. The Seventh-Day church of which he was a part in the late 1650s, which later met in Mill Yard, was the first known seventh-day congregation in England.[9]

---

[9]Peter Chamberlen, *A Discourse Between Cap. Kiffin, and Dr. Chamberlain, about Imposition of Hands* (London, 1654), sig. A2, 1-6, 9-11.

The example of Chamberlen demonstrates how an individual could be a General Baptist, a Fifth Monarchists and eventually a Seventh-Day Baptist. There was a great deal of overlap between such groups. Christopher Feake, the leading London Fifth Monarchist, was never a Baptist, but he had Baptist sympathies by 1646, four years before he expressed his millenarian views in print. Other important Fifth Monarchists such as Vavasor Powell, John Simpson, and John Canne were or became Baptists—at least of the open communion Independent type.[10] A short list of other well-known Fifth Monarchists who were also Baptists would include: Richard Adams, William Allen, Nathaniel Byfield, Edmund Chillenden, John Clarke, John Combes, Thomas Glasse, Francis Langden, Jeremiah Marsden, William Packer, John Pendarves, John Skinner, John Spencer, Nathaniel Strange, John Sturgeon, Thomas Tillam, John Vernon, William White, John Wigan and James Wise.[11]

---

[10]Brown, *Baptists and Fifth Monarchy*, 21; Christopher Feake, *The Genealogie of Christianity and of Christians* (London, 1650), passim. Feake is actually identified as a Baptist in a number of places. See for example Winton Solberg, *Redeem the Time* (Cambridge, Massachusetts: Harvard University Press, 1977), 227. W.T. Whitley casts doubt on this conclusion, "The Fifth Monarchy Manifesto," *Transactions of the Baptist Historical Society* 3 (1913), 152. Vavasor Powell was a radical itinerant evangelist in Wales who spoke out against the Protectorate. He visited Baptist churches, among others, in Wales and was influential in the development of a number of Baptist congregations. He was re-baptized in the 1650s. He was closely associated with Henry Jessey and he was ejected as a licensed Baptist in Wales. See A.G. Matthews, *Calamy Revised* (London: Independent Press, 1959). For John Simpson and Powell see also Nuttall, *Visible Saints,*120; Whitley, *British Baptists*, 86; Tolmie, *Triumph*, 109; Capp, *Fifth Monarchy*, Appendix III, passim. An excellent study of Simpson appears in R. L. Greaves, *Saints and Rebels*, chpt. 4. While many historians deny that John Canne was a Baptist, it is known that he was close to the Broadmead Independent Baptists and he accepted believer's baptism (see Underhill, *Records of a Church of Christ*; Laurence "Army Chaplains," 286; Nuttall, *Visible Saints*, 120, 147). The Fifth Monarchist Anthony Palmer, was the leader of another Independent Baptist congregation. A further example is John Rogers, who became one of the most important Fifth Monarchist. While he never underwent a re-baptism, and believed in infant baptism, for a time his congregation in Ireland had an Independent Baptist character (again, Solberg identifies him as a Baptist, *Redeem the Time*, 227).

[11]For these individuals, see *Biographical Dictionary of British Radicals* and Capp's Biographical Appendix, *Fifth Monarchy*.

While the Baptists and the Fifth Monarchists continued to overlap, the event that forced them to distinguish themselves from one another was the establishment of the Protectorate. This event was to have a profound affect on both the main Baptist movements and the Fifth Monarchists. With the establishment of the Protectorate, the "hotter" saints realized that the Baptists were not going to go into opposition. As long as the Barebones Parliament had existed, the Fifth Monarchists were confident that society would be radically reformed. They assumed that they saw eye to eye with their Baptist brethren. When the Barebones Parliament collapsed and gave its powers to Cromwell, the "hotter" saints were outraged. It quickly became apparent that the majority of Baptists were not willing to go into direct opposition against a post-regnum regime, regardless of its character. As a result, the issue came to a head and believers were forced to chose between obedience and opposition. The eschatology of the Fifth Monarchists made this an easy decision, but the majority of Baptists thought it best not to oppose the government but rather to wait for the manifestation of God's will. In the words of W. T. Whitley, "whole Baptist churches were transformed, many were leavened" as "hotter" saints from the Baptist benches joined the Fifth Monarchists.[12]

As a result of the split, the Fifth Monarchists now defined themselves in contrast to the main Baptist movements, just as the Baptists tried to define themselves against the Fifth Monarchists. Every radical action or declaration on the part of the Fifth Monarchists led the Baptists to a more vehement denunciation of such beliefs and behavior. At the same time, each declaration of obedience by the main Baptist movements further fueled the Fifth Monarchists radicalism and provided proof of the saints' apostasy.

It was, however, their similarities that made them so competitive with each other. Additionally, the Fifth Monarchist effort to define themselves in contrast to the Baptists did not mean a rejection of the validity of believer's baptism. Even after the Baptists and the Fifth

---

[12] Whitley, *British Baptists*, 85.

Monarchists came into open conflict over the Kingdom, Fifth
Monarchists continued to accept believer's baptism and many Fifth
Monarchists later adopted this practice. While many Fifth Monarchists maintained the idea of believer's baptism, they rejected other
parts of the Baptist program. They now saw the Baptists as apostates
who had betrayed the original spirit of the movement. In their view,
the old zeal that had once called the Baptists to witness against the
Beast and decry corruption had faded. The Fifth Monarchists claimed
that the Baptists were afraid to take action in preparation for the
coming of Christ and that they were for that reason not true saints.
As a result, two main differences emerged between the main Baptist
movements and the Fifth Monarchists. The first was in terms of
eschatology, the second was organization.

An example of the distinction between the Baptists' eschatology
and that of the Fifth Monarchists can be seen in the efforts of the
General Baptists to differentiate themselves from the Fifth Monarchists. Employing their new organizational structure, the General
Baptists assembled thirteen messengers and twelve elders in 1654 to
issue their official position on Oliver Cromwell's Protectorate entitled
The Humble Representation and Vindication. This meeting demonstrated not only the growing sense of identity among the General
Baptists, but also the extent to which the Fifth Monarchists were
perceived as a threat and a temptation. It also provided an example
of joint-action among General Baptists with the intended goal of
publicly clearing their name of any wrong doing or malicious intentions. As B. R. White commented, "the beginnings of an established
leadership, together with the publication of certain Confessions and
other representative documents," such as the 1654 *Humble Representation*, reveals the General Baptists' organized effort to rid themselves
of "the term 'Anabaptist'." In their *Humble Representation and
Vindication*, the General Baptist leaders expressed their willingness to
obey "the powers that are in present being," except, of course, when
they contradicted the will of God. They maintained that the saints
would not and should not rule until the return of Christ at the end of
the world. This was becoming the General Baptists' position:

Nor do they [the General Baptist representatives] know any ground for the saints, as such, to expect that the Rule and Government of the World should be put into their hands, until that day in which the Lord Jesus shall visibly descend from Heaven . . . but till then they rather expect it is their portion, patiently to suffer the world.

In other words: not now. The intensity and immediacy that had inspired both the Particular and General Baptists a decade before had faded. They still believed in the apocalypse, but it was now an event placed in the distant future. In the continuing debate over *apocalypse how*, the General and Particular Baptist leadership had become willing to wait and no longer desired that the powers that be should be laid low so that King Jesus could be raised up. For the Fifth Monarchists, on the other hand, it was still an urgently imminent reality.[13]

Eschatology was not the only defining difference between the main Baptist movements and the Fifth Monarchists. The second dissimilarity was their respective organizational structures. Unlike the main Baptist movements, the Fifth Monarchists did not develop an extensive organizational network. The Fifth Monarchy movement was always loosely coordinated. It was deterritorialized and spontaneous. The Fifth Monarchists chose not to establish an organizational structure, despite their knowledge and ability to do so. Their members included numerous proven leaders. Vavasor Powell, for example, was one of the great organizers of his day. Additionally, many Fifth Monarchists had been involved with the army, which had taught them the advantages of a coordinated movement. Finally, the large numbers of Baptists within the Fifth Monarchist ranks meant that the Fifth Monarchists would have known of the Baptists' network and been capable of mimicking it. In other words, the Fifth Monarchists'

---

[13]White, *English Baptists*, 57; *The Humble Representation and Vindication of Many of the Messengers, Elders, and Brethren, belonging to Several of the Baptized Churches in this Nation of and Concerning their Opinions and Resolutions Touching the Civill Government* . . . (London, 1654), 1-5; Underwood, *Baptists*, 84-85.

failure to create a similar network derived from a resistance to doing so. When they published their *Declaration of Several of the Churches of Christ and Godly People* (1654), the Fifth Monarchists intentionally limited the number of signatures that were included. They maintained that they put only enough signatures so that it would not be thought an "inconsiderable testimony." But they limited the number of signatures so that the various Fifth Monarchist "churches in their several Counties" could "bear their own testimony to this suffering cause of Christ and his Saints." They preferred each congregation to have its own voice. The Fifth Monarchists sought to avoid being like the old "Bishops' High-Commission-courts" that compelled everyone to be of the same opinion. They rejected any semblance of "ecclesiastical tyranny" as part of the "Antichristian interest." The Fifth Monarchists implied that a hierarchical organizational system in itself was Antichristian. John Spittlehouse suggested that all organization and officers, while useful, were nonessential for true worship. Thus their eschatology affected their ecclesiology. As Capp concluded, "the saints were preoccupied with the imminent world revolution and probably for this reason failed to create any lasting national organization." Organization was inconsistent with the nature and origins of their movement. Therefore, it is revealing that the two areas of greatest difference between the main Baptist movements and the Fifth Monarchists, eschatology and organization, are the two areas in which the Baptists had undergone a transformation since the 1640s.[14]

The fact that after the demise of their movement many Fifth Monarchists returned to Baptist congregations reveals that there was never a clearly defined break between the Baptists and the Fifth Monarchists.[15] The common practice of believer's baptism and a common past kept the movements close to each other. The Fifth

---

[14]John Spittlehouse, *An Explanation of the Commission of Jesus Christ* (London, 1653), 5-12, passim; *A Declaration of Several of the Churches of Christ, and Godly People In and About the Citie of London; Concerning the Kingly Interest of Christ and The Present Sufferings of His Cause and Saints in England* (London, 1654), sig. a1-2, 5, 7; John Spittlehouse, *Rome Ruin'd by Whitehall* (London, 1650) 291-292; Capp, *Fifth Monarchy*, 175.

[15]Capp, *Fifth Monarchy*, 72, 172, 182, 216, 276.

Monarchists always hoped that the Baptists would join them in their witness against the Beast. Again and again they tried to call the Baptists out of Babylon. A second alliance, like the one between the Levellers and the Baptist movements, was a constant aim for the Fifth Monarchists. During the 1650s a pattern of targeted recruitment can be seen encountering an organized resistance from the main Baptist leaders. An examination of these efforts on the part of the Fifth Monarchists demonstrates the way that they employed apocalyptic language and how the Baptists and Fifth Monarchists defined themselves in contrast to each other.

From their start, the Fifth Monarchists knew that they needed the support of the gathered congregations if their opposition were to be effective. As a result, the Fifth Monarchists put forth a concerted effort to recruit members of the gathered churches to their views. The Fifth Monarchists had two primary methods by which they tried to persuade Baptists to join them. The first was to convince the Baptists that they shared a common enemy, usually the government, but any Antichrist would do. The second method was to confront the Baptists with their own apostasy in the hopes that they would desire to reform themselves and rejoin the fight.

Unlike the Levellers, however, the Fifth Monarchists were unable to mobilize sufficient support from the older Baptist movements. A nascent denominational identity, a distinct core of leaders, and an organizational system all combined to allow the main Baptist movements to distance themselves from the Fifth Monarchists. These developments insured that the Baptists would not be fatally splintered by their new rivals and old friends. Nevertheless, the Fifth Monarchists' repeated efforts to recruit the Baptists demonstrate how close the movements were. Similarly, the amount of energy Baptist leaders had to expend in order to resist the Fifth Monarchists' advances is a further testimony to the sects' inherent connection and their important influence on Baptist development.

From the establishment of the Protectorate, the Fifth Monarchists assumed that their Baptist brethren would follow them into open opposition. As long as Oliver Cromwell ruled in place of Charles I, as king in all but name, then Christ could never be enthroned as the sole "potentate, the King of Kings." The Fifth Monarchists had fought alongside the Baptists in the Civil Wars, "they were stirred up by the Lord to assist the Parliament against the King, for this end, to bring about the destruction of Antichrist, and the deliverance of his Church and people." They viewed their military struggle as a fight for the "destruction of Antichrist, and the advancement of the Kingdom of Jesus Christ." Now that that goal was threatened, and all the blood that had been "poured out for" that cause was to be lost, Baptist support for the Fifth Monarchist cause was taken for granted. As a result, the first apparent alliance between the Baptists and the Fifth Monarchists may have been more of a miscommunication than a general union.[16]

When it was announced that a Parliament would assemble in September 1654, the saints hoped that this Parliament would join them in their criticism of Cromwell. John Spittlehouse published a pamphlet describing the Fifth Monarchy and accusing Cromwell of treason for ruling as a dictator.[17] Spittlehouse's publication was soon followed by Fifth Monarchists' 1654 publication of *Declaration of Several of the Churches of Christ and Godly People . . . Concerning the Kingly Interest of Christ*, issued to coincide with the beginning of Parliament. Fifth Monarchists assumed that the Baptists and others "that are enlightened" would join them in their denunciation of Cromwell's usurpation of Christ's rightful place.

In addition to a violent attack on the government, the *Declaration* contained a forceful denunciation of the apostasy of the godly in the hopes of awakening them from their slumber and recruiting them to the cause: "Oh, did we ever think to see so many hopeful Instruments in the Army, Churches, and elsewhere, to be so fully gorged with the flesh of Kings, Captains, and Nobles . . . so as to sit with ease and comply with Antichrist, the World, Worldly Church and Clergy?"

---

[16]*Declaration of Several of the Churches of Christ* (London, 1654), 8, 16.

[17]John Spittlehouse, *Certaine Queries Propounded to the Most Serious Consideration of those Persons Now in Power* (London, 1654), 4.

How was it that the truth had come to be despised by so many? Even "some godly people and church members, accounted Orthodox, who cannot endure the day of Christ's coming," had become enemies of the truth. The *Declaration* asked those who had previously fought against Antichrist in the Civil Wars "doth not this *Personal Interest* now up, look too much like that which God hath confounded and stamped upon before our eyes?" Further, it made clear that they refused to abandon the goal that they had brought them to the battlefield, that they would have "No King but Jesus." They declared that "Lord Jesus is coming," and that it was time for a divine govern-ment to be established "according to the Word of God."

In line with the English apocalyptic tradition, inherited from men such as John Bale and John Foxe, the Fifth Monarchists saw them-selves as the persecuted "despised remnant . . . that yet cleave close to the cause and interest of our Lord Jesus, so much disowned and rejected in these times." Since Christ's church and cause had always been a small persecuted minority during the tyranny of Antichrist, the Fifth Monarchists could understand the apostasy of their brethren as part of the great falling away foretold in prophecy. Thus their isolation only proved the truth of their struggle: "Yet a little handful of the weak ones may have the Truth (though but the despised persecuted Truth) on their side."

They concluded their *Declaration* by praying that God "would in his due time cast down all those carnal, earthly . . . and political combinations of men (of all sorts) that would not have him to reign over us." Beneath this conclusion were some 150 signatures, some meant to represent entire congregations, which included the names of a number of prominent Baptists. When the *Declaration* appeared in London it seemed that the natural alliance between the Baptists and the Fifth Monarchists had already been established.[18]

Once this *Declaration* appeared in London, Samuel Richardson immediately issued his *Apology for the Present Government* in an

---

[18]A *Declaration of Several of the Churches of Christ* (London, 1654), 1, 4, 6 (misnumbered as 4), 8-10, 17, 19.

attempt to repudiate it. Most importantly, he pointed out that the arrangement of the signatures at the end of the *Declaration* was meant to imply that entire congregations had signed it, when in reality it was only some of their members. Richardson explained that those "opposing the present government" published "a libel, called, a *Declaration* in the names of several churches, with several hands to it, as if it were signed by those said churches, and upon examination it is proved false and counterfeit. I hope that many that oppose this Government shall see their error, and be ashamed." It turned out that while members of their congregations did sign the *Declaration*, men such as Knollys and Jessey did not sign it themselves. The Fifth Monarchists quickly learned that they could not assume the support of even the moderately radical Baptists, let alone the more conservative leaders.[19]

This close call put Kiffin and his circle on the alert. They threw themselves behind a resistance effort. The leaders went to numerous congregations and sent letters denouncing the Fifth Monarchists to some of the congregations that could not be visited.[20] In addition to denouncing the Fifth Monarchists, the London leaders coordinated a show of support for the Protectorate. Kiffin knew that the alliance between the Levellers and the Baptists had existed because of a common enemy, and he was determined to prevent similar circumstances from occurring. The London leaders gathered declarations of support from throughout the realm, declaring, like the one from Yorkshire, that "We profess our subjection to your highness and most honorable Council, as the happy powers ordained of God."[21]

As part of his effort to prevent a closer union between Baptists and Fifth Monarchists, Kiffin attended some of the Fifth Monarchists' meetings. In one instance he was present at a lengthy sermon by

---

[19]Samuel Richardson, *Apology for the Present Government and Governour* (London, 1654), 14.

[20]Nickolls, *Letters and Papers of State*, 159-160. The letters and envoys to Ireland, discussed in the previous section, were part of this effort.

[21]Quoted in Underwood, *Baptists*, 84. Similar petitions were reported from Baptist congregations as far away as Edinburgh.

Christopher Feake. After Feake had rehearsed his persecution at the hands of the state, he declared "I am for rendering and dividing yet more" for "when the churches are gathering corruption, striking in with the antichristian powers of the world, and complying with the interest of Babylon, 'tis high time then to rouze, and rattle them, and give them disturbance." Feake went on and condemned the apostasy of the believers and declared that there was "Babylon civil and Babylon ecclesiastical in this Nation," and God will punish those who "desert that noble cause" for which the wars were fought. After calling all the saints to "come out of them . . . least ye partake of their punishment," Feake warned the congregation against those who preach against such "books as the prophecy of Daniel, and the Revelation," for these men were agents of Babylon who wanted to keep the saints from the knowledge of the Kingdom contained in such texts.

Such division was just what Kiffin feared. He recognized that many of Feake's criticisms were directed against men such as him and when Feake asked if anyone cared to dispute his statements, Kiffin publicly challenged his sermon. Both Kiffin and John Simpson stood and objected to Feake's "fastening the terms Antichristian and Babylon upon civil government," to which the congregation called out that "Mr. Kiffin is a courtier and Mr. Simpson an Apostate." Despite such accusations, Kiffin's consistent, concerted effort proved effective and there was never a mass defection of Baptists to the Fifth Monarchists.[22]

Ironically, the result of the Fifth Monarchists' attempt to recruit the Baptists was to force Kiffin to seek an even closer relationship with the government, accelerating the Particular Baptists' transition from a more aggressive to a more accommodationist movement. But even if a common enemy could have been decided upon, the degree and direction of eschatology required to envision a transformed world, which had been at the heart of the Baptist-Leveller alliance, was no longer a primary concern for leading Baptists, who had become more

---

[22]Thurloe, *State Papers*, vol. 5, 758-759.

interested in differentiating themselves from Anabaptists and maintaining the status quo. As the General Baptists declared in the same year that the Fifth Monarchist *Declaration* appeared, it was preferable to "patiently suffer or humbly entreat favor." In Feake's words, "they do not care to have men looking into the Revelation."[23]

Nevertheless, the Fifth Monarchists continued to try and recruit the Baptists to their cause knowing that leaders aside, many Baptists were still sympathetic. There were reports in 1654 that the Baptists were meeting everyday developing a strategy for the release of General Harrison, a prominent Fifth Monarchist.

Later in the summer of 1655 a pamphlet written by a "well-wisher to the Anabaptists' prosperity," entitled *A Short Discovery of . . . the Lord Protector's Intentions Touching the Anabaptists in the Army*, appeared. While the document claimed to be addressing Cromwell, in reality it was addressed to the Baptists. It appealed to their patriotism, their birthright, and their consciences in an effort to enlist them in the fight against Cromwell. The pamphlet asserted that the Protector, in his effort to reestablish tyranny, intended to purge all the Baptist officers from the army "by degrees," a charge that did not seem unlikely in view of the harsh treatment of the Baptist officers in Ireland. For Baptists passively to allow this to happen would have been a lamentable fate, particularly in light of the Baptists past "integrity," "usefulness" and valiant action in the army. The author of the pamphlet recognized that Cromwell "pretend[ed] a great deal of love" for "Mr. Kiffin," but insisted that this was a subterfuge meant to keep the Baptists at bay.

The general arguments of the pamphlet were a forceful mixture of facts and fantastic fears, and would certainly have resonated with the Baptists. The authorities learned that the pamphlet's author was the Baptist pastor John Sturgeon, who had Leveller connections and was an associate of John Spittlehouse. Sturgeon's Fifth Monarchist sympathies were known and after the appearance of the pamphlet he was promptly arrested and deprived of his place in the army. He

---

[23]Lumpkin, *Confessions*, 223; Thurloe, *State Papers*, vol. 5, 759.

obviously was not detained for long, for within a year he was reported in Reading stirring up opposition to the government. He was jailed again after he had joined Edward Sexby and was caught distributing copies of *Killing No Murder*, a pamphlet that justified the assassination of Oliver Cromwell.[24]

In October 1655, another special appeal to the Baptists appeared under the title, *The Protector (So Called) in Part Unvailed: by whom the Mystery of Iniquity is now Working*. Knowing that the Baptists were always eager to determine the latest manifestation of Antichrist, the author of the text described the apostasy that had allowed the Beast to regain control of England. He was writing during a time "in which season the mystery of iniquity (the spirit of the Beast and false Prophet) doth transform himself into an Angel of light, and is working by the Protector (so called)." As long as the Beast dominated the government, no honest person could with a clear conscience serve the establishment in any capacity, military or civil. The author understood how some foolish people could be seduced into joining the forces of Antichrist "and led away to wander after the Beast," but he was unable to understand how the *Baptists* had been co-opted. He confessed "I thought that if any people in the world would be valiant for God, they would," but now they behave "as once I thought I should never have seen from them, and it grieves my heart." He pitied those baptized believers who have been tricked into doing Cromwell's dirty work of silencing the Fifth Monarchists.

In searching for an explanation of the Baptists' apostasy, he wisely noted the importance of the London leadership. He claimed that the speedy declaration of obedience that came from the Baptists in Kent the previous year was not written there, but in London by Baptists close to the Court, then sent to Kent for signatures. Even then, many of the Baptists in Kent had withheld their consent. Yet, he argued, because one or two eminent Baptists curried the Court's favor and

---

[24]*A Short Discovery of His Highness the Lord Protector's Intentions Touching the Anabaptists in the Army* (London, 1655), 1-8; Thurloe, *State Papers*, vol. 3, 150-151, 291, 738-740; Capp, *Fifth Monarchy*, 113-114, 119, 264.

"wandered after the Beast," the rest of the Baptists were deceived. In reality the goal of the government was ultimately to eradicate the very principles that the Baptists had once fought for. The Baptists must not be deceived any longer, even

> though Mr. Kiffin, and several members of the Baptized Churches, . . . through their simplicity, and ignorance, being led by other men's light, . . . which seeks the riches and honor that comes from man, . . . [do] indeed own the power . . . and therein [join] with the Malignants and others, unsuitable to their principles, to the grieving hearts of many of their brethren.

The author could not comprehend how the Baptist leadership could have come to support a government that maintained a church establishment based on tithes and exercised supervision over its ministry. He did not realize that Kiffin and Richardson, given the choice between anarchy and Antichrist, preferred the Protectorate.[25]

The Fifth Monarchists tried again the next month with *A Ground Voice*. The pamphlet was addressed to the soldiers and to "the Anabaptists in particular that bear any office, either in Court or army, under the present self-created political power." This Fifth Monarchist document referred to Cromwell as a murderer and a traitor. It declared that any Baptists who remained quietly in the army and did not separate from or witness against Babylon retained "the mark of the Beast." Like previous efforts at recruitment, the *Ground Voice* appealed to the Baptists' moral sentiment, asking if it was not an unconscionable violation of their beliefs to associate with the Court.

---

[25]*The Protector, (so called,) in Part Unvailed: by whom the Mystery of Iniquity, is now Working. Or a Word to the good People of the Three Nations of England, Scotland and Ireland, Informing them of the Abominable Apostacy, Backsliding, and Underhand dealing of the Man above mentioned; who having Usurped Power over the Nation, hath most wofully betrayed, forsaken, and cast out the good old Cause of God, and the Interest of Christ; and hath Cheated and Robbed his People of their Rights and Priviledges. By a late member of the Army* . . . (London, 1655), sig a 2, 1-4, 7, 9, 14-15, 19-20, 43, 76, 85-87; Brown, *Baptists and Fifth Monarchy*, 92.

The initial godly goals of the Baptists and "the principle of an Antichristian court are inconsistent, the one with the other." The pamphlet also reiterated the warning to the Baptists that the government was manipulating their leaders to keep the congregations quiet. Once the government became securely established, the author explained, the Baptists would be rejected as speedily as they were embraced. The text ended in asking "whether or no (and in the name and presence of the Lord, we put this question) you ought not to withdraw from, and have nothing to do with the present Court, and also the Army, and return and seek the face of the Lord, and repent, and do your first works, *Rev. 2:5.*" [26]

In 1655 a petition was being circulated in Wales the same month that the *Ground Voice* had appeared. Thurloe's agents had heard of it being read at the largest Fifth Monarchist meeting in the area. It demanded legal reform, the abolition of tithes and justice for the imprisoned saints. "The Anabaptists," it was reported "do generally sign it."

At the same time, the government in London was informed of another larger petition, this time the work of "Vavasor Powell, (who is lately rebaptized)." While Thurloe had commanded his agents to take action, they did not prevent the publication of the petition that was entitled *A Word For God*. The petition contained hundreds of signatures and claimed that it expressed the views of a number of other "churches and saints." Their main concern was how, after fighting for liberty, they could in good conscience endorse tyranny. How had all the godly principles and the cause of the "just civil liberties of Englishmen" become so quickly "forgotten or neglected?" Thus the petition called on readers to weigh their arguments and consider them morally "as you will answer to their great judge, before whose impartial tribunal you (as well as we) shall be very shortly cited to give account." They warned Cromwell that he must repent for his apostasy and return to "doing your first works, . . . lest God's fury break forth like fire upon you, and there be no quenching of it."

---

[26]*A Ground Voice* (London, 1655), 1-8.

Powell's articulate petition was one of the most forceful denunciations of Cromwell:

> Lastly, we do declare and publish to all from our hearts and souls, that those of us that had any hand in joining with the parliament and the army heretofore, had no other design against the late king and his party, save as they were the enemies of our Lord Christ, his kingdom and people, hinders to his work, and oppressors to this nation, and that it never came into our hearts to think or intend the pulling down of one person to set up another, or one unrighteous power to promote another: but we aimed primarily at the glory of God.

The myriad signatures were placed below the words, we "do withdraw, and desire all the Lord's people to withdraw from these men, as those that are guilty of the sins of the later days, and that have left following the Lord, and that God's people should avoid their sin, lest they partake with them in their plagues." Thurloe responded immediately and had several people involved with the petition apprehended. Independent Baptists like John Simpson had to go into hiding after he had been reported for reading the petition at a church meeting.[27]

If such agitation was not worry enough for Thurloe, he was further distressed when a few weeks later he was informed of the capture of "two Anabaptists" who were part of a group spreading "books against his highness" Oliver Cromwell. While the two Baptists were reportedly captured in January 1656, there were several others involved. In March Thurloe wrote again to Henry Cromwell in Ireland to bring him up to date on events in London. He reported:

---

[27]Thurloe, *State Papers*, vol. 4 151, 228, 343, 373, the quotes from the text of *A Word for God* are taken from the copy in Thurloe, *State Papers*, vol. 4, 380-384.

There hath been . . . a meeting of many of the Anabaptist churches in several parts of the nation, whither resorted all the discontented of that party and of the fifth monarchy men, with a full intention to have engaged the churches in blood, many of them having laid their matters beforehand, and prepared both horse and arms; but their intentions being known beforehand, some grave and sober men of their own judgement in matters of religion were sent to meet them, where matters were so handled (through the goodness of God) that these men with their principles were rejected, . . . what course will be further taken with them I cannot yet tell.

The Baptist Colonel Henry Danvers was one of the chief instigators, as was Thomas Buttivant. The identity of the "sober men" who opposed them can be guessed at.[28]

By 1656 Samuel Richardson's pen was again required to defend the Protectorate. His *Plain Dealing* reiterated many of the ideas found in his *Apology for the Present Government* (1654). At the same time it is one of the clearest articulations of the different perspectives on Revelation that separated Independent Baptists like Powell from more conservative Particular Baptists like Richardson. They both still sought the millennium, only Richardson argued that the Beast, for the time being, had been sufficiently defeated. The status quo was an acceptable substitute, if not an avenue for, the Kingdom of Heaven. Powell and his supporters believed there was little good in coming half way out of Babylon.

Like other Baptists, Richardson saw religious persecution as a mark of the Beast. In his pamphlet, he argued such persecution had been undone. "For freedom of religion is so great it is almost unspeakable, for under the present Government we enjoy more liberty than we have" ever before. Christ was now allowed to rule over his church because the machinery of episcopacy had been dismantled.

---

[28]Thurloe, *State Papers*, vol. 4, 412, 629.

Richardson was hard pressed for a justification for the fact that the government still imprisoned people for their religious views, collected tithes, and held discretionary power towards the ministry. To the first, he reiterated his previous position that the Fifth Monarchists were in jail not on account of their religion, but to keep the peace. To the other two, he could only say "I hear they are upon it," and it is best to "hope and wait for a redress therein." The saints should not try and set up a government, for "there is no form of Civil Government in Christ's testament," which they were mandated to establish.

To those who objected that Richardson had not preached such obedience while the king was on the throne and when Richardson was out of favor, he replied that the saints had been obliged by God's law to fight against the king, whereas now they were obliged by the same law to obey the present powers: "The King was one with Antichrist, against whom we are commanded to make war." The Parliamentary forces "sought the destruction of Antichrist [and] this they have done (as for the outward part of it in England) in separating Civil power, and excluding ecclesiastical."

Apocalyptic symbols were still the currency of discourse, and Richardson further elaborated his position. "The late King was one of the ten horns of the Beast, *not as king*, nor as chief governor, but because he gave his power, viz., his horn, his strength, to the Beast, . . . the Lord Bishops and Popes Priesthood, and so became one with Antichrist." By claiming authority over *the church*, Charles had assumed the office of Christ. Despite tithes, Triers, and imprisonments, Richardson maintained that now church and state had been separated, and the saints had done as much as they could to bring in the millennium. Now it was best to accept the status quo. The rest "will be done in God's time and way." He asked whether Cromwell's victory over the Beast was not proof enough that "God hath owned this present Government." To those who retorted to look to Cromwell's head, for Cromwell too had the mark of the Beast, for church and state were not separated and the saints did not rule, Richardson replied "I have looked in his forehead and I saw no such."

Indeed, Cromwell was not the Beast, but in a sense a savior, come to bring God's Kingdom. Richardson argued that it was Powell and his supporters who were the apostates. Like the Jews, Powell's band cries "crucify this government. We cry, 'what evil hath it done?' They cry, 'crucify it, crucify it.' We desire to know what we shall have in stead thereof. They say 'Down with this and trust God.'" Richardson employed equal drama in concluding his defense:

> I, Samuel Richardson, do take God to witness, that I have not written anything herein, but that which I believe with all my heart is true; and if I knew that this should be the last hour that I should live in this world, and so were to have no more benefit by this Government . . . I do believe I should witness to the truth of these things.

As it turned out, it was neither Richardson's last hour nor his last benefit. A few months after penning this pamphlet, Richardson was granted a loan of three hundred pounds from the government.[29]

Powell's petition was still convincing for a number of Baptists of both the Particular and Independent variety, even with Richardson's pamphlet to neutralize it. Thurloe wrote to Henry Cromwell in Ireland informing him of Powell's petition. Thurloe said that while he had detained many involved with its circulation, he had little doubt that they "would endeavor to do the same thing in Ireland, whereof I desire your lordship to take the best care" to prevent such agitation. Henry Cromwell agreed that precautions were indeed in order. He speculated that the Fifth Monarchists would not be behaving in such a manner if they were not confident of support. "Dare they be so bold, if they had not good back?" Henry's guess was that an alliance with the "Anabaptists" was their encouragement. He cautioned Thurloe

---

[29]Samuel Richardson, *Plain Dealing: Or the Unvailing of the Opposers of the Present Government and Governors. In Answer to several things affirmed by Mr. Vavasor Powell and others* (London, 1656), 4, 7-8, 12, 15-17, 20, 24; Bod. Rawl. A38 f. 487. Cf. Knollys, *Mystical Babylon*, 10.

not to be deceived. The sentiment behind Powell's petition was too strong for some Baptists to resist. The call to "withdraw from these men . . . lest they partake with them in their plagues" clearly resonated with the many of the Irish Baptist officers, who late in 1656 resigned their commissions rather than remain in Babylon and partake of her plagues.[30]

The officers' resignation of their commissions was another indication that the Fifth Monarchist effort to win Baptist support was having an effect. There were numerous other signs, many of them from areas outside the direct infuence of Kiffin's circle. For example, at the Midland Association meeting of October 1656, the small church from Tewkesbury inquired "what is the duty of believers at this day towards the present powers, whether in civil things to submit unto them." The lengthy response they received testified to the gravity of the matter. The messengers answered that the New Testament injunctions to obey civil magistrates were still in effect. Additionally, "when the Lord shall make his people a smiting people will he not first clearly put . . . power and authority into their hands?" The signs were still not right. The answer to the messengers' question of *apocalypse how* was to wait.[31]

Most Baptists could be patient for only so long. Soon even the Baptists in London were growing anxious. By spring 1657 *The Humble Petition and Advice* had been put forward as the foundation for a new government. In addition to providing for an "other house" in addition to the House of Commons, the Humble Petition also proposed that Cromwell be named king.

This was too much. Even conservative London leaders like John Spilsbury could not quietly endure this possibility. For a moment an

---

[30]Thurloe, *State Papers*, vol. 4, 348, 374-375, 383.

[31]White, *Association Records*, vol. 1, 30; idem, "The Organization of the Particular Baptists, 1644-1660," 224-225. The messengers added: "We offer it to the serious consideration whether [the true church] be in a low condition till the calling of the Jews and whether it may not be gathered from Mich. 4:8 that the Jewish Church shall have the kingdom and the first dominion. . . . If so, then whether it doth not behoove us with patience and quietness to wait for the time."

alliance between the Baptists and Fifth Monarchists appeared possible. Particular Baptists and Independents drafted a letter urging Cromwell to reject the crown. They maintained that since God's chosen instrument had as recently as 1649 declared that monarchy was "unnecessary, burdensome, and destructive to the safety of the people," then it should not be reinstated. The authors reminded Cromwell of the support that they had given him, both in the pulpit and on the battlefield.

> We beseech you, in the bowels of Jesus Christ, remember what God did for you and for us at Marston Moor, Naseby, Pembroke, Preston, Tredah, Dunbar and Worcester, and upon what grounds, also what boasts we have made of God thereupon, and give not cause for the enemy to say, that because God is not able to perfect his work, therefore we must return into Egypt.

Cromwell refused the crown; no alliance was necessary. It is not known how much this letter affected his decision, but it was certainly signed by well-known London congregational leaders, including, John Goodwin, Henry Jessey, John Spilsbury, Joseph Sansom (Fansom), and Hanserd Knollys. This letter is the only major Baptist document from the period that does not bear Kiffin's signature.[32]

Even if the letter that spring indicated that Kiffin had momentarily lost control of the London Particular Baptists, it was by then already too late for the Fifth Monarchists to capitalize on the Baptists' discontent. By late 1656, the Fifth Monarchists had begun to decline. The failure to win needed support, combined with selective government repression, had severely weakened the movement. Many of its leaders were either in jail or removed from positions of influence.

---

[32]"Addresse of the Anabaptist Ministers in London, to the Lord Protector," in John Nickolls, *Letters and Papers of State*, 142-143.

As the movement waned, some members were driven to even more radical extremes. Already by the beginning of 1657 Thomas Venner's congregation was preparing for a final revolution. Like other saints, Venner had left England for the New World but returned after the calling of the Long Parliament. After his return to England, Venner was briefly employed as the cooper at the Tower of London, but he was dismissed for a number of reasons, including his suspected intention to blow it up.

Venner was one of the leaders of the Fifth Monarchist congregation in Swan Alley, Coleman Street, which formed the nucleus for his theocratic plans. From this center Venner established a covert system of five groups of twenty-five saints. Only the leader of each of the five meetings would be in contact with the other four leaders. This cell organization was soon equipped with a plentiful supply of horses and arms. In addition to this core of supporters, the details of the plan were revealed to varying degrees to other sympathetic groups in hope of gaining further support.

At the start of 1657 Venner was close to recruiting a group of Baptists who he referred to as "the (private mark) rebaptized brethren," who were associated with John Portman. Venner explained that while all the plans were being finalized, his organization endeavored to recruit other like-minded congregations, particularly Baptists.

As part of this effort Venner held meetings with some Baptists, hinting to them at the full scope of his plan. Several additional attempts were made to get these Baptists and others to join Venner's plan. There were a number of Baptists willing to join in Venner's rising, but the timing was wrong. According to their interpretation of Revelation 11, Venner was premature. The Scripture said that the "holy City shall" be "tread under foot, two and forty months." Only then would the reign of Christ begin. Since the Protectorate was the little horn, its time would end on 16 June 1657, but Venner's rising was planned for April. The Baptists refused to sign on.[33]

Venner noted in his journal that "indeed, some of them did judge the time was not yet upon us," and many of the saints refused to join. Before the end of January 1657, Christopher Feake and his followers were excluded from Venner's plans. Later, Venner recorded that he had heard that John Rogers had said "that he would be hanged before he would go out with this spirit . . . and that if we should go out, he would submit to the mercy of the adversary before he would follow us."

There were further objections and defections. Some abstained on the grounds that "the ancient wise Christians are not with us, as Mr. Harrison, Carew [and] Mr. Rogers." Others did not join "because this time is not come by two months." Such feuds forced Venner's faction to break off communication with opposing groups, or else risk both detection and betrayal. As a result, it is difficult to determine his reasons for acting prematurely and not waiting the two months required by the book of Revelation. A likely explanation is that Venner agreed with the sentiment expressed by the authors of *The Banner of Truth Displayed* (1656). These authors addressed those who refused direct action on the grounds that the time was not yet right. Evidently, a number of the saints argued that "the Horn must continue three years and a half . . . But this power hath not been so long standing by a considerable time; and therefore you cannot expect the rise of that smiting work until the said time of continuance be fully accomplished."

The authors of *The Banner of Truth* responded to this argument by saying that it was unlikely that the Scripture actually meant for the saints to wait the entire three and a half years before acting. To do so

---

[33]Burrage, "Insurrections," 723-724, 728-729, 732, 736. With regards to the expression "the private mark," Burrage speculates that "perhaps those associated with Venner, including the Portman Anabaptists, found it of advantage to wear some inconspicious badge or mark . . . such a secret mark also would make their sentiments sufficiently manifest to one another. The use of their names, which they desired to conceal, would thus be less necessary and less frequent" (724-725).

would be to allow the Beast to reign longer than the scripturally appointed time. In other words, Venner agreed with those Fifth Monarchists who believed that "it may be supposed . . . that this work . . . shall begin some considerable time before the end of the said three years and a half." It would take time to prepare the way for the Lord, and Venner was anxious to begin.[34]

In preparation for the rising, the saints determined that "the public seal" for the movement should "be a lion crouching with this motto round it, 'Who shall rouse him up?'," in echo of Genesis 49:9. This seal was placed on the manifesto A Standard Set Up, which was to be distributed shortly before the rising. The Standard claimed the Kingdom in the name of Christ. This new kingdom was to be ruled by a sanhedrin selected by the saints and all laws would be taken from the Bible. Under this pure biblical theocracy, land was to be re-divided and it was agreed that all "precious things" were to "be brought into a common stock and treasury," and "that which is for the brothers, for their particular encouragement" was to "be equally distributed to the whole that hath engaged and those that stay with the stuff." Their manifesto concluded by calling all of the saints to come out of Babylon, for the time of judgment was at hand. The conspirators decided on midnight 9 April 1657 as the date and time to launch their attack. The forces were to make their way towards

---

[34]Burrage, "Insurrections," 725, 729, 732; The Banner of Truth Displayed (London, 1656), 27-28. The Fifth Monarchists' belief that Cromwell's reign would end in accordance with the prophesies of the eleventh chapter of Revelation had allowed many of the most enthusiastic saints to refrain from premature action. For example, in 1655 John Rogers wrote that "were it not to fulfill the word of God (Rev. 11) that this present death is upon us for three years and a half, I should be so astonished at it as not to know what to make of it . . . Yea, the shrill heaven, heart, and earth tearing call of the saints, past, present, and to come from the days of Abel to this day, to maintain their cause, to revenge their blood and the Lamb's, and to be up and doing for the Lord Jesus, King of the Saints, it is now" almost time. John Rogers, from Edward Rogers' Some Account . . . of a Fifth Monarchy Man, 138-139. John Rogers's confessed commitment to apocalyptic dating was, therefore, probably his reason for not participating in the rising. When the forty-two months had passed, and nothing happened, John Rogers did not turn to violence, but he also did not give up hope in the millennium. Instead, he set up a series of weekly meetings designed to discuss the coming Kingdom. Like many millenarians, it is possible that he believed that he had just done his math wrong.

London and reassemble at Mile End Green, from whence they would undertake their final attack on the heart of England. Secretary Thurloe's all pervasive information network got wind of the midnight meeting at seven o'clock that evening. With little time to spare, the authorities acted swiftly and seized the saints while they were still assembling. About two dozen men were captured along with some arms and the lion standard. Their Declaration was also seized and destroyed. Venner was imprisoned in the Tower, where he probably wished that his previous plans for its destruction had been more successful. But his stay was not long and he was freed before the Restoration.[35]

Venner's failed rising did more to bring about the demise of the Fifth Monarchists than both Kiffin and Cromwell's efforts combined. Government administrators were becoming weary of Cromwell's lenient stance towards religious radicals. Henry Cromwell wrote to Secretary Thurloe that the "wild notions" of the Fifth Monarchists "concerning the right of the saints to reign, and the imaginary immediate government of Christ upon earth, must needs call aloud for some settlement both in church and state." Furthermore, the saints had discredited themselves in the eyes of many of their sympathizers.

Internally, they even began to doubt their own cause. John Rogers was no longer certain that Cromwell would be replaced by Christ in the next few months. He noted that many of his fellow saints now speculated that England was not the site of the New Jerusalem and that the millennium, if it were to come, might take place in Germany or somewhere else. Along with his fellow Fifth Monarchist John Belcher, Rogers was arrested the next year, further depriving the movement of able leaders.[36]

---

[35]Burrage, "Insurrections," 726, 738-739; Brown, *Baptists and Fifth Monarchy*, 113.

[36]Thurloe, vol. 6, 222; John Rogers, *Jegar-Sahadutha: An Oyled Pillar. Set up for Posterity Against the Present Wickedness* (London, 1657), 37. This belief would prove to be crucial for the Seventh-Day Baptists and might partially explain why Thomas Tillam and Christopher Pooley began to transport believers to the Palatinate in the latter part of the century.

The failure of Venner's rising in 1657 meant that many borderline Baptists decided against supporting the Fifth Monarchist movement. But the Fifth Monarchists continued to hope that others would come over and a number of Baptists were eager for such a reunion. Venner's supply of arms and numerous supporters put Thurloe on the alert. While Thurloe believed that he had the Fifth Monarchists under control, he was determined not let any information pass him by. As a result, he planted three additional spies at the Particular Baptist Western Association meeting at Dorchester in May 1658.

The spies had traveled to the meeting with such haste that they had arrived earlier than expected. For fear of being discovered, they remained aloof and stashed their weapons in a neighboring town. The Baptists had been denied a meeting place by the mayor of Dorchester and if it had not been for another "trusty and fit agent" already among the Baptists, Thurloe's informants would have had difficulty obtaining information about the proceedings. As it was, there were few hindrances.

The agents reported that the assembly of about 300 spent the morning concerned for the saints' sufferings and praying for both the deliverance of God's people and the destruction of God's enemies. Most of the representatives believed that the suffering of the saints was increasing. They claimed that they were in a season "of apostasy and persecution." The spies description portrays a swelling mass of discontent among the representatives and their respective congregations. Their prayers and letters revealed their frustration with the current state of affairs.[37]

Fortunately for the conservative Baptists, that afternoon William Kiffin and nine other London Baptists arrived at the meeting. The morning after his surprise arrival, Kiffin gave the opening prayer in place of Thomas Collier, who had previously led the meeting. Kiffin appeared to have brought the tumultuous situation under control until another surprise arrival in the afternoon. The new guests were none other than John Carew, John Vernon, and William Allen. John

---

[37]Burrage, "Insurrections," 744; White, *Association Records*, vol. 2, 96.

Carew was a regicide and radical Fifth Monarchist who had recently been re-baptized after his release from prison for opposing the Protectorate. Captain John Vernon and adjutant William Allen were both among the group of Baptist officers who had recently resigned their commissions in Ireland rather than further compromise their principles.[38]

The spies reported that after the arrival of these three radical leaders, "at night there was a private meeting in the George [Inn], where many of the principal ones were and amongst other things there debated, a great contest arose about their joining with the fifth monarchy men." The spies noted that "for the time [this matter was] not concluded by reason of captain Kiffin's opposing it." Since the spies were not within the leadership circle they could not report precise details on this important vote or the private meeting that occurred the next night, but it is likely that Kiffin kept the "principal ones" from voting as to whether or not to join the Fifth Monarchists for fear of the results. From the spies' record, it appears that Kiffin continued to delay discussion "about the fifth monarchy business (broke off the night before)" until at last the meeting ended because the messengers had to disperse "to their respective homes." Once again, Kiffin was able to fend off what he thought were enthusiasms liable to destroy the Particular Baptists. One cannot help but wonder what might have happened if Kiffin had not arrived from London.[39]

The meeting at Dorchester was the last possibility for the Baptists and the Fifth Monarchists to join forces against Oliver Cromwell. Within a few short months, Cromwell was dead and his son Richard had replaced him as Lord Protector. The prospect of a new government meant that the machinery of the London leadership would again be put in motion in order to guide the smaller congregations through the period of confusion. While the Fifth Monarchists were to have one last hurrah in 1659 when the Rump Parliament was

---

[38] Allen and Vernon had both married daughters of James Huish and were apparently very close. See H. Wheeler Robinson, "A Baptist Solider—William Allen," *Baptist Quarterly* 3 (1927): 237-240.

[39] White, *Association Records*, vol. 2, 96-97.

recalled, for the most part their movement was over. Like the Levellers, the Fifth Monarchists were made painfully aware of their dependence on the Baptists. Discontent with the Rump followed hard upon its recall and many Fifth Monarchists were denied the positions they expected and the influence that they would have held. The collapse of the Rump further pulled the Fifth Monarchists' loyalties in varying directions. Once the Fifth Monarchists became hopelessly divided, Baptist support receded as quickly as the apocalypse itself.

Recognizing that the Revolution was unraveling, a meeting of Particular Baptist leaders, prominent Independent Baptists, and General Baptists took place. These representatives from various Baptist movements united in order to issue a joint, blank promise of civil obediency to "whatever Government is, and shall be established in this Nation."[40] The transformation towards greater accommodation, begun in the early days of the Revolution with the 1644 Confession of Faith, now appeared nearly complete as accommodation, on principle, had become almost a tenet of faith.

A few months later, in 1661, another mixed group of Baptists republished sections of their 1659 *Declaration* in a new text entitled *The Humble Apology of some commonly called Anabaptist*, with the "hope and desire that none of us upon the re-establishment of the present government, shall now be judged criminal, . . . but that we may . . . be protected from all injury." This latest statement of obedience reads like a highlight report of the Baptists' efforts to convince the government of their harmlessness. In addition to a newly phrased statement of loyalty and revised effort to distinguish themselves from the Anabaptists, this *Apology* also contained choice quotations from previous statements of obedience issued during all the "revolutions and changes of persons exercised in Government, which hath often happened in these Nations of late years." They began their series of quotations with the article from the Particular Baptists' 1644 Confession of Faith, which declared their submission to the government, moved through the declarations that had

---

[40]*A Declaration of Several of the People Called Anabaptists* (London, 1659), 1.

disassociated themselves from the Levellers—in an effort to make "a good accommodation to men," and ended with their 1659 promise to "live peaceably under the Government established in this Nation." In addition to the predictable signatures of Kiffin, Spilsbury, and Thomas Cooper, the document was also signed by the well known General Baptists Thomas Lambe and Henry Denne.[41]

Quaker Richard Hubberthorn chided the Baptists for their 1659 blanket statement of obedience to any government that might possibly be established in England. He asked:

> And what did you bear arms or fight for, if not for a Government according to the truth, and that righteousness may establish the Nation . . . [for] if now you resolve to live peaceably, and to submit to whatever Government shall be established, then your fighting is at an end: and if Charles Stuart come, or any other, and establish popery and govern by tyranny, you have begged pardon by promising willing to submit and live peaceably under it as the ordinance of God . . . Some did judge that you had been of another spirit.

Hubberthorn wondered, "What, are you about to make a League and a Covenant with Antichrist? Have you for these many years been opposing them in words, and are you now recanting of what you have done when you are sensible of danger upon you? . . . are you turned backwards into love and affection towards them again, and so lost your former principles?" Hubberthorn recognized that in essence, the Baptists had changed. "You are not of the same spirit as once you were." Even if the Baptists no longer recognized it, Hubberthorn warned that "the time of the . . . Kingdom is at hand, behold, behold . . . the sentence of eternal vengeance will pass upon you." Unfortunately for both the Baptists and Hubberthorn, his worst predicted

---

[41]*The Humble Apology of some commonly called Anabaptists* (London, 1661), 14-19.

fears of "Charles Stuart come[ing in] and" establishing "popery and govern[ing] by tyranny," turned into a reality.[42]

---

[42]Richard Hubberthorn, *An Answer to a Declaration put forth by the general Consent of the People called Anabaptists* (London, 1659), 3-4, 17-18, 24. Like the Levellers, the Quakers were angered by the Baptists' denunciation of them in their *Declaration*. They asked, "is it to save yourselves from reproaches" that you have "sought to make us vile that yourselves might appear free" (13). Pages 12-24 of Hubberthorn's text were written by "another hand,"—signed E[dward ?] Burrough—in response to the Baptists' 1659 declaration, and were included by Hubberthorn since he found them useful.

The appearance of a mixed group of prominent Baptists in the 1659 petition led many to see it as a representative statement for all Baptists. Several groups of Baptists objected to this and published declarations distancing themselves from the *Declaration of Several of the People Called Anabaptists* [hereinafter *DSPCA*]. The first such protest was entitled *A Declaration of Several Baptized Believers, walking in all the Foundation Principles of the Doctrine of Christ, Mentioned in Heb. 6.1,2.* It appeared within days of the *DSPCA* in order to "bear Testimony . . . against that Babylonish Antichristian worship still on foot." It stridently declared that the other Baptists had compromised too much to quickly. They had two primary objections. First, the *DSPCA* was too limited in its advocacy of religious liberty. This new declaration retorted that they would "have a full and equal liberty to be granted . . . to all persons whatsoever without exceptions . . . for why should we not give unto another that we would . . . enjoy ourselves?" The *DSPCA*'s limited stance on religious liberty was a symptom of a larger problem, namely that those Baptists had given up witnessing against the Beast by endorsing the national ministry. Unlike the more accommodationist Baptists, those who signed the new declaration vehemently opposed the national ministry. "We do look upon it to be Antichristian . . . we judge it Babylonish, therefore we do in the presence of God . . . declare against it." On 12 January another Declaration appeared distancing a group of Baptists from the previous declarations. The *Declaration of a Small Society of Baptized Believers, undergoing the Name of Free-Willers, about the City of London* had a more apocalyptic tone than the other declarations, speaking of "the great day of account" and using Revelation 13 to support some of its positions. This declaration addressed each of the points made in the *DSPCA* and added certain nuances to each statement, least it be thought that "the Baptists in general" are all of the same opinion. It also declared that since they were a people called out of the world, they should not swear oaths or assume any governmental office. Both of these declarations signed in protest of the *DSPCA* had very few signatories. It was not until January 14th that a prominent Baptist leader protested the *DSPCA*. This time, John Griffith led a number of Baptists in publishing *A Declaration of Some of those People in or Near London, Called Anabaptists.* They maintained that they had further objections to the *DSPCA* that were not expressed in other declarations. The primary reason for bringing this petition forth was that "we cannot in all things close" with the *DSPCA*. "Therefore, for as much as we, who go under the same notion with them of being Anabaptists, thought it out duty to manifest our non-consent with them, in their sewing pillows under the elbows of the Ministers of the Nation; and their want of boldness, to witness against their Babylonish worship; which is also the reason why we declare against those national ministers more than against any other." As for freedom of conscience, "we

Charles Stuart did indeed come back and was proclaimed king on 8 May 1660. The Restoration government did not do the Fifth Monarchists the favor of providing their movement with a martyr's exit. Only John Carew, so recently frustrated in his efforts to form a Baptist-Fifth Monarchist alliance at Dorchester, and Major-General Thomas Harrison were allowed to have a timeless moment on the gallows before being executed as regicides. Both of these men, in addition to being Fifth Monarchists, had also been rebaptized, and their faith and expectation aided them in their final trail. The night before his death, Carew muttered, more in disbelief than in despair, "oh! . . . who would have thought some years since, that popery and formality should have been let in again to these nations?" He was comforted, however, by God and he told the friends who attended him "that this was the last Beast, and his rage was great, because his time was short."

The next day, after he had climbed the ladder to the execution platform, Carew faced the multitude that had gathered for his demise. After reminding them of a few words from Revelation, he declared "[W]hat I have done, I have done it in obedience to the Lord." He then began to address "the kingdom and glorious appearance of Jesus Christ," but was told that he should pray for his soul with the time remaining. This he did and when finished "Mr. Carew said to the executioner, 'stay a while, I will speak one word,' and then he said very solemnly, with a loud voice, 'Lord Jesus, receive my soul: Lord Jesus, into thy hands I commend my spirit.' And then was turned off."

When Carew's companion, Harrison, was taken to his own execution, members of the crowd mocked him and called out "and now—where is your good old cause?" With a resolved smile, Harrison

---

believe, and declare, that all men whatsoever, ought to have their liberty in point of conscience; and that no magistrate hath received power from Christ to punish for, or to compel any to this or that form of Religion." At the same time they also made it clear that they were not Fifth Monarchists. A few months later in March, a nationwide meeting of General Baptists assembled and also declared their obedience to the magistrate in a *Brief Confession or Declaration of Faith*, which later became the primary confession for the General Baptist denomination.

patted his chest and shouted "here it is! And I am going to seal it with my blood!" The other Fifth Monarchists were not so fortunate. Closure eluded the movement, destined to fade rather than expire. A number of Fifth Monarchists were arrested even before the Restoration and more saints were imprisoned with the return of the king. Those who avoided arrest were often harassed; some were banished. Censorship followed Charles's return and the Fifth Monarchists realized that, ironically, the very man whom they had identified as the little horn of the Beast had allowed them to express such views that were now silenced.[43]

Shattered by the Restoration of the king and the failure of all of their prophecies, a group of Fifth Monarchist gathered around the recently freed Thomas Venner. They decided against going gently and opted to make one last bid to bring about the Kingdom of God on earth through force. In their desperation they published *A Door of Hope, Or A Call and Declaration for the gathering together of the first ripe Fruits unto the Standard of our Lord, King Jesus* (1661). It would be the last manifesto of the revolution. Venner and the other saints who had committed to "take up arms for King Jesus against the powers of the Earth," revised their old plans for capturing the capital. They attacked London twice with the rallying cry of "King Jesus, and the heads upon the gate." While their forces were small, they fought with a tenaciousness befitting the death dance of a movement. One contemporary recorded that as they descended on the city and attempted to secure buildings, they encountered a man who, when asked who he was for, said "that he was for King Charles, they answered they were for King Jesus, and shot him through the head, where he lay as a spectacle all the next day."

Fierce fighting broke out, and Venner's army retreated to the woods to regroup. In their second attack, they descended on London with a "mad courage," and for a brief time overwhelmed all resistance, plunging the city into chaos. Venner's small army fought against

---

[43]T. B. Howell, *A Complete Collection of State Trials* (London, 1816), 1234, 1239-1240, 1243-1244, 1247.

disproportionate odds for some time. They refused to take shelter and only after the majority of Fifth Monarchists had been shot or captured was some semblance of order restored. Venner himself had been shot three times before he was captured.

Soon the uprising was crushed and with it the millennial dreams of the Fifth Monarchists. Venner and twelve of his leading disciples were swiftly executed and their heads displayed on London Bridge. In the effort to mop up resistance in the following days, numerous innocent Independents, Baptists, and Quakers were arrested. Within days conventicles were banned.

The Baptists protested that the majority of Venner's followers had supported "infant-baptism, and never had communion with us." They also pointed out that the Fifth Monarchists had labeled the main Baptist movements as "worshipers of the Beast, because of our constant declaring against their . . . interpretations of dark prophecies, and . . . our duty of subjection to the civil magistracy." But the Baptists could not win back the favor they once had with society. Venner's rising was proof enough to most that religious conformity was needed for social stability. A time of great persecution and harassment began for all dissenters. The intensity of this persecution would wax and wane over the next two decades and further transform the Baptist movements. The Fifth Monarchists had extinguished themselves in anything but a blaze of glory. The New Jerusalem had been lost; the cause discredited. For the rest of their existence the Fifth Monarchists were fragmented and hard to recognize. Within a generation the sect had faded from view and many of their members returned to the main Baptist movements.[44]

---

[44]Burrage, "Insurrections," 739-744; Capp, *Fifth Monarchy*, 199; *The Humble Apology of some commonly called Anabaptists* (London, 1661), 8. For an account of the persecution of a number of Baptists prior to Venner's failed uprising, see *The Humble Petition and Representation of Several Peaceable and Innocent Subjects* (London, 1661), 5, the rest of this text is an argument from a group of jailed Baptists, trying to convince Charles II that magistrates have no authority in matters of conscience and justifying their refusal to swear to an oath of supremacy (6-15). Shortly after Venner's rising, a tract appeared entitled *The Last Farewel to the Rebellious Sect Called the Fifth Monarchy-Men . . . .the total Dispersing, Defeating and utter Ruining of that Damnable and Seditious Sect in General* (London, 1661), the

The Revolution had ended. Ernst Troeltsch recognized that this concluded "the last great period of Baptist revolt . . . This advanced sectarianism was the last politically important wave of Chiliasm, the last return of the spirit of the Hussites and of the Peasants' Wars, the last attempt by Christian social reformers to prepare the way for the Kingdom of God by means of the sword." In his view, "from that time forward the revolutionary Baptist movement was over."[45]

---

tract was aptly named, for all though Venner and his rising did not represent the majority of Fifth Monarchists, his failure helped to accelerate their own disappearance.

[45]Troeltsch, *Social Teaching*, vol. 2, 713, 709.

10

SEVENTH-DAY BAPTISTS

Many scholars of apocalypticism agree with Troeltsch's view that the Restoration and the collapse of the Fifth Monarchy movement marked the end of intense chiliasm in the Baptist movements. Christopher Hill points to "a rapid disappearance after 1660" of apocalyptic enthusiasm.[1] The hopeful expectancy of the 1640s had turned into despair by the late 1650s, only to be capped by the Restoration of the monarchy two decades after the calling of the Long Parliament. Millenarian beliefs were already declining when the Fifth Monarchy movement was being born. The dangers presented by their uprisings helped to dissuade responsible leaders from further entertaining millennial dreams. As these dreams turned to memories for the majority of sectaries, there was one last significant manifestation of Baptist eschatology in the seventeenth century. This "godly remnant," the Seventh-Day Baptists, are the focus of this chapter.[2]

---

[1]Christopher Hill, *Antichrist in Seventeenth-Century England* (Oxford: Oxford University Press, 1971), 154.

[2]The Seventh-Day Baptists have received little scholarly attention, but are certainly a part of the earliest English Baptist movements. For a brief historiographical discussion of the materials available for this movement, see Leon Lyell, "Doctrines of the Seventh-Day Men," Dissertation, La Trobe University, Australia, 1981. The first modern study of this group, W. T. Whitley's "Seventh Day Baptists in England," *Baptist Quarterly* 12 (1946-1948): 252-258, serves as a list of some better known Seventh-Day Baptists. Whitley also set out to publish a monographic study of the Seventh-Day Baptists. Unfortunately this book was never published and remains in typed manuscript form in the Angus Library, Oxford, under the title "Men of the Seventh Day or Sabbath Keepers of the Seventeenth Century" (41.e. 1). While this manuscript is helpful, much of its content is available in three recent works: Don A. Sanford's *A Choosing People: The History of the Seventh Day Baptists* (Nashville: Broadman Press, 1992), is a denominational account that contains useful information about

Near the end of the seventeenth century, the Frenchman Henri
Mission gave an illustrative description of the Seventh-Day Baptists
when he observed during his travels in England that he occasionally
encountered a millenarian, but there was one "particular society,"
which he discovered that especially intrigued him. He described them
as an obscure and seldom noticed people who "makes but little noise."
He explained that "they go by the name sabbatarians," and they
"make profession of expecting the reign of a thousand years." Aside
from their millenarianism, Mission described the two most distinguishing features of this sect, namely their Saturday worship and their
pratice of believer's baptism. "These Sabbatarians are so called,
because they will not remove the day of rest from Saturday to Sunday
. . . They administer baptism only to adult people; and perhaps they
are blamable in these two things only because they look upon them
to be more important than they really are." Mission described other
characteristics of the sect, such as their avoidance of pork, but he
noted that they "do not absolutely forbid the use of those meats."
Overall, Mission was struck by the piety of these people commenting
that "their morality is severe, and their whole outward conduct pious
and Christian-like." He ending his description by saying that "were it
only for this one opinion of belief of theirs concerning the absolute
necessity of keeping the Sabbath on Saturday . . . that alone would be
enough to make them unavoidably a society by themselves."[3]

Mission, like other contemporaries called the Seventh-Day
Baptists by a variety of names. Frequently critics simply called them
Jews, Christian Jews, or Judaizing Christians. They used the term Jew
to signify the movement's defining belief, that the word of God gave

---

seventeenth-century Seventh-Day Baptists. David S. Katz's *Sabbath and Sectarianism in
Seventeenth-Century England* (Leiden: E. J. Brill, 1988) provides an excellent account of most
of the major seventeenth-century Sabbatarian thinkers. Katz also draws some provocative
connections and conclusions form his work (see especially his epilogue). The current
definitive work on the movement is Bryan W. Ball's *The Seventh-day Men: Sabbatarians and
Sabbatarianism in England and Wales, 1600-1800* (Oxford: Clarendon Press, 1994).

[3]Henri Mission's *Memories et Observations Faites par un Voyageur en Angleterre* (1689),
trans. by John Ozell as *M. Mission's Memoirs and Observations on his Travels over
England* (London, 1719), 234-235, quoted in Ball, *Seventh-day Men*, 9.

a moral commandment that Saturday be observed as the Sabbath.[4] In the majority of cases, members of this "godly remnant" were not converting to Judaism; rather, out of a deep desire to show proper Christian obedience, they had determined that the Sabbath was on Saturday.[5] Because of their concern over the observance of the Sabbath they have been called Sabbatarians, Seventh-Day Men and Saturday-Sabbatarians. Since nearly all seventeenth-century seventh-day observers came to accept believer's baptism, the inclusive term Seventh-Day Baptists will be used both in preference to Seventh-Day Men and to emphasize the Seventh-Day Baptists' context within the Baptist movements.[6]

There were individual seventh-day Sabbatarian thinkers well before the 1650s when Seventh-Day Baptist congregations began to appear in England. On the Continent, the re-examination of the Scriptures initiated by the Reformation led some to reconsider the nature of the Sabbath and the fourth commandment. In their desire to obey God's word, believers began to discuss the proper day for Christian worship. By the late 1520s, Seventh-Day Anabaptists appeared in Moravia, where they were led by Oswald Glait and his

---

[4]The frequent use of the term "Jew" also shows the widespread confusion about Judaism that followed the discussion of the Jews' re-admission to England—an event in itself that had eschatological underpinnings as well as implications. See Peter Toon, ed. *Puritans, the Millennium and the Future of Israel*, (London: Clarke & Co., 1970), especially chapter 7 as well as Katz's *Philo-Semitism*.

[5]See for example, William Sellars [Saller], *An Examination of a late Book published . . . Concerning a Sacred Day of Rest . . .* (London, 1671).

[6]Whitley, *Baptist Bibliography*, note to item 24-657; Lyell, "Doctrines of the Seventh-Day Men," 20. Throughout the contemporary printed material, the ideas of eliminating "infant baptism and the first day Sabbath" appear together as part of a program for reinstating the pristine church (William Aspinwall, *The Abrogation of the Jewish Sabbath* (London, 1657), 40 in reference to "The Morality of the Fourth Commandment" chapter 7). A rejection of paedobaptism and an acceptance of believer's baptism were standard among seventh-day observers by the 1650s. John Spittlehouse, for example, saw seventh-day observance along with "believers baptism" as "institutions of Christ and his Apostles," *A Manifestation of Sundry gross absurdities* (1656), 6. See also Thomas Tillam, *The Seventh-day Sabbath Sought Out* (London, 1657), 1-5. Ball maintains that there "were some notable exceptions to the general rule that most Sabbatarians were also Baptists," but provides only John Traske and Theophilus Brabourne as seventeenth-century examples and notes that "Baptist Sabbatarians" were "always in the majority" (*Seventh-day Men*, 6-7).

chief assistant, Andreas Fischer.

In addition to reinstating the Saturday Sabbath, these Anabaptists also observed many Old Testament laws that they believed were still mandatory for true believers. In England, after the turn of the century, John Sprint described seventh-day observers as maintaining the opposite practice from Anabaptists. According to Sprint, the Anabaptists rejected the strict observance of any day, claiming that all such empty ceremonies had been undone by Christ. On the other hand, there were the "Sabbatary Christians," who maintained that "the Jewish Sabbath of the seventh day in the week . . . is never to be abolished, being no less necessary for us to observe now than it ever was for the Jews." Sprint was sympathetic to the argument that the Sabbath was a morally binding obligation for Christians, but he explained that it was justifiably moved by the primitive church to Sunday in memory of Christ's resurrection.[7]

Sprint did not mention any of these "Sabbatary Christians" by name and it is not known if there were any such persons in England at that time. The first well-known Saturday observer in England was a man from Somerset named John Traske (1585-1636). Traske saw himself in a prophetic role and he believed that part of his task on earth was to unveil and undo the forces of Antichrist. His eschatological perspective and his re-examination of the Scriptures apparently led him to preach in favor of the recovery and observance of numerous Jewish rites.

In the 1610, Traske began to attract a substantial following. While Traske practiced a strict observance of the Sabbath, he still believed that the Sabbath was on Sunday. Around 1616 one of Traske's followers named Hamlet Jackson had a mystical vision that confirmed his belief that the Sabbath should be observed on Saturday. Jackson soon convinced Traske and the practice was adopted by all of Traske's followers. Shortly after his adoption of seventh-day

---

[7]George H. Williams, *The Radical Reformation* (Philadelphia: Westminster Press, 1962), 257, 410; Kenneth L. Parker, *The English Sabbath* (Cambridge: Cambridge University Press, 1988), 24, 97; John Sprint, *Propositions Tending to Prove the Necessary Use of the Christian Sabbath* (London, 1607), 2-5.

observance, Traske was arrested and imprisoned along with a number of his followers. Following his trial and conviction in 1618, Traske was sentenced to life imprisonment under close watch—a precaution meant to insure that his ideas did not further contaminate the community. He was removed from the ministry and heavily fined. Traske was then publically whipped and his ear was nailed to the pillory he was placed in. After the letter "J" was branded on his head to show his adherence to Jewish opinions, Traske was again publically whipped and his remaining ear was nailed to the stocks. Following this punishment Traske began a life sentence.[8]

A year and a half after his imprisonment began, Traske recanted his errors. He vowed to abandon his Judaizing ways and was released from prison. In 1620 he published A Treatise of Libertie From Iudaisme, which publically recanted many of his previous beliefs, including the Saturday Sabbath. Traske's wife, Dorothy, was not convinced. She remained faithful to the principles for which she was jailed and went to her death observing the Saturday Sabbath. She died in the mid-1640s, some two decades after she had first been imprisoned.

Once free, John Traske soon joined the Jacob-Lathrop congregation. One of the last glimpses of Traske comes from the "Jessey Memorandum," which recorded that at the beginning of 1636 Traske was arrested during a raid on sectaries and held in prison, but released on bail because of his failing health. He died soon afterwards. A few years after Traske's death, Henry Jessey took over the leadership of the Jacob-Lathrop congregation. Jessey would later be one of the most important figures in the debate over Jewish readmission to England. Like Traske and the Jews, he also adopted seventh-day observance, although he did so privately with only a small group of followers. While

---

[8]John Traske, Heaven's Joy, or Heaven Begun Upon Earth (London, 1616), passim; idem, Christs Kingdome Discovered (London, 1615), 3; Sanford, A Choosing People, 50-51; Parker, The English Sabbath, 161-163; Katz, Philo-Semitism, 23-24. Katz maintains that it was Hamlet Jackson who "pushed" Traske "towards Judaizing practices," he quotes one contemporary who commented "Mr. Trask draweth Hamlet Jackson from the Church, accusing it of falsehood both in doctrine and government; and Hamlet Jackson draweth Mr. Trask to points of Judaism, as to the observation of Laws touching meat, drink, apparel, resting, working, building and many other matters" (Katz, Philo-Semitism, 20).

the connection between Jessey and Traske is tenuous, it is reasonable to assume that this enigmatic "Sabbatary Christian," influenced Jessey's later beliefs. Of course, neither Traske nor Jessey were typical of the Seventh-Day Baptists that emerged in the middle of the seventeenth-century, and few seventh-day leaders referred to these two men in their published works.[9]

A decade after Traske adopted seventh-day views, Theophilus Brabourne, a minister in Norwich, published a tract advocating the Saturday Sabbath. His book was the first to appear in the English defending the Saturday Sabbath and a fuller version of its title provides a summary of the work: *A Discourse upon the Sabbath Day. Wherin are handled these particulares . . . 1. That the Lords Day is not Sabbath Day by Divine iustification. 2. An exposition of the 4. Commandment, so farr [as] may give light vnto the ensueinge discourse: and particularly, here it is showne, at what time the Sabbath day should begine and end; for the satisfaction of those who are doubtfull in this point. 3. That the Seaventh-day Sabbath is not abolished. 4. That the Seaventh-day Sabbath is now still in force. 5. The author's Exhortation and reasones, that neverthelesse there be no Rente from our Church as touching practise* (1628). The last line of Brabourne's title is significant, for unlike Traske and later Seventh-Day Baptists, Brabourne was not a Separatist. He was loyal to the Church of England, which he hoped would be reformed to Saturday observance to conform with God's commands.

In his *Discourse* and subsequent work, Brabourne articulated many of the arguments that would become common among Seventh-Day Baptists. The observance of the Sabbath was enshrined in the Ten Commandments and therefore was to be kept holy. Like the other nine commandments, the fourth commandment concerning the

---

[9]Parker, *The English Sabbath*, 163; Katz, *Philo-Semitism*, 32; John Traske, *A Treatise Of Libertie from Iudaisme, or An Acknowledgement of True Christian Libertie, indited and published by Iohn Traske: of late stumbling, now Happily Running againe in the race of Christianitie* (London, 1620), passim; B. R. White "John Traske (1585-1636) and London Puritanism" *Transactions of the Congregations Historical Society* 20 (1968), 229; Burrage, *Early English Dissenters*, vol. 1, 326, vol. 2, 300; Ball, *Seventh-day Men*, 48.

Sabbath was a moral and not a ceremonial law. In literal accordance with the Scripture, this Sabbath was to be observed on the seventh-day, that is Saturday. The Saturday Sabbath was observed both by Christ and the earliest Christians. Therefore, far from relieving the faithful of the their Sabbath obligation, Christ endorsed it. Brabourne also argued that all arguments for the translation of the Sabbath from Saturday to Sunday were without scriptural or divine authority. In fact, the change from Saturday to Sunday was part of the work of the Devil, as prophetically foretold in Daniel 7. While many claimed that the Sunday Sabbath was to commemorate Christ's resurrection, Brabourne insisted that it was to commemorate Creation and that its observance was itself initiated at Creation and set on the seventh day.[10]

Two years later Brabourne published another *Defence of . . . the Sabbath Day* (1632), further clarifying his position. By 1634 he had been arrested for his unorthodox beliefs and was detained for several weeks. At his trial he openly admitted his seventh-day views and was threatened with a punishment similar to Traske's seventeen years before. He was ordered to recant and submitted an ambiguous statement that the authorities regarded as a sufficient recantation. However Brabourne claimed this was only a statement of the beliefs he shared with the established church. Whether or not Brabourne actually recanted, he seems to have escaped with his ears, but was sufficiently frightened to keep his Sabbatarian opinions to himself for the next twenty years. Brabourne never joined a seventh-day congregation, possibly because of differences over baptism or his continued desire to avoid Separatism, but during the liberty of the Interregnum, he again published his views on the validity of the seventh day. He died in Norwich in 1662, leaving ten pounds in his will for "the poor Sabbath-keepers in Norwich," which was to be allocated by Christopher Pooley.[11]

---

[10]Theophilus Brabourne, A *Discourse upon the Sabbath Day* (London, 1628), 62, passim; Sanford, A *Choosing People*, 52-53; Ball, *Seventh-day Men*, 75.

[11]Ball, *Seventh-day Men*, 67-68; Katz, *Philo-Semitism*, 34-36.

While there may have been individuals like Brabourne, or even congregations like Traske's, observing the Saturday Sabbath in the early seventeenth century, the seventh-day movement is traditionally seen as beginning around the mid-1650s, the same time that the main Baptist movements were developing their organizational system. The Mill Yard congregation associated with Peter Chamberlen is taken as the starting point, but it is possible that earlier congregations existed undetected. Men like Traske and Brabourne provide one part of the background for the Seventh-Day Baptists, who emerged out of the interaction between five trends.[12]

First, the Seventh-Day Baptists must be understood in the context of the debate between sixteenth-century Puritans and moderates over the mode of Sabbath observance. While this discussion uses the term "Sabbatarian" to mean a person who observed the Saturday Sabbath, the term is often used to refer to someone advocating a strict observance of the Sunday Sabbath. This meaning was developed during the Sabbatarian controversy between zealous Puritans and more moderate members of the Church of England. The Puritans maintained Christians were morally compelled to observe a strict Sabbath, while others believed that all that was required was church attendance on "Lord's day," that is Sunday.

For the Puritans, the entire day should be spent in spiritual exercises, not physical ones. While the Puritans held that the fourth commandment had never been abrogated—that it predated the Mosaic Law—they did not suggest that the day of Christian observance be moved from Sunday to Saturday. Instead, they thought that all the frolicking and merriment that took place on Sunday should be done away with. They emphasized the first part of the fourth commandment found in Exodus 20:9, "Remember the Sabbath day, [and] keep it holy."

---

[12]Sanford, *A Choosing People*, 57-58. When Chamberlen began to observe the seventh-day is the object of some contention, his tombstone claims it was in 1651, while Thirtle has pointed out that his church record book lists meetings for Sunday and not Saturday, J. W. Thirtle, "Dr. Peter Chamberlen. Pastor, Propagandist, and Patentee," *Transactions of the Baptist Historical Society* 3 (1912): 176-189.

Most Englishmen on the other hand saw the "Lord's day" as different from the Old Testament Sabbath, which they regarded as largely ceremonial and undone by the New Testament. Instead, "Lord's day," was something more akin to a Christian festival, which in addition to morning worship, prayer, and preaching also included a bit of afternoon amusement. Sunday came to be characterized by a great deal of entertainment that was unrelated if not outright offensive to Christian worship. Such amusements included, for example, bear baiting, hunting, and dancing.

James I encouraged such Sunday activities, not only as a means for relaxation, but also as a way of keeping the citizenry prepared for war. In 1618 James issued the Declaration of Sports, which particularly encouraged exercises that had military value, such as archery. When Charles I reissued the Declaration in 1633, he responded to angry Puritan protests by saying that if there were no Sunday sports, then laborers would be deprived of their primary means of relaxation and enjoyment.

But the debate between Puritans and moderates over the manner of observing the Sabbath caused many to re-examine the practice altogether. Soon the question of the correct time of observation was added to the question of the prescribed manner of observation. In addition to a more literal adherence to the first part of the fourth commandment, a few people began to focus on the second part found in Exodus 20:9-11: "Six daies shalt thou labour, and do all thy worke, But the seventh day is the Sabbath of ye Lord thy God: in it thou shalt not do anie worke . . . for in six daies the Lord made the heaven and the earth, the sea and all that in them is, and rested the seventh day: therefore the Lord blessed the seventh daie, and hallowed it." Many saw obedience to the first part of the commandment—to keep the Sabbath holy—as requiring adherence to the second part, which is that it is on the seventh day. It is in this context that the beliefs of men such as Traske and Brabourne must be understood.[13]

The second context from which the Seventh-Day Baptists emerged was related to the first. The Puritan controversy over the Sabbath was partly the result of a close adherence to the Scriptures. The Seventh-Day Baptists continued this tendency almost to the point of imprudence. Their close attention to the Bible and insistence on reviving lost, though still mandated, practices was a common characteristic among the Baptist movements. Additionally, like the Fifth Monarchists, the Seventh-Day Baptists' interest in prophecy also partly stemmed from their intense biblicism.

A third trend, related to the Seventh-Day Baptists' biblicism, was a renewed interest in Judaism. There were many causes behind this interest in God's chosen people, such as a wider study of Hebrew in the universities. Additionally, the apocalyptic enthusiasm of the early seventeenth century drew many Protestants' interests towards the role of the Jews in prophecy. The debate over Jewish readmission was both a product and a further spur towards an renewed interest in Jewish customs and practices. Afer the execution of Charles I, when many of the godly were searching for a new form of governance, some turned to the Old Testament for guidance. This was particularly true of the Fifth Monarchists, who supported subjecting the nation to the Jewish Law to govern the kingdom. As the apocalypticism of the 1640s prompted Englishmen to see themselves as part of the new chosen people working to re-build the New Jerusalem, an interest in the Old Israel was inevitable. As Jewish practices were re-examined, their observance of the Saturday Sabbath was discussed and helped to shape the defense of this practice that later Seventh-Day Baptists would employ.[14]

The fourth important trend that gave rise to the Seventh-Day

---

[13]Katz, *Sabbath*, 6; Parker, *The English Sabbath*, passim. See also, Richard L. Greaves, "The Origins of English Sabbatarian Thought," *Sixteenth Century Journal* 12 (1981): 19-34 and J. H. Primus, *Holy Time: Moderate Puritanism and the Sabbath* (Macon: Mercer University Press, 1989).

[14]See generally, David Katz, *The Jews in the History of England 1485-1850* (Oxford: Oxford University Press, 1994); idem, *Philo-Semitism*.

Baptists was the waning apocalyptic enthusiasm of English society. Like the Fifth Monarchists, the Seventh-Day Baptists refused to relinquish their expectations. One of the defining questions leading to the formation of the Seventh-Day Baptists was how Christians were to prepare for the return of Christ. The Seventh-Day Baptists answered that such preparation required the observation of God's Laws and Commandments, which included the seventh-day Sabbath.

The final influence on the Seventh-Day Baptists was the transformation that the main Baptist movements were undergoing. Again, in this sense, the Seventh-Day Baptists were like the Fifth Monarchists. They were a reaction against the way that the initial enthusiasm of the Baptists had changed. Often, the Seventh-Day Baptists saw the members of the main Baptist congregations as apostates, whose zeal for God was as lacking as their obedience to divine commands. The Seventh-Day Baptists also reacted against the main Baptist leaders' eagerness to accommodate with society. In an effort to continue their opposition, the Seventh-Day Baptists adopted practices that prevented them from merging with the other Baptists. These last three causes, interest in the Jews, apocalypticism, and the reaction against the main Baptist movements will be further examined below in the discussion of Seventh-Day Baptist eschatology.

Though Seventh-Day Baptists remained small in number they were a considerable worry to the leaders of the older Baptist movements. The Particular Baptist leaders cautioned their congregations to avoid the "errors of the times viz. of the people called Quakers and of those that hold the Seventh-Day Sabbath." Scattered throughout the Particular Baptists' Association records during the latter half of the 1650s are reports like that of the congregation at Watford, where "eight . . . were . . . gone off [to] the 7th day Sabbath." The Baptists experienced particular difficulty preventing women from leaving their ranks. Reports of "another sister [who] also went often to hear them" also appear in the records. It is possible that women who had originally joined the sects because of the freedom they offered in the 1640s and early 1650s found that the movements had changed before the Restoration. It was not until 1654 that the West Country

Association officially ruled on the role of women in worship. They decided that "a woman is not permitted at all to speak in the church, neither by way of praying, prophesying, nor inquiring." It is little wonder that women left the Particular Baptists for the "errors of the times viz. the people called Quakers and those that hold the Seventh-Day Sabbath."[15]

By 1659 it was apparent that the losses to the Seventh-Day Baptists were significant. At the twenty-first meeting of the now well organized Abingdon Association, the messengers from Kingston suggested that they still be allowed in communion with the three churches "of the baptized people of Bledlow, most of which do now hold the 7th day Sabbath." Even though the association did not respond positively to this query, "it was desired of diverse of the messengers that in case nothing else should be found amiss but the bare observing of the 7th day Sabbath, then the saying of the apostle in Rom. 14.1,5f., might be well minded." Evidently, some of the messengers considered it necessary to tolerate those who held Sabbatarian views in order to keep communities together.[16]

In many ways the literalist interpretation of Hebrews 6:2, which led to divisions within both Particular and General Baptists over the issue of laying on of hands, might have caused similar divisions when applied to Exodus 20:10 concerning the seventh day. But such divisions occurred only to a limited extent—more a testimony to an

---

[15]White, *Association Records*, vol. 2, 55, vol. 3, 190-191, 209, 211-214. At its formation, Francis Bampfield's seventh-day congregation was also over 60 percent female (Ball, *Seventh-day Men*, 113). For an interesting study of gender and dissent related to the later history of the Mill Yard Seventh-Day Baptist Church, see Timothy Larsen, "How Many Sisters Make a Brotherhood?" *Journal of Ecclesiastical History* 49 (1998): 282-292. Even Kiffin's congregation raised the question of seventh-day observance. See Thomas Edwards, *The First and Second Part of Gangraena* (3rd ed.), 44.

[16]White, *Association Records*, vol. 3, 195. The verses referred to appear in the 1602 Geneva Bible as "Him that is weak in the faith, receive unto you, but not for controversies of disputations"; and "This man esteemeth one day above another day, and another man counteth every day alike: let every man be fully persuaded in his mind. He that observeth the day, observeth it to the Lord: and he that observeth not the day, observeth it not to the Lord. He that eateth, eateth to the Lord: for he giveth God thanks: and he that eateth not, eateth not to the Lord, and giveth God thanks."

increasingly agreed upon set of doctrines than to an ebbing of Baptist biblicism. Nevertheless, both General and Particular Baptist found it necessary to preach and publicly debate against the seventh-day Sabbath.

Many Baptist leaders also produced published texts affirming the Sunday Sabbath and refuting the Saturday Sabbath. The influential General Baptist Thomas Grantham's 1667 treatise titled *The Seventh Day-Sabbath Ceased* aimed to prevent further General Baptist defection to the seventh-day cause. In 1658, the dynamic General Baptist leader, Jeremiah Ives, debated Peter Chamberlen, Thomas Tillam, and Thomas Coppinger on the issue of the Sabbath before a largely Baptist audience in Edmund Chillenden's meeting house. The debate lasted four full days. Henry Denne was also present and supported Ives's arguments against the Saturday Sabbath.[17]

Such activities were part of a concerted effort by the General Baptists to discredit seventh-day beliefs. Just weeks after the debate, Ives brought forth a published version of the four days of proceedings entitled *Saturday No Sabbath*. Even John Bunyan, who usually found himself at odds with other Baptist leaders, joined them in their denunciation of Saturday observance. He set out his objections in *Questions About the Nature and Perpetuity of the Seventh-Day-Sabbath. And Proof, that the First Day of the Week is the True Christian-Sabbath* (1685). Aside from raising numerous smaller criticisms, Bunyan essentially argued that the first coming of Christ had invalidated the Saturday Sabbath and, by implication, those who observed it invalidated the first coming of Christ.[18]

Thomas Collier also leant his support to the anti-Sabbatarian cause, hoping that Baptists would not fall into error. He had long believed that much of Judaic law was abrogated with Christ's first coming. At the Whitehall debates in 1649, Collier defended the Baptist cause of religious liberty against the argument that in the Old

---

[17]Underhill, *Records of the Churches of Christ*, xxvi.

[18]John Bunyan, *Questions About the Nature and Perpetuity of the Seventh-Day-Sabbath* (London, 1685).

Testament governors had been obliged to punish sinners and heretics. In his speech he demonstrated reasons why the Law did not pertain to those "under the Gospel." His politics and theology were unified. Just as he had denounced Jewish laws as a foundation for magisterial power in religion in 1649, so a decade latter he denounced them as a foundation for the observance of the seventh-day Sabbath when he published *The Seventh Day Sabbath Opened and Discovered* (1658). Throughout the latter half of the seventeenth century, the main Baptist movements fought a rear guard action against both the Quakers and the Seventh-Day Baptists.[19]

Despite such efforts, many Baptists continued to be troubled over the Sabbath question throughout the 1650s, as evidenced in 1657 when the Particular Baptist church of Tewkesbury raised the question of the Saturday Sabbath at the Midland Association. The association rejected it, but one messenger was daring enough to declare "himself to be inquiring and not yet fully satisfied." These "undecideds" were to turn increasingly to the Seventh-Day Baptist congregations, so much so that a number of churches began to appear. Within a decade of the Restoration, in a few areas the Seventh-Day Baptists appeared to have come to predominate among the dissenters.[20]

The Seventh-Day Sabbath, the Apocalypse, and resistance to the government were interwoven in the minds of many Baptists. A meeting of the Abingdon Association in 1656 was particularly revealing of these interconnections. In a sense, each of these concerns were questions of *apocalypse how*? The church at Oxford proposed

---

[19]Woodhouse, *Puritanism and Liberty*, 164; see Collier's *The Font-Guard Routed* (London, 1652). The authorship of *The Seventh Day Sabbath opened and Discovered* is uncertain, as the text is only signed T. C. and could have been written by Thomas Chafie, the author of *The Seventh Day Sabbath or a Brief Tract on the IV Commandment* (London, 1652). See also Wing and A. J. Westlake, "Some Rare Seventeenth Century Pamphlets," *Baptist Quarterly* 13 (1949-1950): 109-115.

[20]White, *Association Records*, vol. 1, 32; vol. 3, 209. The Midland Association was thorough in its response to the question concerning the Sabbath, giving three different answers and citing Ex. 3:13, Ezk 20:12, 40:4, Col. 2:16f and Gal. 4:10f (White, *Association Records*, vol. 1, 33).

that all Baptists should seriously consider "what the Beast is that is spoken of in the Revelation of John," and what it means to receive the mark of the Beast. In the next breath they inquired "whether the seventh-day Sabbath, as it was given in Ex. 20.10, be in force to be observed by the saints under the Gospel?" Their next question concerned the "unlawfulness of paying tithes" and "the payment of the church rates." In this context, they wanted to know if a congregation member were punished for non-payment, was it not "the duty of the respective churches concerned in this testimony against the Antichrist to bear a proportional share with the member or members so suffering making it as a public charge." While these issues were not resolved, they show the persistent eschatological concern and the oppositional inclinations among those who were leaning towards Sabbatarian views.[21]

The Seventh-Day Baptists believed that the Sunday Sabbath was a popish innovation on the pristine apostolic practice of observing the Saturday Sabbath. They interpreted the prophecy of Daniel 7:25, that Antichrist shall alter the "Law and the Time," as proof for their argument. In their effort to complete the Reformation and to throw off the veil of Antichristian Rome, they insisted that the Sabbath must be returned to Saturday. Thus, eschatology was at the foundation of the movement, for the observance of the Saturday Sabbath not only complied with Christian obedience, but was also a battle against Rome, in defense of true religion. Rome had usurped God's authority by corrupting the fourth commandment. The "Triple-Crowned-Little-Horn-Changer of Times and Laws" had moved the original primitive Sabbath and lied, saying that "the first day is the Sabbath of the Lord." Moving the Sabbath back was part of the double movement characteristic of Baptist apocalypticism in that it sought return to original purity in order to move forward to the

---

[21]White, *Association Records*, vol. 3, 158.

eschatological end.[22]

Baptist apocalypticism was always concerned with removing the "last stumbling blocks" that were preventing the fulfillment of the Reformation and the millenium. The Baptists frequently saw infant baptism and religious persecutions as the "last bastions of Antichrist." In the doctrine of the Sabbath, the Seventh-Day Baptists recognized another obstruction. They were confident that removing this last design of the Man of Sin would finally allow them to complete the Reformation. They viewed the issue of the Sabbath as the "*last* great controversy between the saints and the Man of sin." In this conflict, the saints were assured of victory over the Beast because the signs of Christ's coming were so visible. The forces of Antichrist had obscured the proper observance of the Sabbath; the saints of Christ were responsible to restore it. It was a necessary preparation for a people awaiting the coming of the Lord.[23]

Another aspect of the apocalyptic importance attached to seventh-day observance concerned the conversion of the Jews. It was widely believed that the conversion of the Jews was a necessary precondition for the return of Christ. William Saller and his Baptist-Fifth-Monarchist-Sabbatarian friend, John Spittlehouse, asked the chief magistrates to enforce the Saturday Sabbath since it would hurry the conversion of the Jews. This in turn would "be a preparative to the accomplishing of those glorious prophecies." Christian observance of the true Sabbath would be "a means to remove a great stumbling block to the Jews, who make it an argument (that Christ is not the

---

[22]James Ockford, *The Doctrine of the Fourth Commandment, Deformed by Popery, Reformed and Restored to its Primitive Purity* (London, 1650), sig a3, 26-30, 36-39 (Ockford's text is the first known text by a seventh-day observer who was also indisputably a Baptist. Ockford was clearly influenced by Brabourne's writings, see for example, 7, 36); Brabourne, *A Discourse Upon the Sabbath day* (London, 1628), 62, passim; Peter Chamberlen, *England's Choice* (London, 1682), 1-3; John Spittlehouse, *A Return to Some Expressions* (1656), 1.

[23]Thomas Tillam, *The Seventh-Day Sabbath Sought out and celebrated, or, the Saints Last Design upon the Man of Sin . . . being a clear discovery of th t black character in the head of the little Horn, Dan. 7.25. The Change of Times & Laws. With the Christians glorious Conquest over that mark of the Beast, and recovery of the long-slighted seventh day, to its ancient glory* (London, 1657), 1-4, emphasis added.

Messiah) because Christians, who profess to be his followers, are Sabbath-breakers." By implication Christ could thus be seen by Jews as a Sabbath-breaker and sinner. The perpetually apocalyptic Thomas Tillam explained that Sunday worship was a great obstacle for the Jews, since it was unscriptural. He reported that "the Jews in London are very much affected with our keeping of the Sabbath, and do frequent our meeting places every Sabbath." This was proof that if the Sabbath were returned to its proper day of the week, the Jews would be more speedily converted.[24]

The Seventh-Day Baptists' call for further Reformation placed them in opposition to a society recently shaken by revolution and desperately searching for stability. The direction of their eschatology was persistently against society. As people sought peace and avoided conflict, the Seventh-Day Baptists refused to be silent. As a result, they were labeled as self-confident trouble-makers. Most glaringly, they stood out because they went to church on the wrong day. Since Antichristian forces had taken the world, they had to somehow separate themselves from it. While many religious movements adopt a standard of dress or some other outward appearance to differentiate themselves from the larger society, the Saturday Sabbath was sufficient to distinguish the Seventh-Day Baptists. By this practice, they actively created a sacred space that separated them from the polluted world. Even if some attended both Sunday and Saturday services, the observance of the seventh day connected them to a select group of saints. In this way, they saw themselves as coming out of Babylon and making themselves a separate people. As Henri Mission observed, observing Saturday as the Sabbath was alone

---

[24]John Spittlehouse and William Saller, *An appeal to the consciences of the chief magistrates of this Commonwealth, touching the Sabbath-day . . . in the behalf of themselves and several others, who think themselves obliged to observe the seventh day of the week, for the Lords holy Sabbath, as in the fourth Commandment of the royal-law of Jehovah, Exod. 20.8,9,10,11* rev. expanded ed. (London, 1679), 13, (this argument was also given by Ockford, *The Doctrine of the Fourth Commandment*, sig. a2); Thomas Tillam, *Seventh-Day Sabbath*, 50. Chamberlen also allegedly associated with "the Jews in London, being a remnant of the numerous people of Israel, scattered into all Countries" quoted in Aveling, *The Chamberlens*, 111; for more on Chamberlen's interest in the Jews, see Froom, *Prophetic Faith*, vol. 4, 911.

"enough to make them unavoidably a society by themselves."[25]

As a result of Venner's Fifth Monarchist uprising in 1661, the authorities made an example of John James, a Seventh-Day Baptist who was arrested in the pulpit for allegedly advocating a change of government. When asked how he would be tried, James answered "by the Law of God." Unfortunately, at his trial, James also chose to quote the eleventh chapter of Revelation in his defense. When one of the authorities scoffingly asked, "What, you are a Jew? . . . James said that in one sense he was a Jew, and in another sense not." Then "the Lieutenant spake something about the fifth kingdom, and asked him, whether it was not his principle?" James "told him he did own the fifth kingdom which must come: whereupon they laughed one upon another and said, 'Now they had it from his own mouth.' " Nevertheless, James disassociated himself from those who had taken part in Venner's attempted coup, saying that he thought it had been a "rash act." His protest fell on deaf ears, for his heterodoxy alone was sufficient proof of his guilt. At his execution James declared:

> I do own the title of a Baptized Believer, . . . the doctrine of Baptisms and the laying on of hands . . . I do not only own the principles and doctrines, declared in the sixth of Hebrews, but I do own the Commandments of God, the Ten Commandments as they are expressed in the 20th of Exodus. . . . I durst not willingly break the least of these Commandments to save my life . . . I would inform persons that I do own the . . . the seventh day of the week to be the Lord's Sabbath.

After this speech, he was brutally executed, with his heart removed and his head skewered on a pole and placed opposite his meeting-house.[26]

---

[25]Mission, *Memories*, 235, quoted in Ball, *Seventh-Day Men*, 9.

[26]T. B Howell, ed., *State Trials* (London: T. Hanserd, 1816) vol. 6, 71-72; W. Cobbett, ed., 2nd ed. *State Trials* (London: R. Bagshaw, 1830) vol. 3, 466-474. John James's trial for high treason reveals another implication of seventh-day worship. Since few contemporaries

The execution of John James demonstrated the degree to which the Seventh-Day Baptists were perceived to be in opposition to society. Frequently when Seventh-Day Baptists were arrested, they were, like John James, involved in the very practice that the authorities most opposed—the observance of the Saturday Sabbath. Gathered together for worship, the believers made an easy target. The way that the observance of the Saturday Sabbath challenged society and conjured up images of anarchy was evident as early as the 1640s when Thomas Edwards recorded one minister's report that in his area the Saturday Sabbath was being observed. As the practice spread in the town, the congregation threatened the Mayor and "told him they would keep the Jewish Sabbath, and hoped before long to see it here as at Amsterdam. But we are gone beyond Amsterdam, and are in our high way to Munster."[27]

Not only was it upsetting that the Seventh-Day Baptists prayed and meditated on Saturday, but also it was even more infuriating that they worked, played, and traded on Sunday. In Durham in 1662 a man and his wife were presented to the authorities for working on Sunday. In 1665 Henry Hallyday was reported for not baptizing his child and for calling people together to dance on Sunday. When John Spittlehouse and William Saller petitioned the government to obey the Saturday Sabbath, they asked the authorities to change the markets and fairs to another day of the week. In 1670 Ann Stroud, "a reputed Jew," refused to have her childreen baptized, kept the Saturday Sabbath, and sold her wares on Sunday.[28]

---

were sympathetic to the practice at all, they frequently failed to see it as a religious matter, instead seeing it as a gathering of undesirables under the pretense of religion. Thus Saturday congregations were often suspected as being little more than assemblies of conspirators plotting the death of the king.

[27]Edwards, *Gangraena*, (1st part, 2nd ed.), 95. The congregation referred to in this passage is not known. While it is likely that such a report was more the product of an active imagination than of fact, it does demonstrate the fears contemporaries associated with seventh-day worship.

[28]Ball, *Seventh-day Men*, 148, 302; John Spittlehouse and William Saller, *An Appeal to the Consciences . . . touching the Sabbath-day* (London, 1657), 12-13; John Hanson, *A short Treatise showing the Sabbatharians confuted by the new Covenant* (London, 1658), 34. Thomas Tillam, who will be discussed below, provides an example of a Seventh-Day leader who

In working on the Lord's day, the Seventh-Day Baptists made it clear that their religious convictions could not be compartmentalized, they accepted their economic as well as theological implications. Joseph Davis admitted that once he was known as a Seventh-Day Baptist, he "could not soon fall into an employment, though I sought very carefully after it." The Seventh-Day Baptists' rigid insistence on remaining in opposition to society hindered the movement's survival. Persistent alienation, economic hardship and constant government harassment meant that they barely survived the seventeenth century.[29]

The Seventh-Day Baptists had difficulty surviving for the same reasons as the Fifth Monarchists. Alienation from society and a lack of organization dug the grave for both of these Baptist-related movements. Like the Fifth Monarchists, the Seventh-Day Baptists were not incapable of organization. They were familiar with the inter-congregational structure of the Particular and General Baptists, but they did not desire to imitate it. Francis Bampfield, a wealthy former clergyman and influential Seventh-Day Baptist, even suggested that Seventh-Day Baptists establish a form of inter-congregational meetings resembling the main Baptists' associations. But the only Seventh-Day Baptist who apparently agreed with Bampfield's proposals for yearly meetings of Seventh-Day messengers was the prosperous physician Edward Stennett.[30]

---

actively encouraged his followers to open their shops on Saturday.

[29]*Legacy of Mr. Joseph Davis*, quoted in Underwood, *Baptists*, 100.

[30]Francis Bampfield believed that yearly association meetings could serve not only as times of "fasting and of Thanksgiving together," but also as an opportunity to prepare a new translation of the Bible, promote poor relief and financial aid to needy members, aid struggling congregations, work for the better education of children as well as ministers, strengthen ties between congregations, further congregational growth, help to resolve theological queries and hurry the conversion of the Jews. He suggested that churches of "brethren in Holland, New-England, or elsewhere" outside of England may have difficulty sending two messengers a year, and so could participate "by letters and messages" (Francis Bampfield, *A Name, an After One, or, A Name, a New One . . . or An Historical Declaration* (London, 1681), 25). For Stennett's support of the idea, see Katz, *Sabbath*, 173. The first association of Seventh-Day churches appears to have been formed in 1696 in Rhode Island (Sanford, *A Choosing People*, 146). Their ability to develop an organizational system in North

Stennett was a Baptist in Abingdon who had been an active Fifth Monarchist in the 1650s before becoming a Seventh-Day Baptist. Evidently, he was a man of some standing and supported himself through his medical practice. In 1672, under the Declaration of Indulgence, he took out a licence as a Baptist preacher. His written work reflects the deeply eschatological nature of his thought and the apocalyptic convictions that led him to embrace Seventh-Day principles. He believed that what God demanded in these days "after so long and great an Apostasy" was a restoration of the Law. The work of the "Mystery of Iniquity" had begun with the lawlessness of "the primitive days," and for that reason "it greatly concerns us therefore, to show ourselves the remnant of the woman's seed, Rev. 12.17, that keep the commandments of God" by "observ[ing] the seventh-day Sabbath."

Once he had adopted seventh-day beliefs, his judicious character allowed him to provide a stabilizing force for the movement. He was one of the movement's ablest leaders and along with Bampfield, Stennett was the most influential Seventh-Day Baptist in the later years of reign of Charles II. He actively published in defense of the seventh-day cause and commanded the respect of other seventh-day leaders. Stennett made an effort to stay in contact with the nine or ten seventh-day churches he knew of in England, as well as the "little remnant of the woman's seed that keep the commandments of God" in Rhode Island. In 1667 he met with some of the best-known advocates of the seventh-day cause to denounce the actions of Thomas Tillam. Together they published a tract entitled *A Further Testimony Against the Teachers of Circumcision,* which disassociated the main seventh-day believers from their more radical elements.

If the seventh-day movement had had more influential members like Stennett, or the organizational system that he and Bampfield advocated, its chances of survival might have been far greater and it certainly would have been able to gain greater numbers of adherents.

America is probably partly responsible for their survival and continued existence today. For an extended discussion of Francis Bampfield, see Greaves, *Saints and Rebels,* chpt. 7.

But such success was never the goal of the movement. Most of its members had little desire to build a denominational network or identity that would benefit them in the future; rather they were interested in pursuing the truth and preparing themselves for the Kingdom in the present.[31]

One of the seventh-day churches that Edward Stennett remained in contact with was the congregation at Bell Lane in London. The Bell Lane church came into being after the Restoration and may have been an outgrowth of an earlier Fifth Monarchist conventicle. The church was founded and guided for most of its existence by John Belcher, a London bricklayer born in Oxfordshire. Belcher was noted as a Fifth Monarchist as early as 1658, when he was arrested at a meeting in Swan Alley. The close affinity between Belcher and Stennett was demonstrated in Belcher's preface to Stennett's 1664 *The Seventh Day is the Sabbath*. Much of Edward Stennett's family was associated with the Seventh-Day Baptists, and his son Joseph Stennett became a dynamic preachers for the movement.

After the death of Francis Bampfield, Joseph Stennett took over the pastorate of the Pinners' Hall congregation of Seventh-Day Baptists that met in London. Still later, after John Belcher's death, the core of the Bell Lane congregation joined with Pinners' Hall. Although his church did not survive long after his death, during his life Belcher had done a great deal to further the seventh-day cause. Most importantly, in 1664 the Bell Lane church had sent Stephen Mumford to America, where he soon established a seventh-day

---

[31]Sanford, *A Choosing People*, 72-73; Capp, *Fifth Monarchy*, 263; Edward Stennett, *The Royal Law Contended for, or, Some Brief Grounds serving to prove that the Ten Commandments are yet still in full force, and shall remain so until Heaven and Earth pass away; also, the Seventh Day Sabbath proved from the Beginning*...(London, 1658) appended to the second edition of this text is the fifteen page "Faithful Testimony Against the Teachers of Circumcision" against Christopher Pooley and Thomas Tillam, signed by John Belcher, George Eve, John Gardiner, Richard Parnham, Arthur Squibb and Edward Stennett, (see Whitley, *Baptist Bibliography*, 14-667); Edward Stennett, *The seventh day is the Sabbath of the Lord* (London, 1664); idem, *The insnared taken in the work of his hands; . . . the truth contained in Gods fourth commandment, is weighed in a just ballance, and sound lighter then vanity, and the seventh-day sabbath of Jehovah stands like a rock against all opposition . . .* .(London, 1677), sig a2, 158-161; Ball, *Seventh-day Men*, 111, 168, 170.

congregation.

In 1668 the Bell Lane church in London wrote a revealing letter to a Seventh-Day church in "a remnant of the Lord's Sabbath-keepers, in or about Newport, New England." They had heard that the congregation was suffering harsh persecution. The letter assured the New Englanders that the English Seventh-Day Baptists were suffering as well, but they consoled them in saying that this only served to confirm that they were "fellow heirs of the kingdom of our Lord, which is now hastening upon us." The Bell Lane church reminded their brethren that the truth always encountered opposition but that in spite of great trials

> great will be the blessings of the Sabbath-keepers, when they shall ride upon the high places of the earth, and have dignity and prosperity, temporal and spiritual. . . . Oh! Then we shall have no more to do with the mother of harlots, nor the beast that carries her, that hath changed times and laws; but shall cast away the carcass of those kings, and defile the coverings of their graven images, that this fourth monarchy has set up (Is. 30:22) to provoke the Lord to jealousy.

At the same time that the Bell Lane church described the apocalyptic punishment of their worldly persecutors, they also asked that while the New Englanders were among "differing brethren," that they be considerate and tender towards them in order to avoid hardening them in their disbelief and ignorance. They added that "the nearer we come to the promised glory, the more will the mysteries of God be opened to us. Then, without doubt, the fallacy of those vain objections (no Sabbath, or a seventh part of the time), will appear."

The persecution of the Bell Lane church only worsened, and three years after writing their letter to New England, much of the congregation was arrested. The occasion of their detainment was not unlike the circumstances surrounding John James, who was executed a decade earlier. The Saturday sermon that Belcher had been preaching was overheard by some and considered seditious. Those who arrested Belcher described him as "a bricklayer, and a Sabbatarian, or Fifth Monarchy" man.[32]

[32]*Calender of State Papers Domestic*, 1671, 156-157; largely as a result of this arrest of some 30 members of the congregation, ten out of eleven names that appeared on the Bell Lane letter to New England, also appear in Capp's appendix of Fifth Monarchists (i.e. John Belcher, Samuel Clarke, Edward [Edmond] Fox, William Gibson, Robert Hopkin, John Jones, John Labourn [Labory], Richard Parnham, Robert Woods [Woodward] and Aaron [Arthur] Squibb). Capp, *Fifth Monarchy*, 121, 239-270; Ball, *Seventh-day Men*, 107, 113. The letter from Bell Lane to New England is reproduced in E. A. Payne "More About Sabbatarian Baptists" *Baptist Quarterly* 14 (1951-2): 161-166. The admonition to be kind to those of a different opinion can be taken as evidence of the pacification of Fifth Monarchist militant-type millenarianism.

11

FIFTH MONARCHIST-
SEVENTH-DAY BAPTISTS
AND
THOMAS TILLAM'S
PALATINATE APOCALYPSE

Identity in the seventeenth century was not as either/or as the agents who arrested John Belcher would have implied. It was not simply that Belcher and his congregation were either "Sabbatarian, or Fifth Monarchy" men; likely they were both. But such evidence raises the question of the connection between the Fifth Monarchists and the Seventh-Day Baptists. This has puzzled Baptist historians for some time, many of whom are hesitant to associate their founders with these radical millenarians.[1] A. C. Underwood admitted that the Seventh-Day Baptists "seem to have been connected in some way with the Fifth Monarchists, though the precise connection has never been made clear." B. S. Capp denied a connection and said that "only a small proportion of the saints were affected."[2]

---

[1]For example, in the 1960's, James McGeachy, semi-pastor of the only remaining seventh-day church in England, publicly apologized for the Fifth Monarchist origins of his Mill Yard Church (James McGeachy, "The Times of Stephen Mumford," *Seventh Day Baptist Historical Society* (New Jersey) 1964, 3, cited in Lyell, "Doctrines of the Seventh-Day Men," 15).

[2]Underwood, *Baptists*, 94; Capp, *Fifth Monarchy*, 224.

The available evidence suggests that there was significant overlap between these two groups. Again, from Capp's biographic appendix of Fifth Monarchists alone, almost fifty of the two hundred forty plus Fifth Monarchists listed have a direct connection with the seventh-day movement. Ten of these men became influential seventh-day leaders as either the heads of congregations or through publications. Since Capp had little interest in the Seventh-Day Baptists, it is possible that many more Fifth Monarchists joined the Seventh-Day Baptists but were not listed as such in the appendix. John Spittlehouse is an obvious example. Thus, there would appear to be a considerable connection between Fifth Monarchists and Seventh-Day Baptists.

In addition to numerous similarities between the movements, the theory behind this study suggests that with the failure of the Fifth Monarchist movement, those Fifth Monarchists who wanted to remain in opposition rather than rejoining the main Baptist movements, joined the Seventh-Day Baptists. This is not to say that the Fifth Monarchy movement turned into the Seventh-Day Baptist movement; the Seventh-Day Baptists had their own internal logic and origins. The Seventh-Day Baptist movement began around the same time as the Fifth Monarchist movement, and for a number of the same reasons. For a time, a number of Fifth-Monarchist-Seventh-Day Baptists seem to have held their Fifth Monarchist and Seventh-Day views concurrently. Once the Fifth Monarchy movement began to fade, a number of members retained their Sabbatarian views. Other members of the Fifth Monarchist who had not previously held such views also joined the Seventh-Day Baptists. In addition to general affinities—high eschatological emphasis, biblicism, gathered ecclesiology, believer's baptism—the Seventh-Day Baptists also offered the Fifth Monarchists a way to remain in opposition and to continue to witness against society to a greater degree than if they had returned to main Baptist movements.[3]

Many seventh-day leaders embraced Sabbatarian views after they had come into conflict with Baptists or Fifth Monarchists who pushed them out of their congregations. This was the certainly the case for John Belcher. According to the Abingdon Association records, he had been excommunicated from the Particular Baptists by 1660.[4] By September 1661 he was reportedly traveling throughout England as a top Fifth Monarchist agent and leading preacher.[5] By 1662, Belcher and Richard Parnham were leading the seventh-day congregation at Bell Lane, which was comprised of a number of former Fifth Monarchists. Of course, this congregation's most noted act was their role in establishing the Seventh-Day Baptists in North America by sending Stephen Mumford from Bell Lane to Rhode Island. It is possible that Belcher's Bell Lane congregation was searching for a place to establish a new colony, much as Thomas Tillam would do in the Palatinate. Through correspondence and sending members and support, the Bell Lane church insured that the fledgling church in the New World would survive, thus providing a connection between modern-day Saturday Sabbatarians and those of seventeenth-century England.[6]

Richard Denton followed a path similar to Belcher's. He began his Baptist career in Hanserd Knollys's London congregation. In 1652

---

[3]Whitley seems to have come to a somewhat similar conclusion, see *British Baptists*, 86; idem, "Men of the Seventh Day or Sabbath Keepers of the Seventeenth Century," section 4.

[4]Belcher is probably the messenger at the Abingdon Association meeting who provoked the recorded discussion over the Sabbath among the messengers. White, *Association Records*, vol. 3, 145, 158, 203. B. R. White is puzzled by the fact that even though "he had been excommunicated by Abingdon . . . there were still people in the district willing to hear him preach and pray" (211). Perhaps this suggests that the decisions of the messengers of the association better represented the views of the leaders than they did of the majority of Baptists in the area.

[5]*Biographical Dictionary of British Radicals in the Seventeenth Century*; Capp, *Fifth Monarchist*, refers to Belcher as "one of the foremost saints" (205) and as one of the "leading missionaries" for the Fifth Monarchist movement (207).

[6]L. E. Froom, *The Prophetic Faith*, vol. 4, 907, 917.

Denton joined the Baptists at Hexham led by Thomas Tillam. The Hexham church book records "the church celebrated a day of praise, and had a love-feast, and after it the holy ordinance of our Lord's supper; to which we admitted Richard Denton . . . a member of one of the London churches." A few years later, Denton was present at John Pendarves's hectic funeral. Like many other Fifth Monarchist Baptists, he ended his spiritual journey as a Seventh-Day Baptist. After the Restoration, Denton joined the Seventh-Day Baptist church led by Francis Bampfield, which had been formed by first baptizing the members and then celebrating the Lord's supper. Bampfield had never been a Fifth Monarchist himself, but he shared many of their beliefs and was in contact with a number of their leaders. Like many of his Fifth Monarchist counterparts and seventh-day brethren, Bampfield was fascinated by the biblical prophesies concerning the conversion of the Jews. He recognized that the conversion of the Jews was the crucial sign for the return of Christ and the end of time. While this sign had not yet come to pass, Bampfield was convinced that the adoption of the seventh-day Sabbath was a step in the apocalyptic process and was necessary before the conversion of the Jews would occur.[7]

---

[7]Capp, *Fifth Monarchy*, 248; Underhill, *Records of the Churches of Christ*, 290; [Whitley], "Bampfield's Plan for an Educated Ministry," *Transactions of the Baptist Historical Society* 3 (1912), 10; Greaves, *Saints and Rebels*, 193, 204; Francis Bampfield, *A Name, an After One, or, A Name, a New One . . . or An Historical Declaration* (London, 1681), 18. Once Bampfield had become convinced of the validity of believer's baptism, he was uncertain of how to obtain his baptism. He found himself in the same dilemma that John Smyth had been in, and proceeded in a similar manner, first baptizing himself and then baptizing his colleague (*A Name . . . a Historical Record*, 14-17). W. Tovey published a little known tract on the seventh-day Sabbath in 1682 entitled *A Letter to Mr. Mead*. His familiarity with the work of Francis Bampfield (8) suggests that he is the same William Tovey who signed the covenant forming Bampfield's congregation (see [Whitley], "Bampfield's Plan for an Educated Ministry", 9). This tract has escaped the notice of the useful bibliographies found in Whitley, *Baptist Bibliography*, and Ball's *Seventh-day Men*, Appendix IV. The tract is important for a number of reasons. As the full-title (given in the bibliography) and the text reveal, articulate detailed sermons were being preached against the seventh-day Sabbath by various ministers, such as the Mr. Mead to whom Tovey addresses his text. Tovey had read and digested many of the arguments advancing the seventh day which allowed him to provide concise rebuttals to arguments such as Mr. Mead's assertion that Christ had moved the seventh day and that

It is significant that around the time the Fifth Monarchists began to fall apart internally, the issue of the Saturday Sabbath was raised in their meetings. It proved to be divisive. Thurloe noted that "their credit declines here very much, many of their party having separated from them." It was true, the absence of Armageddon had drained the saints' enthusiasm. John Simpson, the Fifth Monarchist Baptist, had even started condemning plots and suggesting passive obedience to the government, leading to what Capp described as a "breach between militant and moderate" Fifth Monarchists. Thurloe was informed that Simpson's "work is now to preach against the opinion of the fifth monarchy, which (he says) we are not to look for until Christ coming personally." Simpson also caused a further breach when he began a campaign against seventh-day observance, preaching several influential sermons against its practice and implicitly against John Spittlehouse and other leading Fifth Monarchists who were adopting seventh-day views. William Aspinwall was another Fifth Monarchists who took a staunch anti-seventh-day position. The same year as Venner's frustrated first rising, Spittlehouse asked the magistrates to recognize Saturday as the official Sabbath. The fact that the failed uprising coincided with Spittlehouse's proposal is probably coincidence, but it serves as an illustration of the two paths between which the Fifth Monarchists were choosing. In the absence

---

ecclesiastical history validated Sunday worship. His text also confirms the centrality of eschatology for seventh-day beliefs, stating that the Law of Moses is to be observed until the end of the world and asking "How can our Lord's will be fulfilled, Mat. 5.17,18, if the Sabbath be changed from the Seventh-day to the First?" (12-13). The most interesting aspect of Tovey's text was his argument concerning the toleration of seventh-day views. One of the standard arguments against the seventh-day position was that the Law appointed one day in seven, or a seventh part of the time, to be observed as the Sabbath. If this was the case, Tovey argued, then how could preachers like Mead slander a man who is persuaded that it is on Saturday. For surely from Saturday to Saturday is a seventh-part of the time. "By your doctrine he must be left to his persuasion." Therefore, such ministers should not persecute the Sabbatarians, who like them, observe one day in seven. They should at least tolerantly ignore them rather than actively preaching against them (13). But of course, Tovey demonstrated that even this argument was not enough, for the actual observance of the (not a) seventh day, was what was required by God. This text can be found in the Bodleian Library, under Pamph. C159 item 35.

of the return of Christ, by the late 1650s they had to decide between the desperate radicalism of Venner and the passive eschatology of the Seventh-Day Baptists.[8]

In the wake of Venner's second rising, the choice was even more urgent. As Fifth Monarchists became marked men, many chose to flee abroad. Others melted away into quiet obscurity or rejoined the main Baptist movements. Some joined the Seventh-Day Baptists, still believing in the imminent apocalypse and witnessing against a society that was unreformed and thus ungodly. They did not want to adapt to a society they thought was corrupt. Such beliefs led to the radical decision of Thomas Tillam and his followers that the New Jerusalem could now only be built by God's remnant abroad.

Thomas Tillam was a restless apocalyptic radical. Like John Smyth, his commitment to finding his own truth forced frequent changes in his religious perspective. Tillam was a Particular Baptist, a Fifth Monarchist, and a Seventh-Day Baptist. He was also close to many of the General and Independent Baptists. While he is described as only being "on the fringe" of the Fifth Monarchy movement, Capp believed that a number of his opinions were representative of Fifth Monarchist beliefs. What he had most in common with the Fifth

---

[8]Thurloe, *State Papers*, vol. 4, 545, 698; Capp, *Fifth Monarchy*, 113, 276-278; Greaves, *Saints and Rebels*, 123. Simpson's argument was one frequently employed against seventh-day Baptists, namely that Christians were to observe "one day in seven (or a seventh part of time)" as opposed to strict adherence to the actual seventh day of the week. Spittlehouse defended the practice and insisted that seventh-day observance was necessary for "the Lord's people to come out of the Antichristian practices they now follow." Throughout this response, Spittlehouse often resorted to personal attacks on Simpson, demonstrating the divisions that this issue was causing among the Fifth Monarchists.(John Spittlehouse, *A Manifestation of sundry gross absurdities . . . that naturally ariseth from some expressions in a Sermon, preached by John Simpson . . . in reference to the abrogating of the seventh-day-Sabbath* (London, 1656), 1, 6). In addition to the *Manifestation*, Spittlehouse "returned to some expressions published in a sermon preached by John Simpson" by publishing a tract of that name. Spittlehouse acknowledged that his publication of "a book entitled, *A Vindication of the unchangeable Morality of the Seventh Day Sabbath*, had aroused sharp criticism from the saints (*A Return to Some Expressions* (1656), 2). Aspinwall's, *The Abrogation of the Jewish Sabbath* (London, 1657) reveals the extent to which seventh-day ideas were current in Fifth Monarchist circles, see especially 12-28.

Monarchists was a similar degree of eschatological intensity. It was his eschatology that led him to undertake a fascinating apocalyptic mission to the Palatinate that may have furthered the demise of the Seventh-Day Baptists in England in much the same way as Venner's millenarian uprising harmed the Fifth Monarchists. Both Venner and Tillam demonstrate the different paths men chose to follow in their quest for the Kingdom. Such radicals also influenced the main Baptist movements by convincing them that such intense eschatology was too costly for movements that sought accommodation.[9]

Like other eschatologically inclined members of his generation, Tillam had sought greater religious freedom in New England before returning to London amidst the hopeful expectations of the 1640s. Soon after his return, Tillam joined Hanserd Knollys's Particular Baptist congregation. He was not in London long, however. Knollys immediately recognized Tillam's restlessness, and wisely sent him on a mission to the North Country. There Tillam could not only use his charisma to gather churches, but more importantly he would avoid conflict with the more conservative London leaders. It was recorded that Tillam was given the church's letter of recommendation and sent forth to "preach the gospel, and to baptize them that did the same."[10]

It may have been with the assistance of Paul Hobson, in nearby Newcastle, that Tillam settled in Hexham. Tillam was appointed to the Mercers' Company lectureship, which had been endowed for the support of godly ministers almost a generation earlier. He soon established a small Baptist church, which quickly grew in membership due to his dynamic personality. Tillam's tremendous evangelistic success might have been a source of tension with his Baptist brethren in Newcastle, as they had previously been the only Baptist church in the area.

---

[9]Capp, *Fifth Monarchy*, 137, 140-141, 186, 190, 206, 266; Whitley, "Men of the Seventh Day or Sabbath Keepers of the Seventeenth Century," section 4.

[10]Underhill, *Records of the Churches of Christ*, 320.

Tillam possessed an apparently limitless reservoir of energy. In 1651, in addition to his pastoral duties, he was also able to publish an extensive commentary on the eleventh chapter of Revelation. His commentary, *The Two Witnesses,* interpreted the first and second witnesses as the first and second testaments of the Bible. Additionally, Tillam paid careful attention to the role of the Jews in the eschatological prophecies. But his commentary was far from simply academic; it was also a call to readiness. Tillam opened the text with a proclamation that the "New Jerusalem" is "daily expected." He was certain that the last times had dawned.[11]

While Tillam's vigor was well received up in his "dark corner" of England, he was unfortunately becoming unpopular with the London Baptists. Already, by 1653, the new political environment had made Tillam a liability. At the same time the London Baptists were trying to reassure Cromwell of their loyalty, Tillam had begun associating with undesirables. Tillam had befriended the Fifth Monarchist General Baptist Peter Chamberlen—an action frowned upon by the Particular Baptist leaders in London. Radical politics aside, Chamberlen's theology was resented not only for its Arminianism, but also because of its well-known support of the laying on of hands. Tillam had established his Hexham congregation "under the fourth principle" of the laying on of hands, and while in London he wrote back to Hexham that he had discovered a number of congregations observing the ordinances as he preferred and been fortunate to have met

---

[11]Underhill, *Records of the Churches of Christ,* 289-296, 304; White, *Knollys,* 15-16; Ernest A. Payne "Thomas Tillam," *Baptist Quarterly* 17 (1957) 61; Roger Howell, *Newcastle Upon Tyne and the Puritan Revolution* (Oxford: Oxford University Press, 1967), 249; Thomas Tillam, *The Two Witnesses: Their Prophecy, Slaughter, Resurection and Ascension: or, An exposition of the eleventh chapter of the Revelation, wherein is plainly proved that the scriptures of the Old and New Testaments, are the witnesses there spoken of, who have prophesied in sackcloth one thousand two hundred and sixty years Compleat; that they are already slain, revived, and ascended . . .* (London, 1651), sig. a3, passim. Tillam ends this intriguing commentary in saying "for he cometh, he cometh to judge the Earth; he shall judge the world with righteousness, and the people with his truth: Even so come Lord Jesus, come quickly" (168). Baptist commentators on Revelation, such as Hanserd Knollys, would deny the interpretation that the two witnesses were the two testaments (see for example, Knollys, *An Exposition* (London, 1679), 9).

Chamberlen. He added that he had enjoyed "the blessing of my God, by the laying on of their hands."

Around the same time, Tillam began to associate with other radicals close to the Baptist movements, such as William Saller and John Simpson. He had also been in contact with a number of the churches associated with "Mr. [John] Tombes." Tombes was a well-known open communion, or Independent Baptist, and such an association would have been strongly discouraged by the London closed communion leaders. The Hexham Baptists were closer to the Independent type of Baptists and were unwilling to denounce open communion churches—which was a further source of tension not only between London and Hexham, but also between Hexham and Newcastle. When the Hexham congregation wrote to London to request that Tillam be made their full-time pastor, London promptly washed their hands of the matter, saying that they could not decide and that they were anxious for "brother Tillam" to answer the accusations against him from the Newcastle congregation, for the London church had been upset to hear of these complaints. The matter of Tillam's becoming "pastor, or elder," would have to be resolved by the Hexham congregation. The London leaders recognized that Tillam was a loose cannon, and the deck had begun to pitch.[12]

---

[12]Lyell, "Doctrines of the Seventh-Day Men," 46-47; Capp, *Fifth Monarchy*, 266; Underhill, *Records of the Churches of Christ*, 289, 313-320, 323-324, 349-351. Payne, points out that Tillam's association with the practice of laying on of hands may have forced a break within the Baptists, as this theologically contentious issue was mixed with personal animosity, "Thomas Tillam," 62-63. It is interesting to note that near the end of 1652, "Charles Bond, a member with Dr. Chamberlain, was admitted to communion" with the Hexham church (*Records of the Churches of Christ*, 291). Chamberlen clearly saw the laying on of hands in an apocalyptic light. Thirtle provides a summation of the church records on this point "while the members (of his church) in general accepted the Doctor's practice in regard to the Fourth Principle, one member, Dr. Naudin, objected that the teaching should have been supported from the Book of Revelation by the quotation of passages that he himself gave an entirely different meaning; and he 'admonished' the Doctor thrice for what he had said about the Star, the Angels, the White Horse, and Babylon," Thirtle "Chamberlen, Pastor," 178, cf C. Burrage,"A True and Short Declaration, both of the Gathering and Joining Together of Certain Persons [With John More, Dr. Theodore Naudin, and Dr. Peter Chamberlen]: and also of the lamentable breach and division that fell amongst

In the summer of 1653 a lone stranger found his way to Tillam's church in Hexham. The visitor introduced himself as Joseph Ben Israel, a Jew from the tribe of Judah. He had recently made the twelve mile journey from Newcastle, where he had been with Paul Hobson and the Baptist congregation there. During the Civil Wars, the army had carried Baptist ideas to Newcastle; and later Paul Hobson settled there to become the elder of the Baptist congregation. Thomas Gower, who had signed the 1644 and 1646 confessions of faith with Hobson, joined his old friend in Newcastle and became minister to the congregation. These leaders' distance from London had allowed them to direct their church relatively unhampered, although they always kept in touch with the London leaders. While Hobson may have helped place Tillam at Hexham, Gower resented Tillam's presence.

There were a number of theological differences between Gower and Tillam. The two most important differences were the issues of associating with open communion churches and the imposition of hands. Beyond his friendship with Chamberlen there is also evidence to suggest that it was feared that Tillam might adopt Arminian principles. Furthermore, Tillam devoted almost all of his time and energy to his ministry, and therefore thought it reasonable that a minister should be allowed to receive his living entirely from the congregation. Gower, like other Particular Baptists from the 1640s, may have objected to this idea.

Underlying these theological disputes was also a difference in personalities. Despite an honest effort on both sides to find peace, they inevitably renewed their conflict. As suggested, a certain amount of jealousy on the part of Gower and arrogance on the part of Tillam only exacerbated the situation. The months following Joseph Ben Israel's visit would see the difference between Tillam and Gower widened even further.[13]

---

them" *Transactions of the Baptist Historical Society* 2 (1911), 140. While the Chamberlen-More congregation dissolved for a number of reasons, differences in apocalypticism seem to have been the start of trouble, cf. Burrage, "A True and Short Declaration," 140-145.

[13]Underhill, *Records of the Churches of Christ*, 294-295, 317, 341.

By all accounts Joseph Ben Israel was a striking personality. He was clearly well educated and he had traveled much of the world before arriving in the tiny town of Hexham. He explained that he had been converted to Christianity and had left his home to find out more about the truth of Christ. While traveling through the Protestant heartland on the Continent, he had "heard great things of the Christians in England." In his relentless pursuit of Gospel, he had made his way to England to gain knowledge of their version of the Christian message. While in Newcastle, Ben Israel met Paul Hobson among other ministers there. The Newcastle ministers were not impressed by Ben Israel, but Hobson undoubtedly was. While Ben Israel remained with Hobson, the Newcastle ministers continued to express their reservations about him. Within a month of arriving, Ben Israel could sense the tension he was causing in Newcastle. He had heard of Tillam's congregation and asked to be directed to the Baptists at Hexham. Hobson furnished him with a letter of recommendation in which he noted that "the ministers at Newcastle are discontented at him, and some of them claim that he is no scholar; which I do not believe. I am sure his condition calls for love and pity."[14]

Tillam's success in gaining converts, his recent study of the prophetic texts, and his persistent interest in the Jews all converged with the arrival of Ben Israel. Tillam immediately recognized the apocalyptic significance of the stranger's appearance. Ben Israel was permitted to attend the congregation's meetings and quickly won the trust and respect of the Hexham Baptists. To Tillam's great joy, Ben

---

[14]Tillam, *Banners of Love Displayed over the Church of Christ, Walking in the Order of the Gospel at Hexham* (Newcastle, 1654), 5-6, 14-15; part 2 "The Converted Jew," 5, 7. Ben Israel claimed that he could speak eight languages and that he was a scholar of philosophy (*Banners of Love*, part 2, "The Converted Jew," 3), thus the reference "some . . . claim that he is no scholar." Katz suggests that Hobson's fame as a Baptist leader was known on the Continent and that this could have been the reason that Ben Israel sought him out upon arriving in Newcastle (Katz, *Sabbath*, 26). Given Ben Israel's objectives, "for . . . the army," a more likely explanation is that Hobson's military status was known on the Continent, as Ben Israel explained "he had heard much of the Lieutenant Colonel" while in southern Europe, associating Hobson's reputation with his military status (*Banners of Love*, 14).

Israel decided that he was ready to be baptized. So despite suspicion from the Newcastle ministers, Tillam promptly baptized the convert. In his excitement, Tillam may even have viewed Ben Israel as an "angel of God." Seeing this as a great achievement, and possibly as a sign of the approaching end, Tillam began boasting of his most recent success.[15]

The ministers of Newcastle, however, were still skeptical about Ben Israel. They soon informed Tillam that they suspected the convert was a fake. They had received further information since Ben Israel had left and they requested that Tillam and the converted Jew report to Newcastle to address the evidence and allegations. Among the various people present at the Newcastle meeting was a ship master named Christopher Shadforth. He identified Ben Israel as a passenger whom he had brought to Newcastle from Hamburg aboard his ship. But at that time, Shadforth explained, the man had called himself Thomas Horsley, and not Joseph Ben Israel.

Tillam refused to believe Shadforth's story. He claimed the ship master was himself a liar and used all of his oratorical skills to defend Ben Israel. Tillam was able to put forward a persuasive explanation for Shadforth's statements. However, there were too many gaps in the story. The people present at the Newcastle meeting found it dubious that a Jew, who had supposedly never been to England before, should speak perfect English. Nevertheless, Tillam spoke out for the converted Jew, until, by an uncanny coincidence, a messenger appeared in Newcastle with letters for Ben Israel, written by his mother urging him to return home to Scotland. For this, even Tillam had no defense.

Joseph Ben Israel then confessed. He was not a Jew at all, but had actually been born in London. His real name was neither Joseph Ben Israel nor Thomas Horsley, but Thomas Ramsey, whose father was a Scottish physician. After a bizarre educational odyssey, he had found himself in a Dominican cloister in Rome and then a Jesuit college. It was in Rome that he had learned of Paul Hobson and had been

---

[15]Underhill, *Records of the Churches of Christ*, 289-292; Tillam, *Banners of Love*, 5, 15.

circumcised so that he could pass as a Jew. He was then sent by the Jesuits to England "to use his best endeavors to propagate their ends." He confessed that there were numerous other agents sent from Rome to England, "particularly into the Army . . . sent over for dividing the Army, the troubling of the peace both of the nation and church." He was arrested and the episode proved a scandal throughout England.[16]

Tillam's eschatological expectations had blinded him to Ramsey's wiles. "He seemed to us a real convert." Countless lies and false stories were told about him. Even his own congregation, once so enamored, began to question Tillam's abilities. One member of the congregation challenged him over the issue of the laying on of hands, "blaspheming against Mr. Tillam's doctrine."

If Tillam's support was dwindling within his own church, it had all but vanished from other congregations. Eight regional and one London congregation signed a joint letter to Tillam rebuking and advising him "to look to your garments, that they be kept clean." They hoped that some form of inter-congregational body could be formed for the "approving and sending from the churches, and of signifying to all churches of our communion, who are approved or disallowed as teachers, or in case of removal as brethren, that the churches of God may not be deceived by such impostors as the counterfeit Jew with you." In addition to disapproval from London and the region, the hostilities between Newcastle and Hexham flared. "Great storms and commotions, raised by Mr. Gower more than ever, so far prevailing with the Church in Coleman Street [London], as to the disowning of Mr. Tillam."

Thus, by 1655, Tillam was cast out of the Particular Baptists. Without his energy and character, the Baptist church at Hexham

---

[16]Tillam, *Banners of Love*, 5, 14-15; Thomas Weld, William Durant, Samuel Hammond and Cuthbert Sydenham, *A False Jew: Or, A Wonderful Discovery of a Scot, Baptized at London for a Christian, Circumcised at Rome to act a Jew, Re-baptized at Hexham for a Believer, but Found out at Newcastle to be a Cheat* (Gateshead, 1653), 3-13; Payne, "Thomas Tillam," 62-63; Katz, *Sabbath*, 27-30. Tillam said he believed that Jews were capable of speaking English as well "as a Scot may do Hebrew," especially if trained "from his infancy" (*Banners of Love*, 13). Ben Israel's impeccable English was a persistent point of embarrassment for Tillam in his later retelling of the affair.

soon fell into disrepair. The congregation's record book noted that "the church here began sadly to decline their duties, break off their meetings, and forget their Rock, whereupon miserable effects ensued . . . so that most of them returned to folly." Tillam's spirit had been the cohesive element for the congregation and without him things slowly fell apart.[17]

Tillam realized that his critics were still tainted by the Beast. His charisma, however, insured that he would not be without a congregation for long. In May 1656 an address was sent to the mayor of Colchester from Oliver Cromwell, who "having received good satisfaction of the piety and ability of Mr. Tillam, preacher at Colchester, recommend you to appoint him and his church some convenient place within your town to meet for their religious exercises." It was there, in Colchester, far away from the troubles left behind in Hexham, that Tillam established his seventh-day church. As in Hexham, Tillam enjoyed instant success and before long had baptized almost a hundred new converts. By January 1657, Tillam had begun publicly observing the Saturday Sabbath. He also urged his large congregation to apply their trades on Sunday. Of course such visible dissension would not go unpunished, and Tillam, so recently in favor with the authorities, found himself in jail.[18]

He used his time in prison to write *The Seventh-Day Sabbath Sought out and Celebrated* (1657). In this text, Tillam announced his support for the Saturday Sabbath. The apocalyptic language that pervades the work demonstrates that his eschatological intensity still had not subsided. Like other Seventh-Day Baptists, Tillam associated the Saturday Sabbath with the apocalypse and understood the prophesies of Daniel 7 as evidence that Antichrist was responsible for moving the Sabbath from Saturday to Sunday. Many of his seventh-day brethren agreed with his sentiment that "the signs of his second

---

[17]Tillam, *Banners of Love*, 2-3, 11; Underhill, *Records of the Churches of Christ*, 295, 297, 342-343.

[18]*Calendar of State Papers Domestic 1655-1656*, 342; Payne, "Thomas Tillam," 63; A. Macfarlane, ed., *The Dairy of Ralph Josselin* (London: Oxford University Press, 1976), 368, 388-389.

coming, who is the Lord of the Sabbath, are so fairly visible that, although the day and hour be not known, yet doubtless this generation shall not pass, till New Jerusalem's glory shall crown obedient saints with everlasting rest." In order to be among the "obedient saints," Tillam insisted that Christians had to observe the Saturday Sabbath. Additionally, the adoption of this practice would assist with the conversion of the Jews.

Although Tillam's text presents few arguments not found in other Seventh-Day Baptist publications of the time, it was more widely read than most tracts on the subject. Tillam's enthusiasm, apparent on every page, may have been one reason for the text's popularity. Even Quaker leader George Fox read Tillam's book, although he was not convinced by its argument. Neither was Tillam able to convince the neighboring ministers in Colchester. Edmund Warren, however, thought that Tillam's text was compelling enough to require a response. There was also sufficient interest in the text to warrant a reprinting in 1683.[19]

Upon his release from prison Tillam met Christopher Pooley, who had recently been re-baptized and was one of the most prominent Fifth Monarchists in England. Pooley would soon prove too radical even for their company. In 1656 the Fifth Monarchists in Norwich discussed the "visible reign of Christ and the duty of the Saints towards the governments of the world." They concluded that in the final days there would be "a glorious and visible Kingdom of Christ, wherein the saints should rule." But they agreed that in the meantime they should wait with patience. But not everyone present was willing to wait. There was a faction of "our North Walsham fifth monarchy brethren who were lately dipped . . . and . . . tending to blood." It was

---

[19]Thomas Tillam, *The Seventh-Day Sabbath Sought Out and Celebrated, or, The Saints Last Design Upon the Man of Sin with their Advance of Gods first Institution to its Primitive Perfection . . .with the Christians Glorious Conquest over that Mark of the Beast, and Recovery of the Long-Slighted Seventh Day to its Antient Glory . . .* (London, 1657), sig. a2-a4, 1-5, 12, 26, 47, 50-51. George Fox, *An Answer to Thomas Tillams Book Called the Seventh-Day-Sabbath Wherein It Is Shewed How the . . . Jews Sabbath was a Day Given unto them Since the Fall . . . and this Sabbath was a Shadow and Sign . . .* (London, 1659); Edmund Warren, *The Jews Sabbath Antiquated* (London, 1659); Whitley *Baptist Bibliography*, 40-657.

this group that prayed at the meeting, "the Lord would be pleased to throw down all earthly power and rule and authority, and that he would consume them that they might no more be alive upon the earth and that he would set up the kingdom of his Son." Spies reported to Thurloe, that "Buttephant of the life guard, Ruddock and Pool[e]y" were "the Chieftains of them" that were "high in [such] expressions." Pooley's lack of patience meant that he was not welcome in such company. Soon Pooley found a man who shared his desire for direct action, Thomas Tillam. They became close partners and together they were to lead one last desperate attempt to establish the New Jerusalem before the century of revolution ended.[20]

The greatest impetus behind Tillam's desire to establish a millennial colony was the new atmosphere of Restoration England. While radicals like Venner decided that direct action was needed to clear the throne for Christ, Tillam's apocalyptic beliefs led him to believe that there was no hope of a New Jerusalem in England. Since Tillam could not "violate my conscience by taking the oath" of obedience, he was jailed at the start of the Restoration. He used this prison time to pen another intensely apocalyptic work, *Temple of Lively Stones, or, The Promised Glory of the Last Days*. Despite his latest imprisonment, Tillam signed his work as "a prisoner of hope." His new associate, Christopher Pooley provided the foreword, wherein he described how he had "come to walk in this garden" of obedience and faithfulness to God described by Tillam.

With hindsight, it is easy to see in Tillam's text the thought process that was propelling him towards the Palatinate. Tillam explained that he preferred the liberty of the wilderness to remaining in Babylon. This was not defeat; it was a withdrawal into victory. Once Babylon was abandoned, the remnant would become the rulers of the Kingdom. The idea of a godly remnant had always been present

---

[20]C. B. Jewson, "St. Mary's, Norwich: The Origins of the Church," *Baptist Quarterly* 23 (1969), 174; Thurloe, *State Papers*, vol. 5, 220. "Buttephant" was Captain Thomas Buttevant, who had previously been a member of Hanserd Knollys's congregation and was present at Pendarves's funeral. He seems to have maintained his relationship with Pooley (Underhill, *Records of the Churches of Christ*, 311; *Biographical Dictionary of British Radicals*).

in Baptist eschatology. From the very beginning, English Baptists had not been concerned with winning a large following. All they wanted was to walk in truth with one or two others in Christ's presence. Their small numbers and their persecuted status caused them to see themselves as the remnant of prophecy. This idea had been continued by the Fifth Monarchists, and now in light of the apostasy of the main Baptist movements, it took on a renewed meaning for Tillam and other Seventh-Day Baptists. "The voice of the seventh angel (now sounding) hath produced a small remnant of the woman's seed . . . waiting for the advance of the Law of God, who by their entire separation are become victors over the Beast, his image, his mark, and the number of his name." It was the remnant's obligation to separate from everything Antichristian. In order to do this, they were called into the "wilderness" of the Palatinate to be a people who "have wholly abandoned Babylon's customs and traditions [and] keep the commandments of God." They were "visibly in view of and thereof persecuted by the world . . . having passed already through the baptismal streams of Jordan . . . recovering those precious Times and Laws . . . recovering the sanctified Sabbath from that foot of pride which has so long trampled upon it."

The Restoration was the final blow in the undoing of all the saints' efforts to prepare England for the return of Christ. Now, England was no longer the New Jerusalem, but a new Babylon: "The revived prelacy and English service-book, is a near image of the decayed papacy and Latin mass." The island was drowning and could not be saved. Tillam realized that his present work was to "draw persons now out of Babylon" and "gather them that are sorrowful for the solemn assembly . . . of the enthralled Saints." Only by removing a godly remnant from England and starting a community in the Palatinate could the work of the revolution of the saints be salvaged.[21]

---

[21]Thomas Tillam, *The Temple of Lively Stones* (London, 1660), sig a3, a6-a8, 2-5, 7, 15, 28-29. The chapter of 1 Peter from which Tillam takes the title for his book was often employed by more conservative Baptists to encourage their congregations to accommodate with society. Passing over the later half of the chapter, Tillam intentionally emphasized the first half, viz. "As new borne babes desire that sincere milke of the word, that they may

Tillam was soon freed, but along with Pooley, was constantly under suspicion and closely watched, as were other such "dangerous" men and former Fifth Monarchists. The pair escaped to Holland and not long after Tillam's publication of *The Temple of Lively Stones*, they reportedly went to Germany, evidently to determine a location for the New Jerusalem.[22]

Tillam and Pooley had returned to England by August 1661 accompanied by a mysterious "Mr. Love" who claimed to be a physcian in Rotterdam. It seems that all three of these "seducers of the people" were traveling in disguise and under false names. Tillam, who was calling himself "Mallit (which is Tillam backward)," was recognized as the same man who had preached at Colchester and published in defense of the seventh-day Sabbath. Both Pooley and Tillam now had long unkempt beards that they vainly hoped would conceal their identity, but Pooley was also able to be identified as having been "a grand dipper in Norfolk and Suffolk." Love's identity was more difficult to determine, but he was noted for being present at a "private assembly" of Independents and regicides in Holland.

After attempting to identify the three "dangerous men," the report conveyed that they "gave out that they had been in the Palatinate to settle 100 plantations for so many that would move out of England." The reporter expressed his confusion as to why "a Jew,

---

growe thereby, Because ye have tasted that the Lord is bountiful. To whom coming, as unto a living stone disallowed of me, but chosen of God and precious, Ye also as lively stones, be made a spiritual house, an holy Priesthood to offer up spiritual sacrifices acceptable to God by Jesus Christ. Wherefore also it is contained in the Scripture, Behold, I put in Sion a chiefe corner stone, elect and precious: and he that beleeveth therein, shall not be ashamed. Unto you therefore which beleeve, it is precious: but unto them which is disobedient, the stone which the builders disalowed, the same is made the head of the corner, And a stone to stumble at, and a rocke of offence, even to them which stumble at the word, being disobedient, unto which thing they were even ordained. But ye are a chosen generation, a royall Priesthood, an holy nation, a people set at libertie, that ye should shew forth the vertues of him that hath called you out of the darknesse into his marvelous light, which in times past were not a people, yet are now the people of God" (Geneva, 1602, 1 Peter 2:3-10). Tillam also saw his work as a Baptist evangelist as that of building a temple out of "living stones," Underhill, *Records of the Churches of Christ*, 289.

[22]Public Record Office SP 29/4/18, SP 29/446/40, SP 29/106/11.

a Dipper and an Independent—all three Englishmen of three sundry sects so vast distance from one another should be consorted together to land obscurely in England." Tillam and Pooley do not appear to have remained in England long. As the intellegence report demonstrates, they were obviously being closely watched and may have taken just a small group back to the Palatinate to get the settlement started and make further preparations.[23]

The identity of the enigmatic Mr. Love who came over from Holland with Tillam and Pooley is likely to remain uncertain. On 12 August 1661, however, another intelligence report was sent to the Secretary of State. It noted that Paul Hobson, the Baptist leader from Newcastle, had just arrived again in England from across the sea. The report explained that Paul Hobson was an agent for a German Prince, who had come over to "carry away" supplies.

When Hobson was later apprehended, it was revealed that in addition to going under the alias of "Dr. Smith," Hobson also went by the name "Dr. Love." It is likely that the "Mr. Love" who "gave himself out for a Doctor of Phisick at Rotterdam" and accompanied Tillam and Pooley was Paul Hobson and that the government agent was confusing his intentions with Tillam and Pooley's mission. It is unclear whether or not Hobson helped with Tillam's recruiting efforts, but he was certainly too well known to remain unmolested for long.[24]

Upon his return, Hobson was informed that many of his old allies had been imprisoned and warned of a similar fate. John Joplin, who had been a member of the Hexham church, wrote expressing his despair in saying "neither I nor no honest man can expect our liberty

---

[23]Public Record Office SP 29/41/1. SP 29/40/91 by John Thedam in a note dated 27 August 1661 recorded that Tillam had "landed in Essex in a Dutch small vessel." SP 29/41/1 implies that they may have landed at the end of July. Tillam's *Temple of Lively Stones*, 290-293 implies that his long beard may have been more than merely an attempt at disguise.

[24]*Calendar of State Papers Domestic*, 1661-1662, 62; idem, 1663-1664, 263, 521; Public Record Office SP 29/40/42; Whitley, "Paul Hobson," 307-310. Hobson's reported request that the captain of the vessel "land the other two (i.e. Tillam and Pooley) at a by place and not at Yarmouth amongst the rest," might imply that Hobson was not working with the pair, Public Record Office SP 29/41/1.

or lives one hour, for now the beast doth not only roar but rage . . . and the prisons are full." Hobson himself wrote to some of his imprisoned brethren telling them that "tis not for me to write anything to move thy mind . . . but what is locked up in the will of God. Live there quietly and you will read it and live in it before it's seen. Tis a time to try all our . . . principles . . . stand fast, mind Daniel 3.16. [For] God's faithful, there is no loss in losing for him . . . I dare not write the news; though there is very much good and bad, but most bad."

Hobson was wise not to include revealing information in his letter, for his correspondences were being intercepted. He was soon pursued by the authorities and though he evaded them for a while, he was ultimately apprehended while hiding with his old friend Thomas Gower. The two had led the Baptist church at Newcastle and had signed the 1644 and 1646 Particular Baptist confessions together, but both had long since departed the company of other Baptist signatories such as Kiffin and Richardson. Hobson was released after swearing to a bond of good behavior, but he could not keep his pledge. By August 1663 his name appeared on another arrest warrant for "seditious and treasonable practices." Gower and Hobson managed to elude the authorities in London. Hobson began organizing various radicals and lived in hiding among friends. After a series of aliases and near captures, Hobson's hiding ended in the summer of 1663, when he was arrested for his involvement in the Yorkshire Plot.

Captain Robert Atkinson, who was himself involved in the plot, provided the government with the details of the conspirators' plan. He named Paul Hobson as one of the "chief" and "principal agitators" in the design. Atkinson explained that one of their primary objectives had been "to force his Majesty to preform his promise at Breda to give Liberty of Conscience to all save Romanists." Evidently, Hobson still believed that the Baptists' long-time goal of religious liberty could be achieved through radical action. His capture landed him in the

Tower, where he soon grew ill; he was only released shortly before his death on condition that he go into exile in the Carolinas.[25]

Tillam and Pooley were back in England by 1664 to gather more Sabbatarians for their Palatinate colony. However, fierce pursuit by the authorities forced them to cut their recruiting trip short and return to the Continent. Two years later Pooley returned accompanied by another member of the Palatinate settlement. Pooley was frequently sighted with his new associate, John Foxey. An intelligence report noted that "the party hath been abroad and amongst the Anabaptists and the 5th Monarchy Men . . . They came out of Bohemia; and were sent by their Judge or Leader, one Tillam . . . into England to acquaint all of their judgment, what great favors they receive . . . there, and what a pleasant part of the country" they had found. It was further reported that they had been "ranging in several counties amongst their brethren, endeavoring by all the arguments they can use to persuade them to repair into those parts out of this kingdom, telling them that they must separate because the sins of this kingdom are so great, that our Lord will destroy it; that they hope they must be the people that must restore and set up the kingdom of Christ." The intelligence report ended in saying that Pooley was distributing copies of a "Solemne Covenant" that governed the remnant of saints on the Continent, and given that another shipment of new recruits would soon be leaving for the Palatinate, the informer desired "immediately upon the receipt hereof to let me have your answer, whether or no that I should . . . cause them to be apprehended."[26]

[25]Underhill, *Records of the Churches of Christ*, 293; Public Record Office, SP 29/62/71, SP 29/63/34, SP 29/63/34.I, SP 20/81/32, SP 29/40/42, SP 29/63/2, SP 29/93/11, SP 29/84/64; *Calendar of State Papers Domestic 1661-1662*, 549, 559,564; idem, 1663-1664, 91-92, 244-245, 367; idem, 1667-1668, 369; Whitley, "Paul Hobson," 309-310; Greaves, *Saints and Rebels*, 148-149.

[26]Public Record Office, SP 29/106/11, SP 29/181/116. Ball, *Seventh-day Men*, (304), transcribes "prophets" for "people" in the sentence "they must be the people that must . . . set up the Kingdom" from line 13 of SP 29/181/116; while this is a possible transcription, "people" seems more likely in light of line 21 and the remnant theology of Tillam and Pooley.

A spy obtained a copy of this "Solemne Covenant," which provides the only surviving evidence from the Palatinate theocracy itself. Before Pooley would transport any saints to the Palatinate, they had to agree to the covenant. It declared that all power was given to "Christ our king [and] we do utterly renounce all powers and rulers." They resolved to "separate from all relations who shall continue linked to Antichristian religion." They swore to obey all the laws of God "which he hath commanded for all Israel, and particularly those first foundation truths, the seventh day Sabbath and marriage." The covenant also emphasizes the importance of "a distinct people dwelling alone . . . solemnly separated." It was demanded that all powers other than Christ's be renounced from communion and that "we understand that every person is bound to keep close to all that keep this Covenant, and that is either in Community or propriety as providence shall order." Subscribers were to sign beneath the words, "We . . . do hereby bind ourselves to our sovereign Lord in this covenant breaking day to improve our uttermost power for the destruction of Babylon by separating from the mountain of confusion all the precious children of God which we testify by our hands and seals."[27]

The evidence suggests that their recruiting effort was extensive and covered a number of counties, seeking any like-minded believers who would go with them to the Palatinate. Tillam may even have

---

[27]Public Record Office, SP 29/181/116. See also *Calendar of State Papers Domestic 1667-1668*, 346. There are two copies of the "Solemne Covenant" in the Public Record Office, the sections quoted come from the first copy. Both copies are largely the same except for some minor differences that can probably be attributed to copy errors. The second copy of the Covenant has the "names Christopher Pooley and Mr. Foxey" signed beneath it (SP 29/181/116 f. 197). It appears that the first half of the Covenant was drawn up when Tillam and Pooley first went to the Palatinate, but after some disagreements among the settlers, it was decided that the wording of the Covenant had to be better defined and the Covenant renewed. "Upon the renewing of this Covenant on the 14th day of the first month when we set ourselves consciensciously to inquire into the scope therof more fully than ever . . . by examining each sentence and expression." It is interesting to note, that while the majority of important concepts in the Covenant were further defined, the "first foundation" truth of "the seventh day sabbath," was not reexamined, which implies that it was the only major concept not debated among the Palatinate settlers.

visited Ireland in 1666 as part of the effort, perhaps seeking adherents among the abandoned Baptists congregations left over from the height of the New Model Army's occupation. By June 1667 Pooley had been apprehended and imprisoned. He refused to give his name but was "known to us for formerly he broke prison in this town and escaped." He also refused to swear an oath of obedience to the king or acknowledge himself a subject to the present government. When he was imprisoned he was found to be carrying a substantial amount of literature, probably for use in his recruiting efforts. He must have managed to escape from prison again, for by 1668 he was spotted once more in his efforts to call the saints into the Palatinate.[28]

In March of that year, a report was received that Pooley was again about to return to Germany. The intelligence that came from Harwich noted that Pooley was well supplied and ready to set sail in "a small vessel which by the badness of the weather is still here." The boatload of passengers were waiting "to be transported to a Monastery granted by the Duke of Brandenburg to one Tillam heretofore of Colchester and now settled" in Germany; "where his doctrines are received amongst his disciples of which he hath plenty both males and females. He preaches circumcision; the 7th day Sabbath, Jewish rites; community of goods (and they say of wives) but as many concubines as they please." The report also noted, with a tinge of sadness, that "among these departing (as they say for to enjoy the communion of the saints) is one maid (in appearance) very handsome; and some that have well remarked her say it is a pity she should go." Bad weather continued to delay the ship of hopefuls and even once it departed, they had to return several times because of the seas. It seems finally to have sailed off successfully by the end of March 1668; with it went the last radical remnant of Baptist millenarians.[29]

---

[28]Public Record Office, SP 29/190/104, SP 29/207/1; Payne, "Thomas Tillam," 66; W. T. Whitley "Militant Baptists 1660-1672," *Transactions of the Baptist Historical Society* 1 (1908): 152.

[29]Public Record Office, SP 29/236/14; Katz, *Sabbath*, 45. While uncertain of where exactly they settled, Katz suggests "they may be there still" (47). E. A. Payne postulates that Tillam's group could have influenced the eighteenth-century Church of Brethren that came

How many families Tillam and Pooley ultimately transplanted to the Palatinate is unknown. Reports indicate that they had provisions for 200 families. Men of standing, such as Edward Stennett, claimed that Tillam's views only represented "but . . . a small number of those that keep the Sabbath." John Belcher, Arthur Squibb and Richard Parnham along with other well-known seventh-day leaders joined Stennett in their denunciation of the "teachers of circumcision and the legal ceremonies, who are lately gone into Germany." Nevertheless, contemporaries observed that Tillam had numerous followers and he certainly was esteemed by numerous Baptists.[30] Bryan Ball states that between the number of families transported and Tillam's reputation, the Palatinate scheme had "disastrous consequences for the Sabbatarian movement throughout East Anglia and elsewhere in the country." Transportation of the Sabbatarian community from the North Country to the Palatinate was to the "lasting detriment of several Seventh-day churches in Essex, Norfolk, Suffolk, and countries further north." Tillam and the Palatinate settlers' eschato-

---

from the Palatinate (Ernest A. Payne review of *The Believers' Church*, by Donald F. Durnbaugh, *Baptist Quarterly* 23 (July 1969): 142-143).

[30]Public Record Office, SP 20/41/1; Edward Stennett, *The Insnared Taken*, sig. a3; SP 29/236/14; idem, *A Faithful Testimony Against the Teachers of Circumcision and the Legal Ceremonies; Who Are Lately Gone into Germany* (London?, 1667), Whitley, *Baptist Bibliography* 14-667; Payne "Thomas Tillam," 62. Some Baptists thought Tillam was the most articulate and well-known of the Seventh-Day Baptists. He was referred to as the "great Seventh-day-Sabbath man" (George Whitehead, *The Light and Life of Christ Within* (London, 1668), sig. a2). As mentioned, Jeremiah Ives, took on Tillam, Chamberlen, and others in a four-day debate concerning the Sabbath. Ives's published account reveals not only how urgent the seventh-day Sabbath question was for the Baptist movements, but also how prominent Tillam was among seventh-day believers (Ives, *Saturday no Sabbath* (London, 1659), sig. A2, 1-2, 66-93). Chamberlen, the other major participant in the debate, evidently resisted Tillam's apocalyptic schemes, but maintained his apocalyptic beliefs until the end. A few months before his death in 1683, he wrote to the Archbishop requesting permission to inquire of the leading ministers and university men of England concerning "this one question . . . Who is meant by the Little Horn in Daniel (Chap. 7th) before whom 3 Horn Kings fell . . . Killing & wearing out the Saints of the most high and thinking to change Times and Lawes." John Belcher witnessed Chamberlen's will, and within months of his denied request, he died. The remains of his dilapidated tomb read that he was "baptized about the year 1648, and keeping the 7th day for the Sabbath about 32 years," (Bod. MS Tanner No. 35 (f2); Aveling, *The Chamberlens*, 120, 122-123).

logical convictions had led them far from England and far from the majority of Baptists, but this remnant of believers thought that such action was the only way that they could come out of Babylon and free themselves from the mark of the Beast.[31]

While this accounts for the disappearance of the Seventh-Day Baptists from the North, it does not explain why there were "no new seventh-day churches established in England after c.1680." By the middle of the eighteenth century the movement in England had become virtually extinct.[32] Their primary problems were their high degree of tension with society, lack of organization, and the absence of strong leaders to give the movement both protection and direction. The main Baptist movements simultaneously decreased their distinctiveness from society while they increased their inter-congregational organization. Leaders emerged with both the ability and the desire to guide the main Baptist movements towards accommodation. They established a foundation that could survive adversity and an identity that provided cohesion. As a result they survived.

At the same time, the disappearance of the Seventh-Day Baptists also resulted from a tectonic shift in society's religious outlook. By the end of seventeenth century the kind of exact literalist thinking that the Seventh-Day Baptists were applying to the Bible was being applied by scientists to nature. Rationalism was slowly supplanting the book of Revelation. After 1660 the religious environment of England had changed and the Seventh-Day Baptists were the last to be informed and certainly the least prepared. Their eschatological enthusiasm had

---

[31]Ball, *Seventh-day Men*, 251, 273-274. W. T. Whitley writes that Tillam's Palatinate plan "drained away most of the Fifth-Monarchy men and many Seventh-day Baptists," *Baptist Quarterly*, "Seventh Day Baptists in England" 12 (1947): 253.

[32]Lyell, "Doctrines of the Seventh-Day Men," 4. Ball's excellent study of the movement has shown that this conclusion must be approached with some caution, but agrees that "only in a few instances did seventeenth-century Sabbatarianism in England and Wales persist beyond 1800," (333). For more on the effects of rationalism and the Seventh-Day Baptists' structure on the demise of seventeenth-century Sabbatarians, see Ball, *Seventh-day Men*, 312-313, 317 and his Conclusion generally.

not faded, but the moment for their movement had. In England, the unorthodox Baptists died hoping.[33]

---

[33]The seventh-day movement lasted long enough to set down roots in North America, where as noted, the seventh-day churches did organize. There are four major Christian religious organizations that exist at the end of the twentieth century and observe the Saturday Sabbath. Growing out of the Seventh-Day Baptists that arrived in New England, the Seventh Day Baptists Worldwide Federation had in 1990 a membership of approximately 50,000 Seventh Day Baptists in twenty-two countries on six continents (source: http://www.seventhdaybaptist.org/world.html). The better known Seventh-Day Adventists, organized in 1863, also observe the seventh-day Sabbath. As of 1996, their membership was listed as 9.2 million comprising 42,000 congregations in 204 countries (source: http://www.adventist.org.uk/). The Worldwide Church of God (1939, reorganized and named 1968) has members in over 120 countries and presently its worldwide membership is 69,300 (source:http://www.wcg.ca/aboutus/default.htm and paul_kroll@wcg.org). The Church of God International, formed in 1978, also observes the Saturday Sabbath. At present, it reports just over 2,000 members worldwide (source: contact with CGITYLERTX@aol.com, dir. CGI). There are a number of smaller denominations that observe the Saturday Sabbath. Some of them can be found at http://www.thejournal.org, this includes churches such as United Church of God (UCG), The Church of God Seventh Day (CG7), The Global Church of God (GCG), etc.

CONCLUSION
REFLECTIONS BEFORE THE END OF THINGS

Near the end of his life, William Kiffin sat down and took up his pen since he felt it his "duty to leave behind me some account of those many footsteps of [God's] grace and goodness towards me; (being now arrived to old age, and by the many weaknesses and distempers which attend me, have cause to judge my time is not likely to be long in this world)." His final account was not a history of the movement that he had so profoundly affected, but a reflection on his own remarkable spiritual odyssey.[1]

When Kiffin was born in 1616, the English poet, William Shakespeare, died. In the year of Kiffin's own death in 1701, the Act of Settlement was passed, providing for the birth of the Hanoverian monarchy and the end of the Stuarts. But for the Baptist movements, those years marked more than the death of a dramatist and a dynasty. The former date marked the death of Thomas Helwys, the man who led the first Baptists back to England. The latter date marked the death of William Kiffin, the man who had made the Baptists safe for England. In the year of Kiffin's birth and Helwys's death, John Traske had begun to worship on Saturday and lost his ears for it; his wife lost her life. By 1701 heretics were no longer burnt nor tortured.

Religious plurality had begrudgingly become the accepted reality. The last English witch trial took place in 1712, some hundred years after Thomas Helwys had returned to England and become the first to issue a plea for complete religious toleration. He believed that religious persecution was a mark of the Antichristian Beast and

---

[1]Kiffin, *Remarkable Passages*, 1-2.

should be abandoned. John Locke would issue a plea for religious toleration near the end of Kiffin's life, but it would be for different reasons. Christopher Hill reminds us that in the 1690s when the clergyman John Mason proclaimed the end of the world and the return of Christ, he was regarded as a psychological case rather than as a threat to the church or state. A generation earlier John James had not been so fortunate. More than merely time had passed.[2]

Today, Locke appears reasonable; millenarians perhaps less so. But in the early seventeenth century, millennial dreams were harbored by even the most respectable individuals. King James I spent a great deal of time and ink proving that the pope was the Beast of Revelation; Cromwell had told the Barebones Parliament much the same and urged them to the work of building God's Kingdom. Such dreams were even more prevalent among those on the periphery, hoping for the dawn of a just age. William Kiffin shared in the eschatological excitement of his time. He could "daily see the God of heaven fulfilling his own Word." When Kiffin gathered Particular Baptists together to issue a confession, they declared that Satan had overwhelmed the world, but soon Christ would come "ruling in the world over his enemies, Satan, and all the vessels of wrath, limiting, using, restraining them by his mighty power . . . The kingdom shall be then fully perfected." In an effort to come out of Babylon and into the New Jerusalem, the Baptists had formed gathered churches under the rule of Christ. Here was the Kingdom.[3]

The gathering of the seven churches in London laid the foundation for an organizational system that was to transform the Particular Baptist movement during the century of revolution. The General Baptists followed close behind. Both groups' leaders assumed responsibility for their congregations' well-being. While the leaders looked to heaven for the coming of the Lord, they also laid a founda-

---

[2]Christopher Hill, *The Century of Revolution*, (New York: Norton, 1966), 295; idem, "John Mason and the End of the World" in *Puritanism and Revolution* (London: Secker & Warburg, 1958).

[3]Kiffin, epistle to *Christian Man's Triall*, sig. a2; Lumpkin, *Confessions*, 161. This article (XIX) was altered in the 1646 version.

tion on the earth, just in case Christ's return was delayed. Almost unintentionally, the baptists had grown into Baptists. Near the end of the seventeenth century the Baptist movements had begun to look like denominations. Fundamental beliefs that had been present in the movements from the earliest times were carried forward and articulated in a theology.

This is not to say, by any means, that the Baptists were finished developing; rather it is to suggest that only now could they develop and change as a denomination. The Baptists were not born fully formed, but developed within a historical context. Taking the Reformation heritage of a priesthood of all believers and *sola scriptura*, the Baptists had added their own unique beliefs. Most distinguishing was believer's baptism—a symbol of a life in Christ and the faith of the individual. To the ideas of the gathered congregation under the kingship of Christ as the only authority of the church, the centrality of the Bible and believer's baptism was added the idea of religious liberty. In the midst of Reformation, Revolution and Civil War, they had found these timeless truths which would be the rock from which Baptists would spread throughout the world.

Even so, the fate of the General and Particular Baptists was not secured. Both experienced decline in the following century and underwent further changes and transformation. Today the metamorphosis continues as new generations of Baptists define themselves. But now, many of the societies in which Baptists find themselves have themselves been shaped, at least indirectly, by Baptist ideas. Often it is unacceptable for historians to look to the past for modern concepts, but in the case of the Baptists it is tempting. Words like democracy, liberty, individualism, plurality, and tolerance come to mind. Applying these ideas to the earliest Baptists is anachronistic and, as the Levellers discovered, outright dangerous; but there is the suggestion of some connection.

During the seventeenth century, the Baptists moved from the outermost fringes of society to become an enduring part of British culture. They remained a peculiar people, but their peculiarity was of a type that did not preclude a place in society. This was the Baptists' greatest success, but it had a cost and demanded sacrifice. In order to survive, the Baptists were forced to change. Their variance with society had to be moderated. As society changed and the Baptist changed, a fit was found and preserved. But on the way, Levellers had to be abandoned, witnessing against the Beast had to be tempered, revolutionaries disavowed. As he grew older, Kiffin saw the theological radicalism of the Seventh-Day Baptists and the Fifth Monarchists as dangerous rocks that threatened to wreck the ship. By then he may have forgotten that in his younger days, he believed such radicalism would "prove to be a Haven to our tedious storms." The perspective is always different from the helm.[4]

As the Baptist leaders steered the movements towards greater accommodation, they encountered resistance. The development of the Baptists during the seventeenth century was neither smooth nor constant. It was not the simple progression related in some denominational accounts. It was a struggle in which the outcome was always uncertain. Different Baptists took different paths to the Kingdom. The fact that the accommodationists survived means that there is a denominational family today whose story can be told. But it does not mean that those who had other visions did not struggle with equal faith and passion.

The General Baptists, Fifth Monarchists, Independent Baptists, Particular Baptists, and Seventh-Day Baptists were often mixed and muddled together during the formative period. These various movements all had an equal claim to the name "Baptists," but ultimately the expanse between their competing visions for achieving the Kingdom was as great as the distance between London and the Palatinate. It was similar to the divide between Luther and Müntzer. Building the Kingdom was the goal of all Baptists, of whatever variety. The difficult question was how? The feeling that they were beginning anew, rediscovering ancient truths at the threshold of a new age led individual Baptists to ask what were the true obligations and goals of their lives. It is an important question for any millennium. The story

---

[4]Kiffin, epistle to *Glimpse of Sions Glory*, sig. a3.

of the early Baptist movements would suggest that the answer depends on how one evaluates the question. The orthodox Baptists ultimately cleared themselves of the label "Anabaptists" and outlasted those who rivaled their movements, but to the "godly remnant" fiercely witnessing against the Beast, such criteria were unimportant.

The story of the Baptist movements in the seventeenth century also points to other lessons. It demonstrates the double-edged sword of organization. Both a blessing and a curse, increased organization for the main branches of Baptists allowed survival but forced their transformation. The nascent organizational system was further complemented by effective leaders. If the Seventh-Day Baptist Edward Stennett had been able to benefit from such a system, then the Seventh-Day Baptists might have been subject to a different fate. Organization also fostered a denominational awareness. It provided the opportunity for congregations to speak with authority towards the larger society. Through declarations, confessions, and petitions, inter-congregational organizations provided the Baptists with the means to negotiate how they were perceived. They could declare their criticism of the establishment. They could also publicly differentiate themselves from groups like the Anabaptists and from each other. Thomas Collier issued a Confession of Faith to distinguish himself from the London Baptists in much the same way that the London Baptists had issued a Confession in 1644 to disassociate themselves from the Anabaptists. The flood of petitions that streamed forth after Venner's rising in 1661 demonstrates how important this means of public discourse had become.

The story of the Baptist movements also suggests the possible way that wealth and favor with a society can change one's critiques of it. Millenarianism, or rather religion in general, provides a transcendent foundation from which even the most maligned can have the courage to critique the world. For this reason eschatology often plays an important role in revolutions, from the one that William Kiffin lived through in England to Hong Xiuquan's Taiping rebellion in China two centuries later. But the maneuvers open to eschatological movements are limited. If the world does not end there are few options. The revolution must be postponed, re-evaluated or redefined. While Kiffin spent much of his youth among the "company of poor distressed forlorn people," in his maturity he spent more time at Court, first with Cromwell, then Charles II, then James II, and finally even with William and Mary. After the 1640s, he was no longer a member of the "vulgar multitude." Millenarianism became redundant.[5]

Those who failed to adjust to society were often undone. In this sense, the story of the Baptist movements shows the double-edged sword of accommodation as well, for in the act of accommodating to society, the movement might survive, but it must change. The goal of transforming society becomes secondary. Instead of interpreting their witness by radical criticism aimed at social transformation, the movement may be forced, to some degree, to endorse the status quo. It raises the very question of what the role of religion in society should be.

The actions of Kiffin and others demonstrate that every step toward accommodation is easier than the previous one. Of course, Baptists such as John Smyth showed that the reverse is also true. With each painful rejection came further liberation. Smyth lost a lectureship, had to leave his native country, and was denounced by the English Separatists in Holland. Before the end of his life, he had also been abandoned by his closest friend and pupil, Thomas Helwys. Like Kiffin, Smyth also wrote a final work shortly before his death. He reflected on the "pain of damnation" by his peers, but he would rather endure scorn than have to "shut my ears from" any further truth. "I profess I have changed, and shall be ready still to change, for the better." His further light had not faded. And as for "the number of those men" who pretended to have the answers when they did not, and shortchanged their conscience to impress others: "they may enjoy that glory without my envy, though not without the grief of my heart for them."

---

[5]Goodwin, *Glimpse of Sions Glory*, 6, 9.

In the end, Smyth's journey had taught him that before he could change the world, he had to be transformed himself. He wrote and lived not "to accuse and condemn other men, but to censure and reform myself." Now "I labor to reform myself wherein I see my error, that I continually search after the truth and endeavor myself to keep a good conscience in all things." Smyth had realized that the completion of the Reformation had to begin in his heart. In a sense, his last thoughts echoed those of Origen, in that Smyth now looked forward to the millennium within his soul.

Smyth certainly had not won favor with the world, but the fact that he could justify himself "before the Lord who is my Judge in my conscience," meant that he could "rest having peace at home." In terms of radicalism, Kiffin and Smyth's respective spiritual journeys had led them in opposite directions. Smyth died poor and ridiculed in a foreign land. But he had accumulated inner-wealth in abundance. "Let them think of me as they please." Contemporaries and historians could judge him as they wished, but such judgments would not alter the peace that he had made with his God. Smyth concluded his "last book" in saying "so I rest satisfied."[6]

Almost a century separates the deaths of Smyth and Kiffin. During that time two revolutions had occurred. For the first time in history, a king had been legally tried, found guilty, and executed; England had been ruled by a written constitution; and the institutions of the Monarchy and the House of Lords had been abolished. With the Restoration of the Stuart monarchy in 1660 all of this was undone. Religious persecution followed and turned dissenters into Nonconformists. As popery crept back in, the Baptists were again compelled to protest. When tyranny returned, another revolution was required. Kiffin not only lived through these events, but he had played a role in their unfolding. He had held high positions in government, influenced Parliaments, and aided Kings.

At the end of Kiffin's life, all of these dramatic outward events had begun to fade from his memory. They were comparatively minor

---

[6]Smyth, *Works*, 752-753, 755-756, 760.

details in the story of his salvation and service to God. What mattered was the working of God in his life and the recollection of his earliest moments of enlightenment. He recalled with joy the first time when "I could say with David, 'When I awake I am still with thee.' I found the power of inbred corruption scatter, and my heart set on fire with holy love to Christ." The brightness of such fire forced the rise and fall of monarchs to fade into a distant haze.[7]

Just as modern day Baptists carry a kernel of that initial seventeenth-century radicalism, the apocalyptic fire that had stoked Kiffin's enthusiasm in his earliest days can still be seen in ember form in his last. Kiffin used the final page of his memoirs to warn his descendants:

> I leave these few experiences with you, desiring the Lord to bless you, and to bless them to you. Above all I pray for you, that you may in a special manner look after the great concerns of your souls—To know God and Jesus Christ is eternal life. Endeavor to be diligent. Inquire after, and be established in the great doctrines of the gospel; which are of absolute necessity to salvation. I must expect everyday to leave this world; having lived in it much longer than expected . . .
>
> Yet I know not what my eyes may see before my change—the world is full of confusions—the last times are upon us. The signs of them are very visible. Iniquity abounds, and the love of many in religion waxes cold. God is, by his providence, shaking the earth under our feet. There is no sure foundation of rest and peace but only in Jesus Christ; to whose grace I commend you.[8]

And with that brief apocalyptic admonition, the story of William Kiffin and the earliest English Baptists comes to an end.

---

[7]Kiffin, *Remarkable Passages*, 5.
[8]*Remarkable Passages*, 89-90.

SELECTED BIBLIOGRAPHY

Manuscripts

Angus Library, Regent's Park College, Oxford.

F.P.C.c8 [Benjamin Stinton, "A Repository of Divers Historical Matters relating to English Antipedobaptists," 1712]

1 f.8 [Records and Letters Relative to the Baptist Church at Hexham. October 1651-1680]

36 G. A. e.10 ["An Account of Some of the Most Eminent & Leading Men among the English Antipadobaptists." Pages 1-66 were probably written by Stinton. The rest appears to be the work of Thomas Crosby]

41.e 1 ["Men of the Seventh Day or Sabbath Keepers of the Seventeenth Century." Unpublished book ms. by W. T. Whitley]

Bodleian Library, Oxford University, Oxford.

Rawlinson. A 38 (f. 487) [Note on Richardson]

Rawlinson. D 828 [Register of the acts of an Anabaptist congregation in London (i.e. the Baptist Church at Lothbury)]

Rawlinson. D 859 (f. 162) [Note on Pendarves's death]

Tanner. 35 (f2) [Chamberlen's Request of the Archbishop]

Dr. William's Library, London.

533.B.1 ["Mill Yard Minutes, being the Church Book of the Seventh Day General Baptist Congregation . . ."]

Public Record Office, London.

SP 29/4/18 [Report on Palatinate Colony]
SP 29/40/42 [Notes Relating to Hobson]
SP 29/40/91 [Intelligence Report]
SP 29/41/1 [Report on Pooley]
SP 29/62/71 [Notes Relating to Hobson]
SP 29/63/2 [Notes Relating to Hobson]
SP 29/63/34 [Notes Relating to Hobson]
SP 29/63/34.I [Notes Relating to Hobson]
SP 29/81/32 [Notes Relating to Hobson]
SP 29/84/64 [Notes Relating to Hobson]
SP 29/93/11 [Notes Relating to Hobson]
SP 29/106/11 [Report on Tillam and Pooley]
SP 29/181/116 [Report on Pooley, including Covenant]
SP 29/190/104 [Letter of Sanderson]
SP 29/207/1 [Notes on Recruiting Efforts for Palatinate]
SP 29/236/14 [Notes on Departure]
SP 29/446/40 [Note on Tillam and Pooley]

Dissertations

Brachlow, Stephen. "Puritan Theology and Radical Churchmen in Pre-Revolutionary England." D.Phil. Dissertation. Oxford University, Oxford, 1978.

Land, Richard Dale. "Doctrinal Controversies of English Particular Baptists (1644-1691) as Illustrated by the Career and Writings of Thomas Collier." D.Phil Dissertation. Oxford University, Oxford, 1980.

Laurence, Anne. "Parliamentary Army Chaplains 1642-51." D.Phil. Dissertation. Oxford University, Oxford, 1981.

Lyell, Leon. "Doctrines of the Seventh-Day Men." Dissertation. La Trobe University, Australia, 1981.

Russell-Jones, Iwan. "The Relationship Between Theology and Politics in the Writings of John Lilburne, Richard Overton and

William Walwyn." D.Phil. Dissertation. Oxford University, Oxford, 1987.

Spivey, James Travis. "Middle Way Men: Edmund Calamy and the Crisis of Non-conformity (1688-1732)." D.Phil. Dissertation. Oxford University, Oxford, 1986.

Primary Sources

Allen, William. *The Captive Taken from the Strong*. London, 1658.

_____ . *A faithful memorial of that remarkable meeting . . . at Windsor Castle*. London, 1659.

_____ . *A Word to the Army*. London, 1660.

The Anabaptists' Catechisme. London, 1645.

Archer, John. *The Personall Raigne of Christ Upon Earth*. London, 1641.

Aspinwall, William. *The Abrogation of the Jewish Sabbath*. London, 1657.

Atherton, John. *The Pastor turn'd Pope*. London, 1654.

Bakewell, Thomas. *A Confutation of the Anabaptists and of All others who Affect Not Civill Government*. London, 1644.

_____ . *An Answer or Confutation of Divers Errors Broached and Maintained By the Seven Churches of Anabaptists*. London, 1646.

Bampfield, Francis. *A Name, an After One, or, A Name, a New One . . . or An Historical Declaration*. London, 1681.

The Banner of Truth Displayed: or, A Testimony for Christ, and Against Anti-Christ. Being the substance of severall . . . who are waiting for the visible appearance of Christ's Kingdome, in and over the world; and Residing in and about the City of London. London, 1656.

Barber, Edward. *To the Kings Most Excellent Majesty, and the Honourable Court of Parliament*. London, 1641.

_____ . *A Small Treatise of Baptisme, or Dipping. Wherein is cleerly shewed that the Lord Christ Ordained dipping for those only that Professe Repentance and Faith*. London, 1642.

_____ . *A true Discovery of the Ministry of the Gospell . . . according to that Royall Commission of King Jesus . . . whereby may be clearly Seen* the Great Difference Between the Ministers or servants of the Churches of Jesus Christ and the Ministers of rather Masters of the churches of Antichrist. London, 1645.

_____ . An Answer to the Essex Watchmens watchword. London, 1649.

_____ . Certaine Queries, Propounded to the Churches of Christ. London, 1650?.

_____ . The Storming and Totall Routing of Tythes. London, 1651.

Brabourne, Theophilus. A Discourse upon the Sabbath Day. Wherin are handled these particulares . . . 1. That the Lords Day is not Sabbath Day by Divine iustification. 2. An exposition of the 4. Commandment, so farr [as] may give light vnto the ensueinge discourse: and particularly, here it is showne, at what time the Sabbath day should begine and end; for the satisfaction of those who are doubtfull in this point. 3. That the Seaventh-day Sabbath is not abolished. 4. That the Seaventh-day Sabbath is now still in force. 5. The author's Exhortation and reasones, that neverthelesse there be no Rente from our Church as touching practise. London, 1628.

_____ . A Defence of that most ancient and sacred ordinance of Gods, the Sabbath Day. Amsterdam, 1632.

Bradford, William. Of Plymouth Plantation. Notes and Intro.by Samuel E. Morison. New York: Alfred A. Knopf, 1959.

Brief Confession or Declaration of Faith. London, 1660.

Bunyan, John. A Confession of My Faith. London, 1672.

_____ . Differences in Judgment About Water-Baptism, No Bar to Communion. London, 1673.

_____ . Questions About the Nature and Perpetuity of the Seventh-Day-Sabbath. And Proof, that the First Day of the Week is the True Christian-Sabbath. London, 1685.

Calamy, Edward. England's Looking-Glasse. London, 1642.

Chamberlen, Peter. A Discourse Between Capt. Kiffin and Dr. Chamberlen, About Imposition of Hands. London, 1654.

_____ . England's Choice, &c. To all arch-bishops, and bishops, who are not a shame (to) or ashamed (of) the name of Christ before men, grace, wisdom and truth, from God our Father, and from our Lord Jesus Christ, Amen. London, 1682.

Collier, Thomas. *Three Great Queries Now in Controversie*. London?, 1645.

_____ . *Certaine Queries: or, Points Now in Controvercy Examined, and answered by Scripture*. London, 1645.

_____ . The *Exhaltation of Christ in the Dayes of the Gospel*. 3rd. ed. London, 1647. (With a letter to the reader by Hanserd Knollys). [Wing assigns a date of 1641 to the first edition, which is probably a mistake for 1646].

_____ . *A Discovery of a New Creation*. London, 1647.

_____ . *A Brief Discovery of the Corruption of the Ministry of the Church of England*. London, 1647.

_____ . *The Glory of Christ*. London, 1647.

_____ . *A Vindication of the Army-Remonstrance*. London, 1648.

_____ . *The Font-Guard Routed*. London, 1652.

_____ . *The Pulpit-Guard Routed*. London, 1652.

_____ . *The Right Constitution and True Subjects of the Visible Church*. London, 1654.

_____ . *A Brief answer to Some of the Objections and Demurs Made Against the Coming in and Inhabiting of the Jews in this Commonwealth*. London, 1656.

_____ . *A Confession of Faith of Several Churches of Christ, in the County of Somerset*. London, 1656.

_____ . *A Looking-Glasse for the Quakers*. London, 1656.

_____ . *To All the Churches of Christ, Called to Be Saints*. London, 1657.

_____ . *The Seventh Day Sabbath Opened and Discovered, As it is Brought Forth, and to Be Observed Now in the Days of the Gospel: And the First Day of the Week, the Time of Publique Worship*. London, 1658. [Tract only signed T.C. possibly Thomas Chafie instead of Collier].

_____ . *The Decision & Clearing of the Great Point now in Controversie about the Interest of Christ*. London, 1659.

_____ . *A Body of Divinity, or A Confession of Faith*. London, 1674.

_____ . *A Confession of Faith*. London, 1678.

_____ . *Doctrinal Discourse of Self-Denial*. London, 1691.

Cornwell, Francis. *The Vindication of the Royall Commission of King . . . Against the Antichristian Faction . . . that Enacted by a Decree, that the Baptisme of the Infants of Beleevers, Should Succeed Circumsion . . . Which Doth . . . Oppose the Commission, Granted by King Jesus.* London?, 1644.

———. *King Jesus is the Beleevers Prince, Priest, and Law-Giver . . . or, The Loyal Spouse of Christ hath no head, Nor Husband, But Royall King Jesus.* London, 1645.

Cox, Benjamin, Hanserd Knollys, and William Kiffin. *A Declaration Concerning the Dispute which Should have been in the Publike Meeting House of Alderman-Bury, the 3d of this instant moneth of December; Concerning Infant-Baptisme.* London, 1645.

Cox, Benjamin. *An Appendix to a Confession of Faith, or a more Full Declaration of the Faith and Judgement of Baptized Believers . . . Published for the Further Clearing of Truth, and discovery of Their Mistakes who have Imagined a Dissent in Fundamentals where there is none.* London, 1646.

Coxe, Nehemiah. *Vindicia veritatis, or, A confutation . . . of the heresies and gross errours asserted by Thomas Collier.* London, 1677.

Danvers, Henry. *A Treatise of Laying on of Hands, with the History thereof, both from Scripture and Antiquity. Wherein an account is Given how it Hath been practised in all ages since Christ.* London, 1674.

A Declaration Against Anabaptists. London, 1644.

The Declaration and Proclamation of the Army of God. London, 1659.

A Declaration by Congregationall societies in, and about the city of London; as well of those commonly called Anabaptists. London, 1647.

A Declaration of Divers Elders and Brethren. London, 1651.

A Declaration of Several Churches of Christ, and Godly People and Godly People In and About the Citie of London; Concerning the Kingly Interest of Christ and The Present Sufferings of His Cause and Saints in England. London, 1654.

A Declaration of Several Baptized Believers, walking in all the Foundation Principles of the Doctrine of Christ, Mentioned in Heb. 6.1,2. London, 1659.

A Declaration of several of the people called Anabaptists, in and about the city of London. London, 1659.

The Declaration of a Small Society of Baptized Believers, undergoing the Name of Free-Willers, about the City of London. London, 1660.

A Declaration of Some of those People in or near London, called Anabaptists. London, 1660.

Denne, Henry. Antichrist Unmasked, in Two Treatises: the first, An Answer unto two Pædobaptists, D. Featly and S. Marshall, the second, The Man of Sinne Discovered. London, 1645.

_____ . The Levellers Designe Discovered. London, 1649.

A Door of Hope: or, A Call and Declaration for the gathering together of the first ripe fruits unto the Standard of our Lord, King Jesus. London, 1661.

Edwards, Thomas. Gangraena: or a Catalogue and Discovery of many of the Errours, Heresies, Blasphemies and pernicious Practicies of the Sectaries of this time, vented and acted in England in these four last years . . . the Second Edition Enlarged. London, 1646.

_____ . The First and Second Part of Gangraena: or A Catalogue and Discovery of many of the Errors, Heresies, Blasphemies and pernicious Practices of the Sectaries of this time, vented and acted in England in these four last yeers . . . The Third Edition, corrected and much Enlarged. London, 1646.

_____ . The Second Part of Gangraena or A Fresh and further Discovery of the Errors, Heresies, Blasphemies, and dangerous Proceedings of the Sectaries of this time. London, 1646.

_____ . The Third Part of Gangraena or A new and higher Discovery of the Errors, Heresies, Blasphemies, and insolent Proceedings of the Sectaries of these times. London, 1646.

Erbery, William. The Bishop of London. London, 1652.

Feake, Christopher. The Genealogie of Christianity and of Christians. London, 1650.

Featley, Daniel. A warning for England especially for London in the famous history of the frantick Anabaptists their wild preachings & practises in Germany. London, 1642.

_____ . *The Dippers Dipt, or, the Anabaptists duck'ed and plung'd over Head and Eares*. London, 1645.

Fox, George. *An Answer to Thomas Tillams Book Called the Seventh-Day-Sabbath Wherein It Is Shewed How the . . . Jews Sabbath was a Day Given unto them Since the Fall . . . and this Sabbath was a Shadow and Sign*. London, 1659.

Geneva Bible 1602. facs. ed. Gerald T. Sheppard. New York : Pilgrim Press, c1989.

Goodwin, Thomas. *A Glimpse of Sions Glory*. London, 1641.

Grantham, Thomas. *The Seventh Day-Sabbath Ceased as ceremonial and yet the morality of the fourth command remaineth, or, Seven reasons tending to prove that the fourth command in the Decalogue is of a different nature from the other nine*. London, 1667.

Griffith, John. *A Treatise Touching falling from Grace. Or thirteen arguments Tending to Prove that Believers cannot fall from grace, as they were laid down at a conference at Yalding in Kent*. London, 1653.

A Ground Voice, or some discoveries offered to the view, with certain queries propounded to the consideration of the whole army in England, Scotland, and Ireland, officers and common-souldiers, horse and foot. VVith certain queries to the Anabaptists in particular that bear any office, either in court or army, under the present self-created politick power. London, 1655.

Hanson, John. *A Short Treatise showing the Sabbatharians Confuted*. London, 1658.

Haughton, Edward. *The Rise, Growth, and Fall of Antichrist: Together with the Reign of Christ*. London, 1652.

Helwys, Thomas. *A Short Declaration of the Mistery of Iniquity*. Amsterdam?, 1612.

_____ . *Persecution for Religion Judg'd and Condemn'd*. London?, 1615 and 1620, reprinted 1662.

Hobson, Paul. *The Fallacy of Infants Baptisme Discovered*. London, 1645.

_____ . *Practicall Divinity: or a Helpe Through the Blessing of God to Lead men more to Look Within Themselves*. London, 1646.

_____ . *A Garden Inclosed and Wisdom Justified only of Her Children.* London, 1647.

_____ . *A Treatise Containing Three Things.* London, 1653.

_____ . *Fourteen queries and Ten Absurdities about the extent of Christ's death.* London, 1655.

Hubberthorn[e?], Robert. *An Answer to a Declaration put forth by the general Consent of the People Called Anabaptists.* London, 1659.

Hughes, W. *Munster and Abingdon or, the Open Rebellion There, and Unhappy Tumult Here.* Oxford, 1657.

The Humble Apology of some commonly called Anabaptists. London, 1661.

The Humble Petition and Representation of Several Churches of God in London, commonly (though falsly) called Anabaptists . . . Together with the answer and approbation of the Parliament thereunto. London, 1649.

The Humble Representation and Vindication of Many of the Messengers, Elders, and Brethren, belonging to Several of the Baptized Churches of this Nation of and Concerning their Opinions and Resolutions touching the Civill Government. London, 1654.

Ives, Jeremiah. *Saturday no Sabbath.* London, 1659.

Jacob, Henry. *A Defence of the Churches and Ministry of Englande.* Middelburg, 1599.

_____ . *A Christian and Modest Offer.* Middelburg, 1606.

_____ . *Reasons Taken out of Gods Word.* Middelburg, 1604.

_____ . *An Attestation.* Middelburg, 1613.

_____ . *A Collection of Sundry Matters.* Amsterdam, 1616.

_____ . *A Confession and Protestation of the Faith of Certaine Christians in England.* Amsterdam, 1616.

Jessey, Henry. *The Exceeding Riches of Grace Advanced by the Spirit of Grace.* 2nd ed. London, 1647.

_____ . *A Narrative of the Late Proceeds at White-Hall Concerning the Jews.* London, 1656.

Kiffin, William. epistle to *Christian Mans Triall,* by John Lilburne. London, 1641.

_____ . epistle to *Glimpse of Sions Glory*, by Thomas Goodwin[?]. London, 1641.

_____ . *Certaine Observations vpon Hosea*. London, 1642.

_____ . *To Mr. Thomas Edwards*. London, 1644.

_____ . *A Brief Remonstrance of the Reasons and Grounds of those People Commonly Called Anabaptists*. London, 1645.

_____ . epistle to *Justification by Christ Alone*, by Samuel Richardson. London, 1647.

_____ . *Walwins Wiles: or The Manifestators Manifested viz. Liev. Col. John Lilburn, Mr Will. Walwin, Mr Richard Overton, and Mr Tho. Prince. Discovering themselves to be Englands New Chains and Irelands Back Friends*. London, 1649.

_____ . postscript to *The sufficiency of the Spirits Teaching Without Humane Learning: a Treatise Tending to Prove Humane Learning to be no help to the Spirituall Understanding of the Word of God*, by Samuel How. London, 1655.

_____ . *A letter sent to the Right Honourable, the Lord Mayor of the City of London*. London, 1659. [signed by Kiffin, Gosfright, Hewling, and Lomes]

_____ . epistle to *[Some seri]ous reflections on that part of [Mr]. Bunion's [Con]fession of faith: [t]ouching [church] communion with [unbapti]zed persons*. London, 1673.

_____ . *A Sober Discourse of Right to Church-Communion. Wherein is proved by Scripture, the example of the primitive times, and the Practice of All that Have Professed the Christian Religion: that No Unbaptized Person may be regularly admitted to the Lords Supper*. London, 1681.

_____ . ed. *The Life and Death of that Old Disciple of Jesus Christ . . . Mr. Hanserd Knollys*. London, 1692.

_____ . epistle to *The Simplicity of the Gospel Defended*, by Samuel How. Norwich, Conn. : Alexander Robertson, James Robertson and John Trumbull, [1775].

_____ . *Remarkable Passages in the Life of William Kiffin*. ed. W. Orme. London, 1823.

Killcop, Thomas. *A short Treatise of Baptisme Wherein is Declared that only Christs Disciples or Beleevers are to be Baptised. And that the baptising of infants hath no footing in the Word of God, but is a mere tradition, received from our forefathers.* London, 1642.

_____ . *Seekers Supplied.* London, 1646

_____ . *Ancient and Durable Gospel. Concerning the time of the Perfect and totall Subduing, Washing away, remitting, blotting out, and pardoning, believers sins: and Believers being justified, adopted, Married to Christ; and presented by Christ spotlesse.* London, 1648.

_____ . *The Unlimited Authority of Christs disciples Cleared, or The Present Church and Ministry Vindicated.* London, 1651.

_____ . *The Path-Way to Justification.* London, 1660.

King, Daniel. *A Way to Sion Sought Out.* London, 1650.

Knollys, Hanserd. *A Moderate Answer vnto Dr. Bastvvicks book.* London, 1645.

_____ . *Christ Exalted.* London, 1646.

_____ . *The Shining of a Flaming-fire in Zion. Or, a clear Answer unto 13. exceptions, against the grounds of new Baptism.* London, 1646.

_____ . *Apocalyptical Mysteries.* London, 1667.

_____ . *The Parable of the Kingdom of Heaven Expounded.* London, 1674.

_____ . *The Baptists Answer.* London, 1675.

_____ . *An Exposition of the Eleventh Chapter of Revelation: Wherein All Those Things therein Revealed, which must shortly come to pass, are Explained.* London, 1679.

_____ . *Mystical Babylon Unvailed . . . Also A call to all the people of God to come out of Babylon.* London, 1679.

_____ . *The World that Now is; and the World that is to Come: or the First and Second Coming of Jesus Christ.* London, 1681.

_____ . *An Exposition on the Whole Book of Revelation.* London, 1689.

_____ . *The Gospel Minister's Maintenance.* London, 1689.

_____ . *The Life and Death of that Old Disciple of Jesus Christ . . . Hanserd Knollys.* ed. William Kiffin. London, 1692.

Lambe, Thomas. *The Fountaine of Free Grace Opened . . . Providing the Foundation of Faith to Consist only in Gods Free Love, In giving*

Christ to Dye for the Sins of All, and objections to the Contrary Answered by the Congregation of Christ in London constituted by the baptisme upon the profession of faith, falsly called Anabaptists. London?, 1645.

The Last Farewel to the Rebellious Sect Called the Fifth Monarchy-Men . . . the total Dispersing, Defeating and utter Ruining of that Damnable and Seditious Sect in General. London, 1661.

Lawrence [Laurence], Richard. *The Antichristian Presbyter.* London, 1647.

Lilburne, John. *The Christian Mans Traill.* London, 1641.

Lover, Thomas. *The True Gospel-Faith Witnessed by the Peoples and Apostles, and Collected into Thirty Articles.* London, 1654.

Marshall, Stephen. *A Defense of Infant Baptism.* London, 1646.

Maton, Robert. *Israel's Redemption of the Propheticall History of Our Saviours Kingdome on Earth.* London, 1642.

Ockford, James. *The Doctrince of the Fourth Commandment, Deformed by Popery, Reformed and Restored to its Primitive Purity.* London, 1650.

Overton, Robert. *Mans Mortalitie.* London, 1644.

Patient, Thomas. *The Doctrine of Baptism.* London, 1654.

The Protector, (so called,) in Part Unvailed: by whom the Mystery of Iniquity, is now Working. Or a Word to the good People of the Three Nations of England, Scotland and Ireland, Informing them of the Abominable Apostacy, Backsliding, and Underhand dealing of the Man above mentioned; who having Usurped Power over the Nation, hath most wofully betrayed, forsaken, and cast out the good old Cause of God, and the Interest of Christ; and hath Cheated and Robbed his People of their Rights and Priviledges. By a late member of the Army. London, 1655.

Remonstrance Sent From Colonell Lilburnes Regiment . . . to Thomas Fairfax . . . Wherein They Declare their Resolutions, to Stand and Fall with him. London, 1647.

Richardson, Samuel. *Some Briefe Considerations on Doctor Featley his book, intituled, The Dipper Dipt, Wherein in Some measure is Discovered his Many great and False accusations of divers persons,*

Commonly Called Anabaptists, with an Answer to them, and some brief Reasons for their Practice. London, 1645.

_____ . *Certain Questions Propounded to the Assembly*. London, 1646.

_____ . *Justification by Christ alone*. London, 1647.

_____ . *The Saints Desire*. London, 1647.

_____ . *An Apology for the Present Government, and Governour*. London, 1654.

_____ . *Plain Dealing: Or the Unvailing of the Opposers of the Present Government and Governors. In Answer to several things affirmed by Mr. Vavasor Powell and others*. London, 1656.

Rogers, John. *Jegar-Sahadutha: An Oyled Pillar. Set up for Posterity Against the Present Wickednesses*. London, 1657.

_____ . *A Christian Concertation*. London, 1659.

Saller, [Sellars] William. *A Preservation Against Atheism*. London, 1664.

_____ . *An Examination of a late Book published . . . Concerning a Sacred Day of Rest*. London, 1671.

A Short Discovery of His Highness the Lord Protector's Intention Touching the Anabaptists in Army. London, 1655.

A Short History of the Anabaptists of High and Low Germany. London, 1642.

Some considerations . . . for the . . . uniting of all the Faithful. London, 1654.

Spilsbury, John. *A Treatise Concerning the Lavvfvll Svbiect of Baptisme*. London, 1643.

Spittlehouse, John. *A Treatise Concerning the Lawful Subject of Baptisms*. London, 1643.

_____ . *Rome Ruin'd by Whitehall*. London, 1650.

_____ . *An Explanation of the Commission of Jesus Christ*. London, 1653.

_____ . *The First Address to His Excellencie the Lord General*. London, 1653.

_____ . *Certaine Queries Propounded to the Most Serious Consideration of Those Persons Novv in Power*. London, 1654.

_____ . *Answer's to part of the Lord Protector's Speech*. London, 1654.

_____ . *A Return to some Expressions*. London, 1656.

_____ . *A Manifestation of sundry gross absurditites . . . that naturally ariseth from some expressions in a Sermon, preached by John Simpson . . . in reference to the abrogating of the seventh-day-Sabbath*. London, 1657.

_____ . and William Saller. *An appeal to the consciences of the chief magistrates of this Commonwealth, touching the Sabbath-day . . . in the behalf of themselves and several others, who think themselves obliged to observe the seventh day of the week, for the Lords holy Sabbath, as in the fourth Commandment of the royal-law of Jehovah, Exod. 20.8,9,10,11*. London 1657. [rev. expanded ed. 1679].

Sprint, John. *Propositions Tending to Prove the Necessary Use of the Christian Sabbath*. London, 1607.

Stennett, Edward. *The Royal Law Contended for, or, Some Brief Grounds serving to prove that the Ten Commandments are yet still in full force, and shall remain so until Heaven and Earth pass away; also, the Seventh Day Sabbath proved from the Beginning*. London, 1658.

_____ . *The Seventh Day Sabbath is the Sabbath of the Lord*. London, 1658.

_____ . *The insnared taken in the work of his hands; . . . the truth contained in Gods fourth commandment, is weighed in a just ballance, and sound lighter then vanity, and the seventh-day sabbath of Jehovah stands like a rock against all opposition . . . Whereunto is added, a faithful testimony against the teachers of circumcision, and the legal ceremonies; who are lately gone into Germany*. London, 1677.

Strand, Kenneth A. ed., *Luther's "September Bible" In Facsimile*. Ann Arbor: Ann Arbor Publishers, 1972.

Taylor, John. *A Swarme of Sectaries*. London, 1641.

Tillam, Thomas. *The Two Witnesses: Their Prophecy, Slaughter, Resurection and Ascention: or, An exposition of the eleventh chapter of the Revelation, wherein is plainly proved that the scriptures of the Old and New Testaments, are the witnesses there spoken of, who have prophesied in sackcloth one thousand two hundred and sixty years Compleat; that they are already slain, revived, and ascended*. London, 1651.

_____. *Banners of Love Displayed over the Church of Christ, Walking in the Order of the Gospel at Hexham.* Newcastle, 1654.

_____. *The Fourth Principle of Christian religion: or, the foundation doctrine of laying on of hands.* London, 1655.

_____. *The Seventh-Day Sabbath Sought out and celebrated, or, the Saints Last Design upon the Man of sin . . . being a clear discovery of that black character in the head of the little Horn, Dan. 7.25. The Change of Times & Laws. With the Christians glorious Conquest over that mark of the Beast, and recovery of the long-slighted seventh day, to its ancient glory.* London, 1657.

_____. *The Temple of the Lively Stones, or, The Promised Glory of the Last Days.* London, 1660.

Tillinghast, John. *Generation-Work.* London, 1653.

_____. *Part II.* London, 1654.

_____. *Part III.* London, 1655.

T[ovey], W[illaim]. *A Letter to Mr. Mead, In Answer to Several Unscriptural, and Unsound Sayings of his, in a Sermon against the Seventh-Day-Sabbath, Preached at his Place of Meeting, the Twenty Third of the Second Month, 1682.Wrote the Same Day the Sermon was Preached, refuting his Arguments, and turning them back, making their Unskilfulness and Weakness manifest; and clearly Evidencing, That the Seventh-Day is the Sabbath Day; by clear Scripture-Testimony, and sound Arguments grounded thereon. Published for his Hearers, because he would neither hear an Objection in Publick, nor admit of a Conference in Private.* London, 1682.

Traske, John. *Christs Kingdome Discovered.* London, 1615.

_____. *Heaven's Ioy, or Heaven Begun Upon Earth.* London, 1616.

_____. *A Treatise of Libertie from Iudaisme, or An Acknowledgement of True Christian Libertie, indited and published by Iohn Traske: of late stumbling, now Happily Running againe in the race of Christianitie.* London, 1620.

Walker, Clement. *The Compleat History of Independency.* London, 1661.

Walwyn, William. *The Foundation of Slander Discovered.* London, 1649.

Warren, Edmund. *The Jews Sabbath Antiquated.* London, 1659.

Weld, Thomas, et al. *A False Jew: Or, A Wonderful Discovery of a Scot, Baptized at London for a Christian, Circumcised at Rome to act a Jew, Re-baptized at Hexham for a Believer, but Found out at Newcastle to be a Cheat.* Gateshead, 1653.

Whiston, Edward. *The Life and Death of Mr. Henry Jessey.* London, 1671.

Whitehead, George. *The Light and Life of Christ Within.* London, 1668.

Wilkinson, John. *An Exposition of the 13. Chapter of Revelation.* London, 1619.

Printed Collections of Documents, Tracts and Writings

Abbott, Wilbur Cortez, ed. *The Writings and Speeches of Oliver Cromwell.* 4 vols. Cambridge, Massachusetts: Harvard University Press, 1937-1947.

Birch, T. ed. *A Collection of the State Papers of John Thurloe.* 7 vols. London, 1742.

Cary, H. ed. *Memorials of the Great Civil War.* 2 vols. London: Colburn, 1842.

Cobbett, W. ed. *State Trials* 2nd ed. 34 vols. London: R. Bagshaw, 1830.

Firth, C. H. ed. *The Clarke Papers.* 4 vols. London: Longman's, 1891-1901.

Haller, William, ed. *The Leveller Tracts 1647-1653.* New York: Columbia University Press, 1944.

Howell, T.B. ed. *A Complete Collection of State Trials.* 5 vols. London, 1816.

Lumpkin, William J. ed. *Baptists Confessions of Faith.* Valley Forge: The Judson Press, 1959 revised and reissued 1969.

Macfarlane, A. ed. *The Dairy of Ralph Josselin.* Oxford: Oxford University Press, 1976.

Masson, David, ed. *The quarrel between the Earl of Manchester and Oliver Cromwell: an episode of the English Civil War. Unpublished documents relating thereto, collected by the late John Bruce . . . with fragments of a historical preface by Mr. Bruce, annotated and completed by David Masson.* London: Camden Society, 1875.

Nickolls, John, ed. *Original Letters and Papers of State, addressed to Oliver Cromwell.* London: Printed by William Bowyer, 1743.

Schaff, P. et. al., eds. *A Select Library of Nicene and Post-Nicene Fathers.* vol. 2. New York: Scribner's, 1908.

Tibbutt, H. G. ed. *The Life and Letters of Sir Lewis Dyve, 1599-1669.* Streatley: Bedfordshire Historical Record Society, 1948.

_____. ed. *The Tower of London Letter-Book of Sir Lewis Dyve, 1646-47.* Streatley: Bedfordshire Historical Society, 1958.

Underhill, Edward Bean, ed. *The Records of a Church of Christ Meeting in Broadmead, Bristol 1640-1687.* London: Hanserd Knollys Society 1847.

_____. ed. *Confessions of Faith and Other Public Documents Illustrative of the History of the Baptist Churches of England in the 17th Century.* London: Haddon Brothers, and Co., 1854.

_____. ed. *Records of the Churches of Christ, Gathered at Fenstanton, Warboys, and Hexham. 1644-1720.* London: Hanserd Knollys Society, 1854.

White, B. R. ed. *Association Records of the Particular Baptists of England, Wales and Ireland to 1660.* 3 vols. London: Baptist Historical Society, 1971-1974.

Whitley, W.T. ed. "Debate on Infant Baptism, 1643" [the "Knollys Memorandum"]. *Transactions of the Baptist Historical Society* 1 (1908-1909): 219-230.

_____. "Records of the Jacob-Lathrop-Jessey Church 1616-1641" ["Jessey Memorandum"]. *Transactions of the Baptist Historical Society* 1 (1908-1909): 203-218.

_____. "Rise of the Particular Baptists in London, 1633-1644" ["The Kiffin Memorandum"]. *Transactions of the Baptist Historical Society* 1 (1908-1909): 231-245.

_____ . ed. *Works of John Smyth, Fellow of Christ's College, 1594-8*. 2 vols. Cambridge: Cambridge University Press, 1915.

Wolfe, Don, ed. *Leveller Manifestoes*. New York: Nelson and Sons, 1944.

Woodhouse, A.S.P. ed. *Puritanism and Liberty*. London: J.M. Dent and Sons, 1938.

Wooton, David, ed. *Divine Right and Democracy*. New York: Penguin, 1986.

Secondary Sources

Anderson, Philip J. "Letters of Henry Jessey and John Tombes to the Churches of New England, 1645." *Baptist Quarterly*. 28 (1979): 30-40.

Aveling, J. H. *The Chamberlens and the Midwifery Forceps*. London: J. & A. Churchill, 1882.

Ball, Bryan W. *A Great Expectation: Eschatological Thought in English Protestantism to 1660*. Leiden: E. J. Brill, 1975.

_____ . *The Seventh-day Men: Sabbatarians and Sabbatarianism in England and Wales, 1600- 1800*. Oxford: Clarendon Press, 1994.

Barkun, Michael. *Millennialism and Violence*. London: Frank Cass, 1996.

Barnes, Robin Bruce. *Prophecy and Gnosis*. Stanford: Stanford University Press, 1988.

Bell, Mark R. "The Revolutionary Roots of Anglo-American Millenarianism: Robert Maton's *Israel's Redemption* and *Christ's Personall Reign on Earth*." *Journal of Millennial Studies*. 2 (2000): 1-8.

Brown, Louise Fargo. *The Political Activities of the Baptists and Fifth Monarchy Men in England During the Interregnum*. Washington, D.C.: American Historical Association, 1912.

Brachlow, Stephen. "John Smyth and The Ghost of Anabaptism." *Baptist Quarterly*. 30 (1984) : 296-300.

_____ . *The Communion of Saints: Radical Puritan and Separatist Ecclesiology, 1570-1625*. Oxford: Oxford University Press, 1988.

Burgess, Walter H. "James Toppe and the Tiverton Anabaptists." *Transactions of the Baptist Historical Society*. 3 (1913): 193-211.

Burrage, C."The Fifth Monarchy Insurrections." *The English Historical Review*. 25 (1910): 722-747.

_____ . "A True and Short Declaration, both of the Gathering and Joining together of Certain Persons [With John More, Dr. Theodore Naudin, and Dr. Peter Chamberlen]: and also of the lamentable breach and division that fell amongst them." *Transactions of the Baptist Historical Society*. 2 (1911): 129-160.

_____ . *The Early English Dissenters in the Light of Recent Research*. 2 vols. Cambridge: Cambridge University Press, 1912.

Burrage, Henry S. *Religious Liberty in the Sixteenth Century*. Philadelphia: American Baptist Publication Society, 1892.

Butterfield, Ruth. "The Royal Commission of King Jesus: General Baptists Expansion and Growth 1640-1660." *Baptist Quarterly*. 35 (1993): 56-81.

Capp, Bernard S. *The Fifth Monarchy Men: A Study in Seventeenth-century English Millenarianism*. London: Faber and Faber, 1972.

Christanson, Paul. *Reformers and Babylon*. Toronto: University of Toronto Press, 1978.

Coggins, James R. "The Theological Positions of John Smyth." *Baptist Quarterly*. 30 (1984): 247-264.

_____ . *John Smyth's Congregation: English Separatism, Mennonite Influence, and the Elect Nation*. Waterloo, Ontario: Herald Press, 1991.

Cohn, Norman. *The Pursuit of the Millennium*. rev & exp. ed. Oxford: Oxford University Press, 1970.

Crosby, Thomas. *A History of the English Baptists*. 4 vols. London: Printed for the Author, 1738-1740.

Dowley, T. "John Wigan and the First Baptists of Manchester." *Baptist Quarterly*. 25 (1973): 151-162.

Evans, B. *The Early English Baptists*. 2 vols. London: J. Heaton& Son, 1864.

Firth, K. R. *The Apocalyptic Tradition in Reformation Britain.* Oxford: Oxford University Press, 1979.

Froom, L.E. *The Prophetic Faith of Our Fathers: The Historical Development of Prophetic Interpretation.* 4 vols. Washington D.C.: Review and Herald, 1946-1954.

Gardiner, Samuel. *History of the Commonwealth and Protectorate 1649-1656.* 4 vols. New edition. London: Longmans, Green and Co., 1903.

Gimelfarb-Brack, Marie. *Liberte, Egalite, Fraternite, Justice! La vie et l'oeuvre de Richard Overton, Niveleur.* Berne: P. Lang, 1979.

Gillett, Charles Ripley, ed. *The McAlpin Collection of British History and Theology.* New York: Union Theological Seminary, 1927-1930.

Gooch, G.P. *English Democratic Ideas.* Harper: New York, 1959.

Greaves, Richard L. and Robert Zaller. eds. *Biographical Dictionary of British Radicals in the Seventeenth Century.* 3 vols. Brighton: Harvester Press, 1982-1984.

Greaves, Richard L. "The Origins of English Sabbatarian Though." *Sixteenth Century Journal.* 12 (1981): 19-34.

_____ . *Saint's and Rebels: Seven Nonconformists in Stuart England.* Macon, Ga. : Mercer University Press, 1985.

_____ . *God's Other Children: Protestant Nonconformists and the Emergence of Denominational Churches in Ireland 1660-1700.* Stanford: Stanford University Press, 1997.

Hardacre, P. H. "William Allen, Cromwellian Agitator and 'Fanatic'." *Baptist Quarterly.* 19 (1961-1962): 292-308.

Haller, William *The Rise of Puritanism.* New York: Columbia University Press, 1938.

_____ . *Liberty and Reformation in the Puritan Revolution.* New York: Columbia University Press, 1955.

Hill, Christopher. *Puritanism and Revolution.* London: Secker & Warburg, 1958.

_____ . *The Century of Revolution 1603-1714.* New York: The Norton Library, 1961.

_____ . *Society and Puritanism.* London: Secker & Warburg, 1964.

_____ . *Antichrist in Seventeenth-Century England*. Oxford: Oxford University Press, 1971

_____ . *World Turned Upside Down*. London: Penguin Books, 1972.

_____ . *Milton and the English Revolution* . London : Faber and Faber, 1977.

_____ . *The Experience of Defeat Milton and Some Contemporaries*. London: Faber and Faber, 1984.

_____ . *A Turbulent, Seditious, and Factious People: John Bunyan and his Church*. Oxford: Oxford University Press, 1988.

_____ . *English Bible in the Seventeenth-Century Revolution*. New York: Penguin, 1994.

Howell, Roger. *Newcastle Upon Tyne and the Puritan Revolution*. Oxford: Oxford University Press, 1967.

Jewson, C. B. "St. Mary's, Norwich: The Origins of the Church." *Baptist Quarterly*. 23 (1969): 170-176.

Johnson, Benton. "A Critical Appraisal of the Church-Sect Typology." *American Sociological Review*. 22 (1957): 88-92.

_____ . "On Church and Sect." *American Sociological Review*. 28 (1963): 539-549.

Jordan, W. K. *The Development of Religious Toleration in England*. Cambridge, Massachusetts: Harvard University Press, 1932-1940.

Katz, David S. *Sabbath and Sectarianism in Seventeenth-Century England*. Leiden: E. J. Brill, 1988.

_____ . *Philo-Semitism and the Readmission of the Jews to England, 1603-1655*. Oxford : Oxford University Press, 1982.

_____ . *The Jews in the History of England, 1485-1850*. Oxford: Oxford University Press, 1994.

Lamont, William. *Godly Rule: Politics and Religion: 1603-1640*. London: Macmillan and Co. LTD, 1969.

Larsen, Timothy. "How Many Sisters Make a Brotherhood?" *Journal of Ecclesiastical History*. 49 (1998): 282-292.

Laurence, Anne. *Parliamentary Army Chaplains 1642-1651*. Woodbridge, Suffolk: Boydell Press, 1990.

Mack, Phyllis. *Visionary Women: Ecstatic Prophecy in Seventeenth-Century England*. Berkeley: University of California Press, 1992.

Matthews, A.G. *Calamy Revised.* London: Independent Press, 1959.

Mauss, Armand L. and Philip Barlow. "Church, Sect, and Scripture: The Protestant Bible and Mormon Sectarian Retrenchment." *Sociological Analysis.* 52 (1991): 397-414.

McGregor, J. F. and B. Reay, eds. *Radical Religion in the English Revolution.* Oxford: Oxford University Press, 1984.

Mommsen, Theodor E. "St. Augustine and the Christian Idea of Progress: The Background of the City of God." *Journal of the History of Ideas.* 12 (1951): 346-374.

Morgan, D. Densil, "John Myles (1621-83) And the Future of Ilston's Past: Welsh Baptists after three and a half centuries." *Baptists Quarterly.* 38 (1999): 176-184.

Nuttall, Geoffrey F. *Visible Saints: The Congregational Way 1640-1660.* Oxford: Blackwell, 1957.

_____ . "The Baptist Western Association 1653-1658." *Journal of Ecclesiastical History.* 11 (1960): 213-218.

_____ . review of *The Fifth Monarchy Men,* by B.S. Capp, *Journal of Theological Studies.* 24 (1973): 309-312.

_____ . "Abingdon Revisited 1656-1675." *Baptist Quarterly.* 36 (1995): 96-103.

Parker, Kenneth L. *The English Sabbath.* Cambridge: Cambridge University Press, 1988.

Payne, Ernest A. "More About Sabbatarian Baptists." *Baptist Quarterly.* 14 (1951-1952): 161-166.

_____ . "Thomas Tillam." *Baptist Quarterly.* 17 (1957): 61-66.

_____ . review of *The Believers' Church,* by Donald F. Durnbaugh. *Baptist Quarterly.* 23 (1969): 142-143.

Ploger, Otto. *Theocracy and Eschatology.* trans. S. Rudman. Richmond: John Knox Press, 1968.

Primus, John H. *Holy Time: Moderate Puritanism and the Sabbath.* Macon, Ga: Mercer University Press, 1989.

Robinson, H. Wheeler. "A Baptist Soldier_____ . William Allen." *Baptist Quarterly.* 3 (1927): 237-240.

Rogers, Edward. *Some Account of the Life and Opinions of a Fifth Monarchy Man.* London: Longmans, 1867.

Rogers, P. G. *The Fifth Monarchy Men*. Oxford: Oxford University Press, 1966.

Sanford, Don A. *A Choosing People: The History of the Seventh Day Baptists*. Nashville: Broadman Press, 1992.

Seaver, Paul S. *The Puritan Lectureships: the Politics of Religious Dissent, 1560-1662*. Stanford: Stanford University Press, 1970.

Sellers, Ian. "Edwardians, Anabaptists and the Problem of Baptist Origins." *Baptist Quarterly*. 30 (1981) : 97-112.

Smith, J. *Anti-Quakeriana*. London, 1873; reprinted New York: Kraus Reprint Co., 1968.

Solberg, Winton U. *Redeem the Time*. Cambridge, Massachusetts: Harvard University Press, 1977.

Sprunger, Keith L. *Dutch Puritanism. A History of English and Scottish Churches of the Netherlands in the Sixteenth and Seventeenth Centuries*. Leiden: E. J. Brill, 1982.

Swatos, William H. Jr. *Into Denominationalsim: The Anglican Metamorphosis*. Ellington, Connecticut: K & R Printers, Inc., 1979.

Taylor, Adam. *History of the General Baptists*. London: T. Bore, 1818.

Thirtle, J. W. " A Sabbatarian Pioneer_____ . Dr. Peter Chamberlen." *Transactions of the Baptist Historical Society*. 2 (1910-1911): 1-30; 120-117.

_____ . "Dr. Peter Chamberlen. Pastor, Propagandist, and Patentee." *Transactions of the Baptist Historical Society*. 3 (1912): 176-189.

Tolmie, Murray. *The Triumph of the Saints: The Separate Churches of London 1616-1649*. Cambridge: Cambridge University Press, 1977.

Toon, Peter ed. *Puritans, The Millennium and the Future of Israel: Puritan Eschatology 1600 to 1660*. London: James Clarke & Co. LTD., 1970.

Troeltsch, Ernst. *Die Soziallehren der Christlichen Kirchen und Gruppen*. Tubingen: J. C. B. Mohr (P. Siebeck), 1923.

_____ . *The Social Teaching of the Christian Churches*, Trans. by Olive Wyon. New York: The Macmillan Company, 1931.

Underwood, A.C. *A History of the English Baptists*. London: The Carey Kingsgate Press Limited, 1947; 3rd. impression 1961.

Underwood, T. L. *Primitivism, Radicalism and the Lamb's War: The Baptist Quaker Conflict in Seventeenth-Century England.* Oxford: Oxford University Press, 1997.

Wainwright, Arthur W. *Mysterious Apocalypse: Interpreting the Book of Revelation.* Nashville: Abingdon Press, 1993.

Walton, Robert C. *The Gathered Community.* London : Carey Press, 1946.

Watts, Michael R. *The Dissenters.* Oxford: Clarendon Press, 1978.

Weber, Max. *The Sociology of Religion.* trans. Ephraim Fischoff. Boston: Beacon Press, 1993.

Westlake, A. J. "Some Rare Seventeenth Century Pamphlets." *Baptist Quarterly.* 13 (1949-1950): 109-115.

White, B.R. "The Organization of the Particular Baptists, 1644-1660." *Journal of Ecclesiastical History.* 18 (1966): 209-226.

_____ . "John Traske (1585-1636) and London Puritanism." *Transactions of the Congregations Historical Society* 20 (1968): 223-233.

_____ . *The English Separatist Tradition.* Oxford: Oxford University Press, 1971.

_____ . "Thomas Collier and Gangraena Edwards." *Baptist Quarterly.* 24 (1972): 99-110.

_____ . "Henry Jessey: A Pastor in Politics." *Baptist Quarterly.* 25 (1973-1974): 98-110.

_____ . "John Pendarves, the Calvinist Baptists and the Fifth Monarchy." *Baptist Quarterly.* 25 (1973-1974): 251-271.

_____ . *Hanserd Knollys and Radical Dissent in the 17th Century.* London: Friends of Dr. William's Library, 1977.

_____ . "Henry Jessey and the Great Rebellion." In *Reformation, Conformity and Dissent* ed. R. B. Knox. London, Epworth Press, 1977.

_____ . *The English Baptists of the Seventeenth Century.* rev. & exp. ed. London: The Baptist Historical Society, 1996.

Whitley, W. T. "Baptists and Batholomew's Day." *Transactions of the Baptist Historical Society.* 1 (1908) : 24-37.

_____ . "Thomas Collier." *Transactions of the Baptist Historical Society.* 1 (1908) : 121-122.

_____ . "Militant Baptists 1660-1672." *Transactions of the Baptist Historical Society*. 1 (1908): 148-155.

_____ . "Salisbury and Tiverton about 1630." *Transactions of the Baptist Historical Society*. 3 (1912-1913): 1-7.

_____ . "Bampfield's Plan for an Educated Ministry." *Transactions of the Baptist Historical Society*. 3 (1912-1913): 8-17.

_____ . "The Fifth Monarchy Manifesto." *Transactions of the Baptist Historical Society*. 3 (1912-1913): 129-153.

_____ . *A Baptist Bibliography*. 2 vols. London: The Kingsgate Press, 1916-1922.

_____ . "The Plantation of Ireland and the Early Baptist Churches." *Baptist Quarterly*. 1 (1922-1923): 276-281.

_____ . *History of British Baptists*, 2nd ed. London: Kingsgate Press, 1932.

_____ . "Rev. Colonel Paul Hobson Fellow of Eaton." *Baptist Quarterly*. 9 (1939): 307-310.

_____ . "Henry Denne." *Baptist Quarterly*. 11 (1942): 124.

_____ . "Seventh Day Baptists in England." *Baptists Qu~* (1946-1948): 252-258.

Wilson, Bryan A. "An Analysis of Sect Devel *Sociological Review*. 24 (1959): 3-15.

_____ . *The Social Dimensions of Sectarianism: Sects Movements in Contemporary Society*. Oxford: (1990.

Wilson, John F. "A Glimpse of Sions Glory." *Churc* (1962): 66-73.

_____ . *Pulpit in Parliament*. Princeton: Princeton Unive. 1969.

Willams, George H. *The Radical Reformation*. Philadelphia: W ster Press, 1962.

Yinger, J. Milton. *Religion and the Struggle for Power*. Durham: L University Press, 1946.

_____ . *Religion, Society and the Individual*. New York: Macmillan 1957.

_____ . *The Scientific Study of Religion*. London: Macmillan Company, 1970.

INDEX

Act of Settlement, 255

Adams, Richard, 172

Allen, William, 103, 104, 150, 151, 158, 172, 196-197

Allhallows the Great, 65, 168-169

Amsterdam, 101, 223; and the first General Baptists, 35

Anabaptist, 2-3, 21, 31, 34, 74-76, 86, 97n, 100, 111, 114, 116, 163, 184-186, 189, 193n, 198, 259; baptism, 21; Baptists Falsely Called, See General and Particular Baptists; communism, 87, 89; Continental Anabaptists, 3, 55, 74, 88-89; English, 2-3; Munster (and its negative association), 2, 21-22, 23, 30, 37, 62n, 89n, 147, 149, 223; Seventh-Day Anabaptists (Continental), 207-208

Antichrist. See Antichristian

Antichristian and Antichrist, 17, 18, 23, 26, 27, 34, 36, 79, 116, 178, 181, 184, 199-200; as altering the Sabbath, 219, 242, 252n; Baptism and, 26-27, 35; Church of England as, 39n, 84, 176, 188, 200; the Court as, 24-25, 185, 188; and the Last Stumbling blocks, 26-28, 44, 137, 220; Levellers as, 117; Persecution as, 39, 79, 171, 187; as Pope, See papacy; Succession of ministers as, 37-39, 146n; two swords (civil and religious authority) as, 30-31. See also Beast, Christ, and Tithes

apocalypticism, 14-15, 17-18, 20-21, 23, 31, 70, 129, 159, 205, 218, 262;
definition, 5n; Baptism and 51; literature of 13-14, 70, 170, 188. See also Christ, and New Jerusalem

Archer, John, 70, 167n

Armageddon, 233

Arminian Baptists. See General Baptists

Arminianism, 44, 86, 236, 238

Arminius, Jacobus, 3

Aspinwall, William, 233, 234n

Assembly of Divines, 49-50

Associations. See Baptists, Particular Baptists, General Baptists, Fifth Monarchists, and Seventh-Day Baptists

Atkinson, Captain Robert, 248-249

Augustine, St., 15-16, 24

Axtel, Daniel, 113-114, 149, 158

Babylon, 19, 20, 26, 28, 29, 70, 85, 113, 147, 171, 177, 181, 184, 187, 190, 194, 200, 221, 237n, 244, 245, 250, 253, 256

Bale, John, 19, 23, 179

Bakewell, Thomas, 80n

baptism, 2-3, 13, 50, 63, 77, 207n, 220; believer's baptism, 3, 26, 27, 45-46, 60-61, 62n, 84, 137, 151, 167n, 169, 176, 257; infant baptism, 26-27, 28, 29, 46, 49, 60, 83, 102, 113, 139, 203; re-baptism, 3, 27, 60-61, 62n, 167n, 172n, 197, 243

Baptist, John the, 36

Baptists, 2-4, 20, 88, 97n, 146n, 183, 245, 262; and accommodation with society, 173, 204, 253, 260; apocalyptic perspective, 23-31, 105, 108, 118, 129, 174, 190, 205, 219-220, 244-245; and army, 105, 112, 117, 152, 182, *See also* Parliamentary Army; eschatology, 5, 6, 23, 29, 117-118, 205, 235, 244-245; Fifth Monarchists, 164-167, 173-204, *See also* Fifth Monarchists, General Baptists, Independent Baptists, and Particular Baptists; and Levellers, 108-111, 113, 118-119, 150, 177, 180, *See also* Levellers; new light and further light, 25-26, 118; organization, 121, 256, *See also* Particular and General Baptists; and Presbyterians, 104-106; Seventh-Day, *See* Seventh-Day Baptists; women, 170, 215-216

Ball, Bryan, 206n, 207n, 252, 253n, Bampfield, Francis, 216n, 224-226, 232
Barber, Edward, 44, 46-48, 87, 102, 171
Barebones, Praise-God, 62, 168
Barrow, Robert, 98n, 158
Barrowists, 56
Baxter, Richard, 98
Beast, 20, 25, 28, 29, 183-184, 188, 193-194, 202, 218-219; bear witness against, 29, 171, 177, 219, 252n, 253, 259; Cromwell, Oliver as, 31, 189; Infant Baptism as, 26-29; Luther, Martin as, 20; Persecution as, 26-29, 171, 187, 255-256; Succession of ministers as, 26-27, 37-39, 146n. *See also* Antichristian
Beaumont, Richard, 98n
Bedfordshire, 123
Belcher, John, 158n, 168, 195, 226, 228, 229, 231, 252
Bell Alley congregation, 42-46

Ben Israel, Joseph, 238-240
Bible, 4, 17, 18, 26, 30, 34, 44, 46, 47, 63, 65, 153, 164, 194, 214, 224n, 236, 253, 257. *See also* Old Testament and New Testament
Blackwood, Christopher, 26, 149, 151
Blackwood, Thomas, 98n
Bockelson, Jon. *See* John of Leyden
Bohemia, 17, 249
Brabourne, Theophilus, 207n, 210-212, 214, 220n
Brachlow, Stephen, 34
Bradford, William, 33
Bramston, John, 156
Brandenburg, Duke of, 251
Broadmead congregation (Bristol), 67, 144, 172n
Brown, L. F., 166
Browne, Robert, 2
Brownists, 2, 55, 100
Bunyan, John, 68, 90, 132-133, 217
Burrage, Champlin, 41, 101
Burrough, Jeremiah, 69n
Buttivant (Buttevant/Buttephant), Thomas, 187, 244n
Byfield, Nathaniel, 172

Calvinism, 33, 55, 61, 62, 64, 74, 76, 90-91, 142
Calvinist Baptists. *See* Particular Baptists
Cambridge, 33, 35, 49, 59, 62, 84, 90, 124-125
Canne, John, 172
Capp, Bernard S., 164-165, 166, 167n, 175, 228n, 229-230, 233, 234
Carew, John, 167n, 196-197, 201
Catholic Church, 15, 17, 19, 21, 85, 106. *See also* papacy
Chafie, Thomas, 218n

Chamberlen, Peter, 29, 168-171, 212, 217, 221n, 236-238, 252n

Charles I, 25, 31, 46, 75, 85, 98, 102, 104, 106, 107, 110-111, 113, 118, 132, 134, 139, 165, 169, 177, 188, 200-201, 213, 214

Charles II, 202, 203, 225, 260

Cheshire, 168

Chillenden, Edmund, 98n, 103, 168, 172, 217

Christ   3, 4, 17, 18, 19, 28, 38, 43, 45, 49, 63, 64, 68, 69, 71, 76, 77, 78, 83n, 89, 91, 92, 94, 112, 116, 129, 133, 139, 140, 141, 143, 148, 153, 176, 188, 211, 221, 239, 246n, 262; first coming, 15; first coming and the Sabbath, 217; as King, 25, 28, 31, 41, 44, 46, 47, 55, 57, 68, 69, 70, 71, 78, 80n, 102-103, 104, 117, 122, 136, 138n, 141, 156, 159, 163-165, 171, 175, 177-79, 186, 192, 201-202, 215, 244, 250, 257; Kingdom of 25-26, 47, 50, 57-58, 68, 70, 72, 78-79, 80, 85-86, 89, 94, 102, 107, 109, 136, 139, 140, 147, 153, 187, 194-195, 202, 204, 243-244, 249, 256, 258; second coming, 15, 18, 24, 27, 29, 46, 50-51, 55, 65, 66, 70, 85, 92, 109, 137, 141, 142, 154, 157, 166, 174, 220, 215, 232, 233, 245, 256; spirit of, 34; thousand year reign, 4, 13, 15, 41, 63. See also Apocalypticism, eschatology, Millenarianism and New Jerusalem

Christian Jews. See Seventh-Day Baptists

Church of England, 2-3, 24, 33, 56, 59, 60, 62n, 83, 84, 210, 212

Civil Wars, 97-98, 104, 113, 178-179, 238, 257. See also Revolution of the 1640s and Parliamentary Army

Clarendon, Earl of , 132

Clarke, John, 172

Clarke, Samuel, 228n

Colchester, 168, 242, 243, 246, 251

Collier, Thomas, 27, 84, 98, 108-110, 138-46, 196, 217-218, 259; Somerset Confession of Faith, See Particular Baptists; Western Association, See Particular Baptists

Commons, House of, 83n, 91, 103, 113, 114-115, 190

Combes, John, 172

Congregationalists, 4, 64-65, 67n, 86-87, 99n, 111, 113, 144, 148, 165-166, 169, 191, 203; Savoy Confession, 144

Cooper, Thomas, 156, 199

Coppinger, Thomas, 217

Corinthians, Book of, 89n

Cornwell, Francis, 43, 44n, 45, 55, 149

Cox, Benjamin, 81n, 90

Coxe, Nehemiah, 143

Cradcock, Walter, 63

Crawford, Major General, 97

Cresset, Edward, 130

Cromwell, Henry, 148-9, 150, 155, 156, 158-159, 186, 189, 195

Cromwell, Oliver, 31, 97, 110, 123-124, 130, 132, 147, 148, 150, 153, 157, 173, 177-178, 182-186, 188-189, 190-191, 195, 197, 236, 242, 256, 260. *See also* Protectorate

Cromwell, Richard, 197

Daniel, Book of, 13, 164, 181, 211, 219, 242, 248, 252n

Danvers, Henry, 46n, 187

Davis, Joseph, 224

Declaration of Indulgence, 225

Declaration of Sport, 213

Denne, Henry, 24, 48-51, 104, 118-119, 199, 217; apocalypticism of, 49-51

Denton, Richard, 231-232

Dorchester, 150, 196, 197, 201

Dublin, 149, 150n, 151, 155

Dunning's Alley Congregation, 46

Duppa, John, 59, 62n

Durham, 223

Eaton, Samuel, 60-61, 62n, 68, 72, 83

Edward I, 66

Edwards, Thomas, 42, 44, 48-49, 73, 82, 93, 94, 101, 105, 223

Elizabeth I, 106

Ephesians, Book of, 89n

episcopacy, 25, 39, 187

eschatology, 5-6, 13-14, 16, 17-21, 23-26, 29, 68, 106, 110, 181, 208, 259-260; definition, 5n; Puritan, 34-35. *See also* Antichrist, Apocalypticism, Christ, Millenarianism, and New Jerusalem

Eve, George, 226n

Exodus, Book of, 212, 213, 216, 219

Fansom, Joseph, 154, 191

Feake, Christopher, 65, 133, 157, 171, 181-182, 193

Featley, Daniel, 49-50, 87-88, 89n

Fenstation. *See* General Baptists

Fenton, John, 168

Fifth-Monarchists, 4, 5, 6, 8, 29, 65, 85-86, 112, 126, 129, 141, 145, 150, 154, 157, 160, 163-204, 205, 222, 224, 225, 226, 228, 229-235, 258; accommodation and opposition, 173-175, 224; baptism and re-baptism, 167n, 172n, 173-174; and Baptists, *See* Baptists; eschatology, 86, 160-166, 169, 172-176, 193-195, 203; Lothbury Square, 168, *See also* Chamberlen, Peter; organization, 168-169, 175-177, 224; and Seventh-Day Baptists 164, 214-235, *See also* Seventh-Day Baptists; Stone Chapel Congregation, 168, *See also* Chillenden, Edmund; Swan Alley Congregation, 192, 226, *See also* Venner, Thomas

Fischer, Andreas, 208

Fleetwood, Charles, 148, 149n

Fox, Edward (Edmond), 228n

Fox, George, 91n, 127, 243

Foxe, John, 23, 179

Foxey, John, 249

Friends, Society of. *See* Quakers

Fulcher, Samuel, 101

Galway, 150n

Gardiner, John, 105, 226n

Gathering of churches, 55, 57, 64, 67-68, 70, 99n

General Baptists, 3, 4, 33-52, 55, 58, 68, 74, 121-132, 135-138, 169,171, 173-175, 182, 198, 201n, 234, 256-258; and Antichrist, 40, 48, 50-51; apocalypticism of, 43,

45, 48-51, 174-175; Arminianism, 3, 44; army, 98n, 102, 105, 125, *See also* Parliamentary Army; baptism, 43-44, 45-46, 49-51; Bell Alley Congregation, *See* Bell Alley; church communion (open versus closed), 124-125; Confession of, 122-123, 201n; dipping, 28, 47; Fenstation, 48; Fifth Monarchists, *See* Baptists, and Fifth Monarchists; laying on of hands, 45-48, 52, 125,171, 216; Levellers, 97n, 99-104, 110, 118-119, 121, 126, *See also* Levellers; marriage, 124-125; missionary efforts, 44, 45, 51, 121; mortalism, 102n; organization, 121-127, 138, 174, 224; Sabbath, 125, 217

Genesis, Book of, 194
Gibson, William, 228n
Glait, Oswald, 207
Glasse, Thomas, 146, 172
Glazier's Hall congregation, 135-136
Goodgroom, Richard, 158n
Goodwin, John, 191
Goodwin, Thomas, 68-70, 160
Gower, Thomas, 81n, 82, 238-239, 248
Grantham, Thomas, 217
Griffith, John, 46, 87, 125, 171, 200n
Groome, Benjamin, 105
Gunne, Thomas, 81n, 136n

Hallyday, Henry, 223
Harrison, Edward, 98n
Harrison, Thomas, 167n, 182, 193, 201-202
Harriman, Anne, 170
Heath, Edward, 81n

Hebrews, Book of, 216, 222
Helwys, Thomas; 35-40, 42, 45, 46, 49, 51, 52, 255-256, 260; and episcopacy, 39; confession of faith, 73-74
Hexham Baptists. *See* Tillam, Thomas
Hill, Christopher, 108, 118, 133, 205, 256
Hindes, Arthur, 124
Hobson, Paul, 64, 81n, 82, 91, 93--94, 97, 100, 104, 105, 112, 129, 155-156, 235, 238-240, 247-249; Mr. Love, 246-247
Holms, Thomas, 81n
Holland, 35-38, 69, 131, 224n, 246, 247, 260
Hopkin, Robert, 228n
Horsley, Thomas. *See* Joseph Ben Israel

Hubberthorn, Richard, 199, 200n
Huish, James, 197n
Huntingdonshire, 123
Hus, Jan, 16-17
Hussites, 17, 204
Hut, Hans, 21

Independent Baptists, 4, 67, 68, 84, 90, 136, 144-145n, 166, 167n, 169, 172, 186, 187, 189, 198, 234, 237, 258; and Anabaptists, 86; baptism, 67; church communion, 4; eschatology, 65, 166. *See also* Broadmead Congregation, Henry Jessey, and Thomas Tillam
Independents. *See* Congregationalists
infant baptism. *See* baptism
Instrument of Government, 153
Ireland , 81, 129, 138, 148, 149-51, 172n, 189, 197, 251
Irish Baptists, 148-159, 182, 190. *See also* Ireland

Ives, Jeremiah , 98n, 101, 217, 252n

Jackson, Hamlet, 208-209
Jacob, Henry, 56-61, 62n, 72. *See also* Jacob-Lathrop Congregation
Jacob-Lathrop Congregation (and Jacob-Lathrop-Jessey Congregation), 56n, 59-60, 62-65, 68, 83, 92, 209; debate over infant baptism, 63-65
James I, 40n, 213, 256
James II, 213, 260
James, John, 222-223, 227-228, 256
Jessey, Henry, 62-68, 83, 84, 90, 166n, 167n, 168, 172n, 180, 191, 209-210
Jesuits, 106, 240-241
Jesus of Nazareth. *See* Christ
Jews, 16, 55, 65, 92, 142, 147, 189, 190n, 207, 214-215, 218, 220-222, 223, 224n, 232, 243, 246, 251; False Jew, 239-241; Judaic Law, 212, 217-218; readmission to England, 65-66, 67n, 139, 207n, 209, 214; Sabbath, 66, 206
Joachim of Fiore, 16-18
Johnson, Francis, 35
Jones, John, 228n
Joplin, John, 247-248
Judaizing Christians. *See* Seventh-Day Baptists
Katz, David, 67n, 208n, 209n, 239n, 251n
Kent, 59, 124, 125, 183
Kiffin, William, 6, 28, 63, 64, 68, 72-73, 75, 81, 82, 84, 90, 91, 92n, 99, 100, 102, 112-113, 114-119, 127, 128-134, 135-136, 137, 143, 148, 149, 151, 153-154, 155-158, 160, 171, 180-184, 190, 191, 195, 196-197, 199, 248, 255-256, 259-262; Apocalypticism of, 70-72, 116-119; Closed Communion, 90; and Confessions of Faith, 73, 75, 90; Gathering of Churches, 68-69; Jewish Readmission, 67n; Laying on of Hands, 171; seventh-day observance, 216n; wealth and trade, 129-134
Killcop, Thomas, 82, 91-94
Kilkenny, 149, 150n
King, Daniel, 137, 168
Knollys, Hanserd, 28, 64, 69, 81n, 83-6, 100, 112, 130, 166n, 168, 180, 191, 231, 235, 244n; and Apocalypticism, 25, 29, 55, 236n

Laborn (Labory), John, 228n
Lambe, Thomas, 42-46, 48, 76, 98n, 101, 123, 199
Langden, Francis, 167n, 172
Langley, Captain, 159
Larner, William, 102
Lathrop, John, 59-60, 62, 72. *See also* Jacob-Lathrop Congregation
Laud, William, 82
Lawrence, Richard, 100, 106-108
laying on of hands. *See* General Baptists, Particular Baptist, and Seventh-Day Baptists
Le Barbier, Denis, 81n
Le Burer, Christoph, 81n
Leicestershire, 122, 123
Levellers, 8, 45, 48, 51, 71, 73, 82, 95, 98-119, 121, 127, 177, 182, 198, 200n, 258; beliefs, 99, 104, 105; eschatology and Baptist support, 110; and General Baptists, *See* General Baptists; and Particular Baptists, *See* Particular Baptists; and Presbyterians, 105-106, 110;

Networks and Congregations, 102-104
Leyden, John of, 21, 22
Lilburne, John, 71-72, 99-100, 102, 103, 104n, 107, 110, 114, 115, 117, 132
Lincolnshire, 122, 123
Locke, John, 256
Lollards, 17
London, 127-129, 132, 135-136, 141, 168, 179, 183, 186, 202, 235, 256
Lords, House of, 261
Love, Mr. See Paul Hobson
Luther, Martin, 18-21, 258; Anabaptists, 21; baptism, 21; eschatology, 18-19; papacy, 19, 20; Lutherans, 21, 22

Mabbat, Thomas, 136n
Mabbatt, John, 81n
Manchester, 168
Mark, Gospel of, 13, 30
Marsden, Jeremiah, 172
Marshall, Stephen, 49
Mason, John, 256
Maton, Robert, 92, 93n
McGeachy, James, 229n
McGregor, J.F., 68, 163n
Mede, Joseph, 23
Mennonites, 37-38
Merchant Adventurer, 131
Middelburg, 58
Middlesex, 131
Miles, John, 135-136
millenarianism, 5-6, 13, 16-18, 20-26, 29-31, 41, 78, 146, 159, 205, 251, 256, 259-260; definition, 5n; and the gathering of churches, 70. See also Apocalypticism, Antichrist, Christ, Eschatology, and New Jerusalem
millennium. See millenarianism
Mission, Henri, 206, 221-222

Monk, Thomas, 132
More, John, 170, 237-238n
Mumford, Stephen, 226-227, 231
Munday, Thomas, 81n, 83
Munster, 2, 21-22, 23, 30, 37, 62n, 89n, 147, 149, 223
Munter, Jan, 37n
Müntzer, Thomas, 19, 20-21, 29, 258
Murton, John, 39n, 40, 41

Naudin, Theodore, 170, 171, 237n
New England, 60, 64, 67, 74, 84, 149, 151, 227, 235, 254n
New Jerusalem, 19, 21-22, 25, 28, 108, 195, 203, 214, 224, 234, 236, 244-245, 256. See also Apocalypticism, and Christ
New Model Army. See Parliamentary Army
New Testament, 13, 36, 77, 89n, 190, 213
Newcastle, 235, 237, 238-241, 248
Newport (New England), 227
Norwich, 168, 210, 211, 243
Northhamptonshire, 123
Nottingham, 168

Oates, Samuel, 28, 45, 76, 101, 123
Ockford, James, 220n, 221n
Old Testament , 28, 36, 66, 208, 213, 214, 217-218
organization. See Particular Baptists, General Baptists, and Seventh-Day Baptists
Origen, 14, 261
Overton, Richard, 73-74, 99, 100-102, 104n, 114-115, 167
Owen, John, 63
Oxford, 16, 23, 67, 122, 218-219
Oxfordshire, 123, 226

Packer, Robert, 97n

Packer, William, 172
Palmer, Anthony, 172n
Palatinate. See Tillam, Thomas
papacy, 20, 26, 29, 98, 106; as Antichristian, 17, 19, 24, 85, 98, 106-107, 188, 219, 256, 261. See also Apocalypticism, and Catholic Church
Parliament, 25, 45, 46, 52, 75, 98, 104, 107, 112n, 113, 114, 115-6, 131, 178, 261; Long, 79, 192, 205; Barebones, 151, 153, 165-166, 173, 256; Protectorate, 158; Rump, 197-198. See also House of Commons, House of Lords, and Parliamentary Army
Parliamentary Army, 49, 51, 82, 93, 97-99, 102, 105, 111-112, 118, 135, 145-146, 149-150, 152, 153, 155, 175, 182-185, 188, 238, 241, 251
Parnham, Richard, 226n, 228n, 231, 252
Particular Baptists, 4, 5, 6, 52, 55-72, 84, 95, 97n, 110, 132-133, 135-160, 168, 187, 189, 191, 198, 215, 231, 234, 235, 236, 238, 256-258; Abingdon Association, 129, 130, 137, 146, 168, 216, 217, 225, 231; and accommodation with society, 79-80, 81-82, 91, 93, 94-5, 110, 117-118, 132-134, 136, 141-143, 157-158, 160, 175, 198; and Anabaptism, 75-77, 79-80, 86-88, 113-115, 160, 163; and Antichrist, 69, 71, 84; apocalypticism, 74, 85, 94, 106, 112; baptism, 77, 83, 84, 89, 90, 92, 136; Calvinism, 76, 90-91; Church communion (open versus closed), 90, 138, 144, 216; Confession of 1644, 28, 73-88, 122, 128, 136,

142, 160, 163, 198-9, 238, 248, 259; Confession of 1646, 88-93, 122, 238, 248; Confession of 1677, 144; Confession of 1689 ("Second London Confession"), 144, 145; Dipping, 136-137; eschatology, 55, 60, 68-69, 71-72, 78, 85-86, 89-90, 92, 93n, 98, 103, 105, 139-146, 151-153; Fifth Monarchists, 166, 177-199, See also Fifth Monarchists; General Baptists, 76-77, 87, 90, 115, 122, 126, See also General Baptists; Independent Baptists, 90, See also Independent Baptists; laying on of hands, 138, 171, 216, 241; Levellers, 95, 100, 113-116, 118, 121, 126, 139, 160, 198-199; London Leadership, 81, 137, 141, 144, 148-153, 180, 191, 196-197, 236, 241, 259; Midland Association, 136-137, 168, 190, 217; military, 82, 97-99, See also Parliamentary Army; organization, 80-81, 121, 127-134, 135-139, 148, 160, 224, 256; Sabbath, 215, 217; Somerset Confession of Faith, 142; Western Association, 137, 138, 142, 144, 146, 163n, 196, 215-216; Wexford, 149
Patient, Thomas, 81n, 87, 100, 137, 151-154
Peasants' War, 20, 21, 204
Pendarves, John, 146-147, 168, 172, 232, 244n
Penn, William, 127
persecution. See religious persecution
Peter, First Book of, 245n
Phelpes, Joseph, 81n
Pooley, Christopher, 168, 195n, 211, 226n, 243-247, 249, 250n, 251-252

Pope. *See* papacy

Popery. *See* papacy

Portman, John, 192, 193n

Powell, Vavasor, 84n, 167n, 168, 171-172, 175, 185-187, 189-190

Presbyterians, 2, 49, 104-108, 113, 143, 164, 171; as Beast, 105-108, 143, 171; Westminster Confession, 144

Pride, Thomas, 113

Protector, Lord. *See* Cromwell, Oliver, and Cromwell, Richard

Protectorate, 93-94, 130, 132, 150-151, 153-155, 157, 160, 172, 173, 174, 177, 180, 184, 187, 192, 196

Protectorate Parliament. See Parliament

Puritan, 33, 104, 212, 213-214; eschatology, 34-35; New England, 64; preachers, 25, 74, 98; Sabbath, 212-214

Putney and Putney Debates, 49, 108, 110, 138-9, 140

Quakers, 2, 91n, 124, 133, 135n, 163, 199, 200n, 202, 214, 215, 216, 217, 243

Ramsey, Thomas. *See* Joseph Ben Israel

Ranters, 163n

Raworth, Francis, 168

Reading, 168, 182

Religious persecution, 24, 26, 28, 187, 203, 220

Restoration of the Stuarts, 9, 65, 93, 126, 132, 137, 143, 150, 195, 201, 202, 205, 215, 218, 226, 232, 243-245, 261

Revelation, Book of, 13, 14, 23, 29, 41, 66, 74, 84-5, 89n, 91, 106, 140, 147, 185, 187, 193, 201, 219, 225, 236n, 237n, 253; as history, 16-17, 19, 23, 29, 85; Revelation 11, 55, 85, 192, 194n, 222, 236; Revelation 13, 200n; Revelation 20, 13, 14

Revolution of 1688, 84, 132

Richardson, Samuel, 81, 88, 91, 92, 110, 114-115, 127, 129-130, 156-158, 179-180, 184, 187-189, 248

Rhode Island, 224n, 225, 231

Rogers, John, 151, 157, 167, 172n, 193, 194n, 195

Romans, Book of, 30, 216

Rutland, 122, 123

Sabbatarians. *See* Seventh-Day Baptists

Sabbath. *See* Jews, Puritan, and Seventh-Day Baptists

Salisbury, 118

Saller, William, 220, 223, 237

Saltmarsh, John, 43n

Sansom, Joseph. *See* Fansom, Joseph

Satan, 25, 78, 89, 116, 256. *See also* Antichristian

Saturday-Sabbatarians. *See* Seventh-Day Baptists

Savoy Confession. *See* Congregationalists

Scotland, 81, 138, 152n, 240

Scottish Baptists, 138n, 159

Separatists, 33, 34, 35, 41, 55-57, 60, 62n, 130, 210, 211, 260; confession of faith (1596), 74; Holland, 35-39, 260; semi-Separatists, 55-56, 59

Seventh-Day Baptists, 4, 5, 6, 8, 129, 158n, 163-4, 167n, 171, 195n, 205-228, 229-254, 258, 259; and Antichrist, 234n, 245; baptism,

206; Bell Lane, 168, 226-228, 231; eschatology, 160, 206, 214-215, 218-221, 225, 230, 232-237, 239, 252-254; and Fifth Monarchists, 164, 166, 168, 168, 205, 229-234; as Jews, 206-207; laying on of hands, 222, 236-237, 238, 241; Mill Yard, 171, 212, 216n, 229; organization, 225; Pinners' Hall, 226; Saturday Sabbath, 206-207, 209-214; women, 215-216. *See also* Tillam, Thomas

Sexby, Edward, 183

Shadforth, Christopher, 240

Shakespeare, William, 255

Sheppard, Thomas, 81n, 83

Shropshire, 123

Simon, Menno. *See* Mennonites.

Simpson, John, 63, 65, 169, 171, 181, 186, 233, 234n, 237

Skinner, John, 172

Smyth, John, 3, 5, 26-27, 30, 31, 33-39, 45, 105, 232, 234, 260-261; self-baptism, 35, 36; baptism, 27; believer's baptism, 26; confession of faith, 73-74; further light eschatology, 5, 31, 33-35; General Baptists, 33-45; religious transformations, 34, 36, 38

Spencer, John, 172

Spilsbury, John, 61, 62, 74, 80, 81, 82, 87, 91, 115, 127, 128-129, 137, 154, 155, 190-191, 199

Spittlehouse, John, 133, 176, 178, 182, 207n, 220, 223, 229, 233, 234n

Sprint, John, 208

Squibb, Arthur (Aaron), 226n, 228n, 252

Steele, William, 130

Stennett, Edward, 98n, 224-226, 252, 259

Stennett, Joseph, 226

Stinton, Benjamin, 56n

Straffordshire, 123

Strange, Nathaniel, 105, 145-146, 172

Stroud, Ann, 223

Stuarts, 255. *See also* Charles I, Charles II, James I, and James II

Sturgeon, John, 168, 172, 182

Taborites, 17

Taiping Rebellion, 259

Taylor, John, 61

Tew, Nicholas, 102

Tewkesbury, 190, 217

Thirtle, J.W., 212n, 237n

Thomason, George, 91, 115n, 118

Thurloe, John, 150, 155, 156n, 159, 185-187, 189-190, 195-196, 233, 243

Tillam, Thomas, 5, 138n, 168, 171, 195n, 217, 221, 225, 226n, 232, 234, 235-253; Apocalypticism, 5, 234-238, 242-245, 252; Hexham Congregation, 138n, 232, 235-242, 247; Jews, 221, 236, 238-241, 251; Palatinate Plantation, 5, 6, 195n, 225-226, 231, 234, 244-253, 258; 'Solemne Covenant', 249-250

Tillinghast, John, 133, 141

Tipping, George, 81n

tithes, 46, 48, 94, 99, 102, 103, 109, 138, 158, 184, 185, 188, 219; as Antichristian, 26, 46, 102, 184

Tiverton Congregation, 41

Tolmie, Murray, 57, 60n, 62n, 83n, 99n, 112n, 114n

Tombes, John, 67, 136, 237

Tomkins, John, 130

Toppe, James, 41, 165

Tovey, William, 232n-233n
Traske, Dorothy, 209, 255
Traske, John, 207n, 208-212, 214, 255
Triers, 130, 188
Troeltsch, Ernst, 6, 204, 205; church-sect typology, 6-8
Turner, John, 105

Underwood, A.C., 229

Venner, Thomas, 167, 192-196, 202-203, 204n, 222, 233-234, 235, 244, 259
Vernon, John, 158, 172, 196-7
Virginia, 59

Waldensians, 16, 17
Wales, 81, 135-136, 138, 152n, 168, 172n, 185
Walwyn, William, 99, 100, 114, 115-116
Warner, Lieutenant Colonel, 97
Warren, Edmund, 243
Warren, H., 148-149
Warwickshire, 123, 168
Waterlanders, 36-42, 73. See also Mennonites
Webb, John, 81n, 82, 83, 93, 105
Wesley, John, 127
Westminster Confession. See Presbyterians
Whalley, Edward, 67n
White, B.R., 34n, 42, 63, 67n, 126, 146, 166, 174, 231n
White, William, 172
Whitehall, 66, 67n, 217
Whitley, W. T., 56n, 127, 166, 173, 205n, 231n, 253n
Wigan, John, 168, 172
William and Mary, 132, 260
Wilson, John, 55, 69n-70n
Winthrop family, 63

Wise, James, 172
Woods (Woodward), Robert, 228n
Wycliff, John, 16

Xiuquan, Hong, 259

Yinger, J. Milton, 7
Yorkshire Plot , 82, 248